Democracy, Authoritarianism and Education

Also by Russell F. Farnen

CIVIC EDUCATION IN TEN COUNTRIES: An Empirical Study (*co-author*)

DEMOCRACIES IN TRANSITION: Political Culture and Socialization – Transformed in East and West (*co-editor*)

DEMOCRACY, SOCIALIZATION AND CONFLICTING LOYALTIES IN EAST AND WEST (*co-editor*)

EUROPEAN NATIONS AND NATIONALISM: Theoretical and Historical Perspectives (*co-editor*)

INTEGRATING POLITICAL SCIENCE, EDUCATION AND PUBLIC POLICY

NATIONALISM, ETHNICITY AND IDENTITY (*editor*)

THE POLITICS, SOCIOLOGY AND ECONOMICS OF EDUCATION: Interdisciplinary and Comparative Perspectives (*co-editor*)

RECONCEPTUALIZING POLITICS, SOCIALIZATION AND EDUCATION: International Perspectives for the Next Century (*editor*)

Also by Jos D. Meloen

IT IS ONLY A QUESTION: An Investigation of Response Effect in Questionnaires for Minorities (*co-author*)

POLITICAL PSYCHOLOGY IN THE NETHERLANDS (*co-editor*)

PROVIDING SHELTER FOR REFUGEES: An Investigation of Government Sponsored Support for Sheltering Asylum Seekers (*co-author*)

Democracy, Authoritarianism and Education

A Cross-National Empirical Survey

Russell F. Farnen
Professor of Political Science
University of Connecticut
USA

Jos D. Meloen
Senior Researcher
University of Leiden
The Netherlands

First published in Great Britain 2000 by
MACMILLAN PRESS LTD
Houndmills, Basingstoke, Hampshire RG21 6XS and London
Companies and representatives throughout the world

A catalogue record for this book is available from the British Library.

ISBN 0–333–74079–3

First published in the United States of America 2000 by
ST. MARTIN'S PRESS, LLC,
Scholarly and Reference Division,
175 Fifth Avenue, New York, N.Y. 10010

ISBN 0–312–23464–3

Library of Congress Cataloging-in-Publication Data
Farnen, Russell Francis, 1933–
Democracy, authoritarianism and education : a cross-national empirical survey /
Russell F. Farnen, Jos D. Meloen.
p. cm.
Includes bibliographical references and index.
ISBN 0 312 23464 3
1. Authoritarianism—Cross-cultural studies. 2. Democracy—Cross-cultural
studies. 3. College students—Attitudes. I. Meloen, Jos. II. Title.

JC480 .F37 2000
321.9—dc21

00–027826

This book is printed on paper suitable for recycling and made from fully managed and sustained
forest sources.

10 9 8 7 6 5 4 3 2 1
09 08 07 06 05 04 03 02 01 00

Printed and bound in Great Britain by
Antony Rowe Ltd, Chippenham, Wiltshire

Table of Contents

Lists of Figures and Tables

LIST OF FIGURES

LIST OF TABLES

Preface

This project was initiated and conducted from its beginning in 1991 as a cooperative international endeavor between the authors. Colleagues in more than 44 countries were included in this research project. Our list of acknowledgments mentions those responsible for translations, survey administration, and data collection in their respective countries. Without their assistance, this research project would not have been completed. Our study would also not be either as complete or as interesting.

We also want to thank others responsible for the many successes we experienced along the way. For example, we acknowledge the financial assistance the University of Connecticut Research Foundation provided for manuscript preparation for publication and thank the Universities of Connecticut and Leiden (LISWO) for their overall support for this research effort.

Although both authors collaborated on the entire project and book, Russell Farnen was primarily responsible for chapters 3, 4, 5, 6, and 12, and Jos Meloen primarily for chapters 2, 7, 8, 9, 10, and 11. For chapter 1, which states the research problem, and chapter 13, that states the conclusions, we share joint responsibility. The general editing of the manuscript was Russell Farnen's responsibility, one shared with Mrs. Martha Bowman, our professional editorial assistant, word processing expert, indexer, and overall caretaker of the book. Special editing was done by Jos Meloen.

Both authors developed the project and jointly produced the questionnaire. Russell Farnen contacted many colleagues who sent contributions from India, Central and Eastern Europe, Finland, China, and Hong Kong. Jos Meloen contacted additional colleagues who provided samples from Western and Southern Europe, Asia, Africa, Latin America and the Caribbean, Australia/New Zealand, Canada, and Serbia, while joint efforts were made in the US, The Netherlands, Germany, France, Russia, Turkey, and Lithuania.

With enthusiasm high for this international research, we received hundreds of letters, faxes, e-mails, and packages. Jos Meloen also coded and stored all the data of the almost 10 000 questionnaires for computer analysis, created and double checked the system file, and performed the statistical analyses. Finally, both authors share the responsibility for the project management and interpretation of the data, as well as for the overall results.

This work borrowed time from already full schedules, often preventing us from being with our loved ones, Christa and Carmen. Since it robbed us of our free time with them (which was scarce enough to begin with), we dedicate this book to them. Finally, we hope we have done enough to create progressive, multicultural, democratic and internationally oriented, tolerant personalities, rather than closed-minded ideological authoritarians, out of the

Ted's and Monika's in this world, also trusting they will have that same positive influence on their spouses and progeny in years to come.

While we are willing to accept any small credit accorded us for our scholarly efforts, we also accept responsibility for any unintended errors or omissions in the text which, even in this tolerant era of probabilistic logic, we are certain have unavoidably crept into our work.

February 10, 2000

Russell F. Farnen, Ph.D.   Jos D. Meloen, Ph.D.
Farmington, Connecticut, USA   Velserbroek, The Netherlands, EU

ACKNOWLEDGMENTS

We would especially like to thank the many colleagues who joined our project and collected data for us from their students. Their generous contribution to our project was of the greatest importance. Without their assistance and involvement, we would never have be able to expand our survey to student groups in 44 countries.

Orlando Jorge D'Adamo, and Virginia Garcia Beaudoux (University, Buenos Aires, Argentina), Rasa Alisauskiene (Baltic Surveys, Vilnius, Lithuania), Ruben Ardila (National University of Colombia, Bogota), Elena Bashkirova (ROMIR, Moscow, Russia), Irina Bekeshkina, Ilko Kucheriv (Democratic Initiatives, University of Kiev, Ukraine), Erkki Berndtson (University of Helsinki, Finland), S. Bhattacharya (University of Calcutta, India), Mircea Boari (Manchester University, UK; University of Hawaii, Honolulu, USA), Teresa Botelho (Universidade Nova de Lisboa, Lisbon, Portugal), Tom Bryder (University of Copenhagen, Denmark), Olga Bustos-Romero (National Autonomous University of Mexico, Mexico City, Mexico), R.A. Byaruhanga (Makerere University, Kampala, Uganda), Sajal Chattopadhyay (University of Connecticut, USA), C. Y. Chang, and Jaqueline Mou (The Chinese University of Hong Kong, Hong Kong), Antonello Chirumbolo (University of Rome, Rome, Italy), Georgyi Csepeli, and Agnes Kende (Eötvös Loránd University, Budapest, Hungary), Justin Daniel (University of the Antilles, Martinique), Suresh Deman (University of Connecticut, USA), Ignacio Dobles Oropeza (Universidad de Costa Rica, Costa Rica), John Duckitt (University of Auckland, Auckland, New Zealand), Edward Erhagbe (University of Benin, Nigeria), M. Cecilia Gastardo-Conaco (University of the Philippines, Quezon City), Ömer Faruk Gençkaya (Bilkent University of Ankara, Turkey), Daniel German (Appallachian State University, USA), Javier Grossi, Anastasio Ovejero (Universidad de Oviedo, Spain), Léon Gúzman, Xavier Vanni (University Diego Portales, Santiago, Chile), Sophia Grodzinskaya-Klemetti (University of Helsinki, Finland), Michael Haas (University of Hawaii, USA), Maryam Hassan (Kuwait University, Kuwait), Romuald Holly (University of Warsaw, Poland), J. Michael Innes (James Cook University, Townsville, Australia), Tetsuro Kato (Hitotsubashi University, Tokyo, Japan), Suna Kili (Bogazici University, Istanbul, Turkey), Cees Klaassen (University of Nijmegen, the Netherlands), Jan Kleinnijenhuis (Free University Amsterdam, the Netherlands), Sam McFarland (Western Kentucky University, USA), Jon Massaro (Tunxis Community College, Farmington, USA), Czeslaw Mojsiewicz, and Agnieszka Ladziak (University of Poznan, Poland), Claus Montag (Universitaet Potsdam, Potsdam, Germany), Rüdiger Meyenberg (Universitaet Oldenburg, Germany), Paul Nesbitt-Larking (Huron College, London, Canada), Eric Otenyo (University of Nairobi, Kenya), Robert Patman, and Sabina Lautensach (University of Otago, Dalmore Dunnedin, New Zealand), E. D. Prinsloo, Z. Postma de Beer (University of South Africa, Pretoria, South Africa), Patrick Rayou (University of Paris, France), Isabel Rodriguez Mora, Ricardo Sucre Heredia (Universidad Simon Bolivar, Caracas, Venezuela), Vladimir Rukavishnikov (University of Moscow, Russia), Andrus Saar (University of Tallinn, Estonia), Jose Manuel Sabacedo (University Santiago de Compostella, Spain), Stephanie Schulze (Humboldt and Brandenburg Universities, Berlin and Potsdam, Germany), Chih-Yu Shih (National Taiwan University, Taipei, Taiwan), Ivan Siber (University of Zagreb, Croatia), Leonard Suranski (University Durban-Westville, Durban, South Africa), Laura Tedesco (Warwick University, UK), Larissa Titarenko (Belarus State University, Minsk, Belarus), Vucina Vasovic (Belgrade University, Serbia), Hilde Weiss (University of Vienna, Austria), Hans de Witte (University of Leuven, Belgium), Chrisanthi Zafiratou, Mika Haritos-Fatouros (Aristotle University of Thessaloniki, Greece).

Other colleagues tried hard to participate, but circumstances beyond their control did not allow them to do so. Finally, we thank still other colleagues who prefer to remain anonymous because of current political circumstances in their countries. For example, in China and Cuba, we were not able to obtain any further cooperation, despite our repeated efforts to do so and the willingness of some interested colleagues there to join this project.

About the Authors

RUSSELL F. FARNEN

Professor of Political Science at the University of Connecticut (Hartford/Storrs), Russell Farnen received his Ph.D. in 1963 from the Maxwell School of Syracuse University, Syracuse, NY, in political and social science. His academic specialties include mass media and politics, national defense, and cross-national political socialization. Between 1990 and 1997, he chaired the Research Committee for Political Socialization and Education of the International Political Science Association (IPSA). He presented numerous papers at international conferences and authored and/or edited many articles and books. Recently, he published *Nationalism, Ethnicity, and Identity* (1994), *Democracy, Socialization, and Conflicting Loyalties in East and West: Cross-national and Comparative Perspectives* (1996), *Politics, Sociology, and Economics of Education: Interdisciplinary and Comparative Perspectives* (1997), and co-authored *Civic Education in Ten Countries: An Empirical Study* (1975). He is managing editor of *Politics, Groups, and the Individual* (International Journal of Political Psychology and Political Socialization).

JOS D. MELOEN

Senior Researcher at the University of Leiden, The Netherlands, Jos Meloen received his Ph.D. in 1983 in social science from the University of Amsterdam based on an extensive review and meta-analysis of *The Authoritarian Personality* (Adorno et al., 1950) studies. As social science researcher and project leader at the universities of Leiden (LISWO) and Rotterdam (ISEO), he conducted studies on authoritarianism, ethnic minorities and discrimination, and cross-cultural surveys. He presented papers at many conferences and published numerous scientific reports, articles, and books. He co-edited *Political Psychology in The Netherlands* (1986). In Russell Farnen's *Nationalism, Ethnicity, and Identity* (1994), he contributed a chapter on 'A Critical Analysis of Forty Years of Authoritarianism Research'. His chapter on 'The F Scale as a Predictor of Fascism: An Overview of 40 Years of Authoritarianism Research' appears in *Strength and Weakness: The Authoritarian Personality Today* (Stone, Lederer, and Christie, 1993). He is co-founder of the Dutch Society of Political Psychology (NVPP) and editor of *Politics, Groups, and the Individual.*

1 Theoretical Introduction: Education and Political Attitudes

INTRODUCTION

The relationship between political education and democratic attitudes is the focus of this worldwide cross-national survey (see Appendix). Prior cross-national investigations (Torney, Oppenheim, and Farnen, 1975) left some major issues unaddressed. Our primary focus is on the relation between ideological content, style of education, and political attitudes. We ask: What effects do liberal and conservative-nationalist educational choices have on university students' political attitudes, preferences, and self-ratings? When do students see themselves as multicultural, democratic citizens and when do they express authoritarian or extremist preferences? Is educational policy relevant to such attitudes despite a decline in worldwide ideological polarizations?

We tried to answer these questions by surveying almost 10 000 students from 44 countries; by analyzing a vast literature on political attitudes, political socialization, and education; and by conducting secondary analyses of previous international surveys. Some preliminary results were reported earlier (Meloen, Farnen, and German, 1994a & b). This final report on our survey begins with a description of the theoretical propositions that guided us.

THEORETICAL CONTEXT

Political Culture

A nation's political culture is revealed by examining citizen attitudes about their political system on three levels: system, process, and policy. The systemic level relates to values and organizations that sustain the system (political legitimacy based on tradition, ideology, participation, and/or policies).

The process level includes political involvement, obedience, supports, and demands. It includes informed and involved participants, passive and uninvolved subjects, and unaware parochials (see Figure 1.1, box E). In a typical industrial democratic country (the Netherlands or Australia), most citizens will be informed participants, minority subjects, and a few parochials. In an authoritarian industrial society (the former USSR), there would be mainly subjects, with a few elite participants and some parochials. A democratic pre-industrial system (India) would have few informed participants, many subjects, and mainly parochials in its rural, largely illiterate population.

1

Another process division is the societal degree of perceived social divisions, unity, trust, hostility, conflict, violence, and aggression.

The level of policy outcomes is another important part of a political culture and its view of the 'good' society. Examples of such values include privacy, nationalism, equality, competition, security, liberty, individualism, commercialism, redistribution, and conflict resolution. Some political cultures are consensual, others are conflictive. There are either societal agreements or divisions over regime legitimacy or how to decide politically (means) and what the major problems or goals (ends) are. Some societies are more centrist-oriented (US, UK, and FRG), while others are more polarized (France, Italy, and Greece). These issues help define political subcultures, coinciding with ethnic, national, religious, immigrant, linguistic, historical, geographical, and other polarities (Almond and Powell, 1996, pp. 36-41).

Our approach is consistent with Inglehart's (1997) 'postmodern shift' and the 'authoritarian reflex' which apply to the pattern of political cultural development in today's world. Inglehart et al. (1998) examined the interrelationships of modernism and postmodernism, materialism and postmaterialism with democracy, order, authority and educational levels in 43 countries. His findings are of special interest for our studies. In some countries, respondents support greater respect for authority as a social value (Nigeria, South Africa, Chile, US), while others favor less (Japan, Sweden, China, FRG). Some (Finland, Canada, Poland, US, Netherlands) highly value social order, others less (China, Russia, Baltics). More open government also is supported (Hungary, Belarus, China), but others want less (US, Belgium, France, Japan, the Netherlands). Overall, the most advanced postindustrialist countries (Finland, the Netherlands, FRG, Canada, France) stand in contrast with the least advanced (China, Russia, Estonia, Hungary). Countries high in postmaterialism are also pro-democratic and anti-authoritarian. Those with the highest mean educational levels tend to have less regard for authority and order and more for democratic participation, open government, and postmaterial values.

Political Socialization

One generation transmits its political culture to the next via political socialization. This lifelong process also resocializes adults. Directly (education) or indirectly (family), it affects a person's political values and behaviors. Certain views on nationalism, ethnicity, class, religion, ideology, rights, obligations, and subcultural loyalties are formed early and last long, especially if repeatedly reinforced. The family mainly shapes one's views on authority, obedience, participation, class loyalties, educational worth, job values, and gender roles (Farnen, 1994a, b, c; Farnen et al., 1996).

Education also has cross-national political effects. The educated person is more involved politically, has more information, thinks differently about politics, and is more attentive. Schools provide political information, transmit basic social values, and teach patriotism and the unwritten rules of democratic politics such as compromise, participation, equality, rights, and duties (values often reinforced at home). Certain religious values (especially those of fundamentalists in the US, India, and Nigeria) often clash with secular political ones. Peer group pressures also influence socialization. Occupation, class, and status (US working class Democrats versus upper-SES Republicans) influence the growth of political orientations as do the mass media. The press encourages the rise of a cynical, negative, bored, passive, and alienated citizenry. Political parties' political socialization efforts have not yet overcome these sentiments. Some political parties (US Republicans) specialize in degrading government, politics, politicians, bureaucrats, and public life in general. Unfortunately, citizens' direct contacts with many government agencies may not be positive, reinforcing their bad press. When citizens vote for lower education/school budgets or support downsizing the government staff while expecting high-quality education and efficient service, they fail to see (or refuse to admit) the contradictions between their personal behaviors and beliefs.

Additional factors which influence political socialization, systems, and actors include trends such as secularization and fundamentalism, democratization and authoritarianism, modernization and postmaterialism, ethnicity and nationalism, and social welfare and marketization. Forces such as these (with the aid of global communications and increasing international interdependence) have a clear, if indeterminate, impact on political cultures and their socialization processes (Almond and Powell, 1996, pp. 41-51).

Democratic Education

Political socialization is about what is being taught or learned about politics, to or by whom, under what conditions, and with what consequences for current or future political behaviors, cognitions, attitudes, opinions, or beliefs. It is related to political education, psychological and sociological research, and behavioral 'persistence' in political orientations over a lifetime. Recent political socialization research in the US, Europe, and elsewhere dealt with the growth of partisanship, party identifications, postmaterialism (support for environmentalism, civil liberties, self-government, and so on), and economic beliefs (Farnen, 1990, 1993a-c, 1996, 1997a-c).

Political socialization research measures the relative value of schooling in politics contrasted with family, media, peer group, and other influences. It studies students and adults learned values that support or oppose democratic government and political processes. These values include toleration, equality, civic virtue, political participation, and reasoned patriotism. Such research also shows how youth develop personal and national political identities, how they perceive minorities, how minorities view the general society, and how a person integrates such political constructs to define one's political self (one's cognitive map) (Farnen, 1993c).

Competence as a democratic citizen stems from one's political socialization experiences. Political socialization links the individual and the political system. Individuals and groups develop political orientations either directly/intended or indirectly/unintended from their lived experiences. Direct socialization occurs when one develops specific political orientations; indirect socialization occurs when one forms a nonpolitical orientation (personal efficacy) which influences one's social dispositions (subjective political efficacy). Political socialization occurs in a particular cultural context. To maintain the stability of a political system/culture, it must directly or indirectly transfer political knowledge, beliefs, opinions, attitudes, values, ideologies, and behavioral intentions or predispositions from one generation to another.

One's political behavior, in general, and intention to participate or vote, in particular, are products of the political socialization experiences a person learns and lives with. Parents, schools, and mass media influence one's political knowledge, interest level, sense of institutional salience, party and candidate preferences, sense of political self-identification, efficacy, attitudes about voting, and opinions about gender equality. All of these factors are learned within a given political system through the political socialization process (Dekker, 1996).

THE MAJOR SURVEY CONCEPTS

We will describe some key concepts used in our survey design to provide a common framework for analyzing and interpreting results. This leads to a discussion of our general theoretical model (see Figure 1.1). Some concepts are explained more fully in later chapters. For example, Riggs (1998) defines political terms such as democracy, ethnicity, globalization, hegemony, modernism, multiculturalism, nationalism, racism, regionalism, and Westernization.

Democracy

By 1997, of the nearly six billion people living on the Earth, more than half lived in democracies, leading some observers to proclaim the 'end of history' (Fukuyama, 1992) and the universalization of Western-style liberal democracy as the 'final form of human government'. If true, this finding would be significant in and of itself not only for the people so governed, but also for peacemakers since other scholars have maintained that democracies, while fighting in self-defense, do not make war against other democracies.

Schlesinger (1997) describes modern democracies as having representative government, party competition, a secret ballot, and guaranteed personal rights and freedoms. While disclaiming the need for a 'pure democracy' through elective plebiscites, he reasons that private ownership and capitalism are required under democracy, but that capitalism does not presuppose democracy as China, Singapore, Malaysia, Spain, Italy, and Germany have shown at times in the past. Capitalism, itself, unless checked, may be a threat to the continuing existence of democracy. Invoking so-called Asian values in favor of the group, order, authority, solidarity, discipline, and stability may be effective in advancing capitalism, but they also support authoritarianism, not democracy. Islamic fundamentalism is also hostile to free expression, women's rights, and religious toleration: all democratic values. Even current democracies face their own threats in the form of religious fundamentalism, racism, nationalism, multiculturalism, and a crisis of leadership. But most of all, Schlesinger says, democratic leaders have to use government in a positive way to offset what the free market will not solve on its own, namely workplace democracy, educational reform, environmental safeguards, health care, urban renewal, and infrastructure repair. Democracy would then both have a future and help to make the world a safer place for everyone.

While most of the world's regions claim to adhere to democratic principles, there is widespread debate and confusion about the phrase 'rule by the people'. Opinions and approaches differ about basic elements of democracy such as self-rule, participation, equality, liberty, justice, law observance, and individual rights. Democracy must be concerned with both the continual reform of state power and the simultaneous restructuring of civil society. But there are also limitations to nation-based democracies in our era of global interconnectedness. Problems of health, environment, communications, and technology cross national boundaries and require international democratization processes, institutions, and agreements for their resolution (Held, 1993).

Authoritarianism

Political scientists are less interested in studying authoritarian personality traits or the authoritarianism syndrome than in examining authoritarian or totalitarian political regimes, systems, theories, or ideologies. This is true despite any convergence between political regime structures and individual personality traits. Alternatively, psychologists mainly have been interested in attitudes rather than in political regimes, with the exception of research on authoritarianism, dogmatism, and extremism. Some of the political psychological parallels are aggression, political indoctrination by a stronger (dominance over a weaker) person, unquestioning support or submission, nationalistic and militaristic traditions, disregard for civil rights/liberties, rabid anti-'enemy' fervor, intolerance toward 'other' ethnic groups, chauvinistic nationalism, and right-wing extremist party support (see Figure 1.1, box F).

At the personal level, research has confirmed that authoritarians accept a ruler's authority, embrace middle class conventions and extol sexual morality (Altemeyer, 1981, 1988, 1996; Meloen, 1983, 1991, 1993, Meloen, Farnen, and German 1994a; Farnen 1996, pp. 69-72; Meloen, van der Linden, and de Witte, 1996). They exert power over those from whom they expect obedience; revere hierarchy, authority, and status; exploit women (whom they see as inferior); demand homage and withhold praise; and view education as elitist. On the job, they are the 'boss' or 'tyrant'; humorless, they reject challenges to their authority. They employ Machiavellian intrigue, often use ethnic stereotyping, and express anti-Semitism. Authoritarians are less politically interested or informed, distrust or oppose democracy, use national symbolism, approve of capital punishment, prefer a 'strong leader' and the 'good old days', see society as 'degenerated', and reject aid to poorer countries. They lack interest in environmentalism, admire their betters (the elite), and worship social conventions. Authoritarians oppose economic changes, equal opportunity, and affirmative action. They call themselves 'conservatives', 'right-wingers', and 'anti-socialists'; condone stern police measures, dislike homosexuals, and want strict child rearing and family discipline; they support racially discriminatory views, are nativists, and share similar parental values. Their views are dogmatic, ethnocentric, distrustful, paranoid, and ambivalent. In foreign affairs, they endorse *Realpolitik*.

'Ideal' authoritarians vary from society to society because of differences in political culture, child rearing, average amounts of education, level of economic development, type of political system, extent of urbanization, and other factors. For example, in the Soviet Union, authoritarians were anti-democratic and anti-capitalistic, yet shared their ethnocentrism, ethnic prejudice, anti-Semitism, rabid nationalism, and sexism with their Western counterparts (McFarland et al., 1993).

Altemeyer (1996) claims there are many authoritarians and that the 'psychology of fascism' already thrives in North America. Other countries could follow the path Germany took in the 1930s. Altemeyer (1996, p. 5) concluded it would outrage conservatives who condemned the Oklahoma City bombing to learn they differ more in degree than kind from the militiamen and neo-Nazis out to overthrow the 'American government'. Therefore, Altemeyer (1988) called right-wing authoritarians 'enemies of freedom'.

Authoritarianism is a major impediment to democratic learning or decision-making processes in schools, workplaces, or other group settings because it depends on factors (stereotyping, rigid, impulsive thinking, conformism, and field dependence) which stifle adaptive or creative learning and refining strategies. Authoritarians are poor information processors, faulty decision makers and problem solvers, and lack critical thinking skills because their talents are both restricted and maladaptive (see Figure 1.1., box C).

Nationalism

Both nationalism and patriotism require obligatory loyalty and devotion to a nation state or ethnonational group. Patriotism is a more neutral term; nationalism is more negative. Nationalism often exalts one's nation above all others. It espouses 'we-ness' or ethnocentrism ('us' versus 'others'). Nationalists often claim their culture's superiority and promote their vital national interests. They ignore the interests and concerns of other national or supranational groups, organizations, or institutions, all considered to be of lesser value.

Nationalism's key elements include the existence of a sovereign nation-state with a defined territory, government, and population. The citizen demonstrates loyalty or allegiance to the nation in exchange for guarantees of security and protection. Nationalists believe in an alleged common community, history, traditions, ethnicity, origins, language, territory, identity, and independence. Nationalism builds and destroys nations. Its effects are both healthy and malignant. Two types of nationalism are national-liberation (American and French revolutions) and ethnocentric/expansionist (19th century American conquest of Mexican and Spanish territories).

A nationalistic population has a sense of common identity, group sovereignty, solidarity, and supreme attachment, loyalty, or patriotism. Nationalism requires a sentimental tie with a homeland, 'race', people, or mother country. Nationalists define their self-worth via national identity and are willing to die for their land, people, and nation/national group. They believe nations are natural, timeless, unique; reflect elements of the 'collective will' in a drive for liberty, self-governance, self-determination; and create a state to which citizens can give their highest loyalties and patriotism (Russet and Starr, 1992, pp. 46-72; Rourke, 1995, pp. 175-204; Bayer, 1995; Farnen, 1994b).

Reasoned patriotism and a citizens' rights to actively support or oppose state action are compatible with a democratic political system. One example is conscientious objection to the military draft for religious reasons. The definition of national identity and citizenship in countries such as the Netherlands, Canada, the US, and Germany allows for this sort of exception to the general rule that the citizen should risk his/her life to protect the nation.

Militarism

This term means the excessive or illegitimate influence of military institutions, policies, and values on civilian society. The military may exercise too much control over national life. A militaristic society immediately uses armed force to settle international disputes or quiet domestic disturbances. Militarism was a prime feature of 20th century fascist regimes in Italy, Germany, Spain, and Japan. More recently, because of the strong role the military industrial complex played in national policy, both the US and the former USSR were accused of militarism. The influence of defense interests over the economy was so significant that critics believed civil society was too dependent on militarists. Opponents thought military requirements predominated and social emphasis on military demands, considerations, spirit, ideals, and values was excessive. Classical militarism was also seen in the cold war era when the US and USSR intervened in third world conflicts. This phenomenon was also independently demonstrated in Africa, Asia, and Latin America when military elites discarded democracy and civilian rule. A 1989 report showed that more than 50 per cent of 120 third world countries were then ruled by military-controlled governments using martial law at will. Often, these regimes supported favored elites to prevent income redistribution, routinely using a reign of terror to quell civilian unrest (Krieger, 1993, pp. 586-9).

Multiculturalism

Regardless of the country, the problem of undemocratic, intolerant, and inhumane views and discriminatory behaviors toward different or minority religious, immigrant, ethnic, racial, and other groups is a major impediment to fulfilling the democratic promise. In the US, advocating multiculturalism, supporting pluralism, celebrating difference, and promoting unity in diversity have been derisively labeled 'politically correct' (P.C.) thinking. Thus, counterpropagandists from the right callously negate efforts to further multiethnic and multicultural programs and projects in American society, falsely claiming that racism is dead and integration/equality are accomplished facts.

Immaterial culture means patterns of human behavior which are transmitted by symbols, values, and ideas reflecting a group's ways of life. An ethnic group is a (sub)cultural group whose origin may precede the nation state in which they live (American Indians in the US). It is assumed to be an involuntary association, but individuals may or may not identify with it. Members share a sense of tradition, 'we-ness', or belonging together as a common group of interdependent people. The group has distinct ethnic values, behaviors, and interests. Members and outsiders jointly identify the particulars of ethnicity and group membership. Especially important for democratic school-ing and ethnic and cultural diversity is that the relevance of ethnic/(sub)-cultural factors is recognized and should be respected at all levels. The atten-dant or resultant diversity thus supplied enriches the larger society and fur-thers its vitality. All ethnic/cultural group members deserve equal social opportunity and the right to participate fully, but their own choices as to group identification must be made optimal in a democratic society. Demo-cratic ideals and cultural diversity are consistent so the total education-al/school/classroom environment should reflect all of these propositions; educational objectives and curriculum guidelines can be used to implement these basic principles (NCSS, 1992).

THE THEORETICAL MODEL

The theoretical model of Figure 1.1 serves as a cognitive map that depicts some dependent and independent variables we describe in this book. It shows how these factors interact and illustrates various patterns of possible influ-ence. The interactive processes produce waves, patterns, and variations in the map charting the ebb and flow of political authority/democracy, conserva-tism/liberalism, and nationalism/internationalism. The map shows some of authoritarianism's major features (item a, box F) and its positive relationship to nationalism, militarism, conservatism, pro-dictator, and anti-democrat-ic/multicultural orientations (items b-g, box F). Probable connections exist among the degree of authoritarianism (box F), the level of political culture (box E) in the context of generational/cohort/period effects (box B) on its development, combined with the influence of significant socialization agents (box A) (parents, media, and schools). There is also a connection between it and stage, developmental, information-processing, and problem-solving edu-cational formats (box C). Box D lists information and research sources useful in this type of project; these factors also influence the description/analysis of a political culture or identification of a society's authoritarian characteristics.

THE RESEARCH PROBLEM

Our main goal was to investigate the relationships between political education on the one hand and authoritarian, democratic, and multicultural attitudes on the other. We wanted to test hypotheses that related both level and content of education to these democratic indicators. Thus, we had to reassess these con-cepts' validity and reliability. We chose a cross-national framework to enlarge the political and cultural scope in which these concepts could be played out.

Figure 1.1. Theoretical, multivariate, and interactive (multiple causality) model of three political culture types and authoritarian personality characteristics

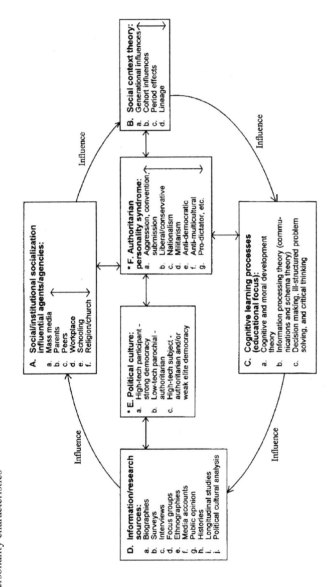

Figure 1.1 (continued)

Notes: Determinants of authoritarianism and political culture/environment of a given 'age', time (1, 2, 3, or past, present, future). Dynamic influences and interactive processes produce political patterns, waves, figures, and chaotic outlines of political cultures regarding authority/democracy-conservatism/liberalism. Double-headed arrows indicate interacting forces/influences for political stability and change. (*) Since the authoritarian personality reinforces an authoritarian political culture and vice versa, these two factors may be considered as either independent or dependent variables in different research designs. Source: Farnen, 1996, pp. 70-1.

Education and Authoritarianism

Education is one of the most oft-cited social variables associated with authoritarianism (Lederer, 1982 and 1983; Albinski, 1959; Hesselbart and Shuman, 1976; McFarland and Sparks, 1985; Photiadis, 1962; Shaver, Hofmann, and Richards, 1971; Wrightsman, 1977; Stone, Lederer, and Christie, 1993; Raaijmakers, Meeus, and Vollebergh, 1986). Since no previous study related education's ideological content to democratic or authoritarian attitudes, our thesis presents alternative proposals about education's effects internationally.

The basis for previous research in this field, conducted since the publication of *The Authoritarian Personality* (Adorno et al., 1950), has often been psychological. In the 1950s, a relationship between educational level and authoritarianism was often reported (Christie and Cook, 1958). High school students scored higher on authoritarianism than university freshmen, who scored higher than college seniors. This inverse relationship between general level of education and authoritarianism was reported in other studies (Brown, 1965; Bethlehem, 1985; Kirscht and Dillehay, 1967; Dillehay, 1978; Sanford, 1973; Christie, Havel, and Seidenberg, 1958; Alfert, 1959; Greenberg and Fare, 1959; Plant, 1966; Perioe, 1970; Middendorp, 1978; Meloen and Middendorp, 1991; Meloen 1983, pp. 44-45; Meloen, 1993). These correlations mostly range between -.30 and -.40 (Meloen, 1993; Meloen and Middendorp, 1991). Christie (Christie and Jahoda, 1954) estimated that this relationship was much stronger, but this was never proven. Unfortunately, this relationship seldom was analyzed critically. It was a consistent finding, but was not incorporated into a theoretical framework. Its face validity was apparent since in the post-WWII period, most of the better educated did not support authoritarianism, but embraced democratic attitudes.

This relationship suggested that lack of support for democracy was a result of insufficient schooling, especially for the poorest educated in a society. Apart from the parallel controversy on presumed 'working class authoritarianism' (Lipset, 1959; Lipsitz, 1965; Dekker and Ester, 1987; Middendorp and Meloen, 1990), this relationship led to the unproven assumption that antidemocratic tendencies could easily be countered by furthering general education and general learning processes (Goldstein and Blackman, 1978; Altemeyer, 1981 and 1988; Kirscht and Dillehay, 1967). It also implied that increasing democratic attitudes depended just on staying longer in school, learning more about the world in general. Also, it meant anti-democratic attitudes were 'only' incorrect cognitions. Nonauthoritarians were considered cognitive, rational individuals who understood the world and could make wise decisions. This contradicted approaches stressing nonrational and emotional group superiority as a basis for attitudinal anti-democracy, the most pronounced of which was the authoritarianism/ethnocentrism paradigm (Fromm, 1941/1965; Adorno et al., 1950; Rokeach, 1960; LeVine and Campbell, 1972).

Questions such as 'where was it that authoritarianism was taught after WWII, when the main authoritarian political movements were militarily defeated and politically dead?' were not asked. This was the 'optimistic' general learning approach to anti-authoritarianism (Altemeyer, 1988). How did children acquire authoritarian attitudes if teachers since 1945 did not teach authoritarianism, favoring democracy? Many believed democracy was a product of rationality and the Enlightenment and seemed amenable to rational learning processes. But how could anti-democratic tendencies result from such learning processes? Just which learning processes are meant here?

This approach of 'low average level of education - high risk for democratic society' is not entirely satisfactory despite previous empirical support for the negative correlation between a general higher level of education and a lower level of authoritarianism (Christie and Cook, 1958; Christie, Havel, and Seidenberg, 1958; Alfert, 1959, Greenberg and Fare, 1959; Plant, 1966; Perioe, 1970; Meloen, 1993; Meloen and Middendorp, 1991). A closer look at this corroborative research reveals at least three weaknesses.

Three Weaknesses

Most research about authoritarianism was psychological. Lacking funds for nationwide random sampling, psychological researchers often restricted their efforts to social science or other student samples. Sociological researchers, using a few random samples, developed scales which were too short and unreliable. Both these 'short cuts' resulted in a lack of studies of truly anti-democratic groups. However, these social science (mainly psychology) student groups were among the most pro-democratic in Western society (Meloen, 1983, 1993). This 'student bias' restricted generalizations based on these findings. Nevertheless, results were often extrapolated because more adequate studies were unavailable. For instance, social science students appear to become more democratic and less authoritarian during their 4-5 years at US universities (Christie and Cook, 1958; Sanford, 1973). One might hardly expect otherwise. Also, university students appear to be more democratic and less authoritarian compared to secondary school students. However, this relationship became accepted as an universal phenomenon. The faulty, misleading resultant proposition was that any education would make people less authoritarian and more democratic, no matter what was taught. Worse yet, exceptions to these results were often ignored. Despite prolonged education, students other than social science majors seemed less democratically influenced (Meloen, 1983, pp. 44-5; Ayers and Rohr, 1977; Athanasiou, 1968; Christie et al., 1958; Greenberg and Fare, 1959; Martoccia, 1964; Lee and Warr, 1969; Sherwood, 1966; Hogan, 1970; Dunham, 1973; Granberg and Corrigan, 1972; Libo, 1957; Peabody, 1961; Stuart, 1965; Arnett, 1978). Some studies had no positive findings; some results contradicted conventional wisdom. Social science, natural science, and humanities (but not business or engineering) students became less authoritarian over time (Ayers and Rohr, 1977; Meloen, 1983). But Lambley (1980) and Liebhart (1970) found higher mean authoritarianism scores after retesting the same social science students.

Thus, we have three reservations about the inverse relationship between education and authoritarianism as a useful cross-national generalization:
1. The education-democracy connection was found in North America and most of Western Europe (Middendorp, 1978; Meloen, 1983; Simpson, 1972), but not in developing countries such as Costa Rica and Mexico (Simpson, 1972; Lindgren and Singer, 1963) or in certain authoritarian cultures (Duckitt, 1992) such as Afrikaans-speaking white South Africans. Culture makes a difference for acquiring political attitudes. The so-called 'non-Western' higher educated (in Simpson's and Duckitt's analyses) were almost as authoritarian as the lower educated, despite their presumed educational advantages. But what teachers conveyed to students in educational interactions made a difference. It seems implausible that any type of general education would diminish authoritarian attitudes.
2. Historical examples from totalitarian and authoritarian regimes clearly show education almost always promotes the prevailing extremist right- or left-wing or some empowered ideology. The Nazis used education to create the new nationalist 'Aryan' German (Blackburn, 1985). Other authoritarian regimes also used their ideology or nationalism to influence educational systems, teachers, and curricula. Much more education or higher levels of education to produce less authoritarianism is not likely in such situations. In South Africa, Duckitt (1992) showed that most intellectuals who protested against these undemocratic regimes were censured immediately. This also happened if they spoke out publically for democracy or, worse, taught it to their students (such as in Serbia, Croatia, China, or Cuba today). One likely effect is that in these cases, educational level was positively related to authoritarianism, the opposite of the Western post-WWII

experience. But we lack suitable comparative studies from anti-democratic regimes. Western studies cannot be generalized to apply to such countries.
3. No one has adequately formulated the connection, transformation, or intermediary process of just what happens between the general level of education and authoritarianism. Altemeyer (1988) suggests general learning processes instead of a psychoanalytical explanation, but he does not tell us precisely how authoritarianism is learned. What makes students more democratic? Do they benefit only from general education courses instead of a specific pro-democracy curriculum? At least two mutually exclusive explanations have been suggested. More education may lead to a better understanding of the world in general and, therefore, to more democratic attitudes: Gabennesch's (1972) 'breath of perspective' hypothesis. But the opposite is just as likely: the most authoritarian students may find it difficult to accept or understand the higher and more complex content of advanced education. They may become annoyed, bored, and drop out ('school selection process' hypothesis). They may remain more authoritarian and more supportive of strong leadership, having acquired less strong democratic attitudes and a lower capacity for abstraction.

Content of Education

The relation between educational level and authoritarianism may be just a coincidence or a result of factors not considered previously. We suggest that this effect may be not just an 'automatic' product of general education, but also (perhaps even predominantly) of one's preference for a certain style, philosophy, ideology, and/or content of education. That is, a preference for realistic, highly democratic content (multicultural, liberal, international) is associated with more democratic attitudes and more democracy in the overall educational system (among teachers, in curricula, with procedures, and in the 'hidden curriculum') as well as among students. Intensive democratic education will also be more available in more democratic countries and in more democratically inclined sections of a given society. In general, one's preference for a certain content/style/process/philosophy of education may even be more important than just the average level of education, although both (content and level) may result in less authoritarianism and stronger pro-democratic attitudes, at least in democratic political systems.

This relation becomes important if one wants to teach students to become less authoritarian and more democratic. If a higher level of education is the sole prerequisite, it may be useless to teach democracy, especially to the already most receptive groups (university social science students). This elite view also writes off the majority of the population destined for a lower level of education, those never to become educated democrats who oppose authoritarianism.

THE MAJOR RESEARCH QUESTIONS

Focusing on relationships between educational and democratic and authoritarian attitudes, we address the following research questions:

1. What is the relationship between political education and relevant attitudes in cross-national surveys?
2. How universal is the relationship between level of education and authoritarian (inverse) and democratic and multicultural (positive) attitudes?
3. How universal is the relationship between content of education and authoritarian (inverse) and democratic and multicultural (positive) attitudes?
4. What are the empirical results detailing democratic/authoritarian concepts, scales, and ratings in this cross-national survey?
5. What are the characteristics of the educational and political systems in the countries and world regions in this survey?
6. What are the results of reported recent research on democracy, multiculturalism, authoritarianism, and political socialization/education?
7. What is the distribution of democratic, multiculturalist, and authoritarian attitudes over the world regions?
8. How universal is the relationship between level of education and authoritarian (inverse) and democratic and multicultural (positive) attitudes in some large international surveys?
9. Are there any exceptions to the almost universal relationship between level of education and authoritarian (inverse relation) and democratic and multicultural (positive relation) attitudes (that is, Simpson's thesis)?
10. How universal is the relationship between content of education and authoritarian (inverse relation) and democratic and multicultural (positive relation) attitudes?
11. What is the distribution of preferences for liberal-progressive and conservative-nationalist teaching content and styles in the world regions?
12. How universal are the relationships between liberal and conservative-nationalist teaching style preferences and political attitudes (the Farnen/Meloen thesis)?
13. What can we conclude from this survey about civic and political education for (pro)democracy and (anti)authoritarianism?

OVERVIEW OF THE BOOK

Chapter 2 explains our empirical framework, questionnaire, operationali-
zations, analyses, and scales used. Chapter 3 provides country and regional
educational and political summaries. Chapters 4, 5, and 6 summarize recent
research on democracy, authoritarianism, and education, respectively. Chapter 7 presents results over world regions about democratic and authoritarian
attitudes and ratings. Chapter 8 investigates the universality of the inverse
relationship between education and authoritarianism by re-analyzing international surveys. Chapter 9 provides a test of Simpson's thesis in a secondary
analysis of a worldwide survey. Chapter 10 presents results about liberal and
nationalist-conservative teaching orientations over the world regions. In
Chapter 11, the Farnen/Meloen thesis is tested regarding relationships between education and political attitudes. Chapter 12 applies our studies' results
to the field of political education. Chapter 13 summarizes our overall results
and draws conclusions for political education, public policy, and future
research. The survey, itself, is reproduced in the Appendix.

2 An International Project on Democracy, Authoritarianism, and Education

INTRODUCTION

This chapter describes how we conducted this survey. The main questions and key concepts (as operationalized in the questionnaire) are presented. Our general strategy for this international survey is explained. In the second part, the results and initial statistical analyses of the concepts included are presented. This chapter provides the conceptual and statistical foundation for the analyses in the following chapters.

AN INTERNATIONAL PROJECT

In the early 1990s, we became interested in conducting an international survey, including the issues of democracy, authority, and education. With the cold war ended, apartheid fast crumbling, and democratization rapidly rising worldwide, we believed a new empirical study would be very important for democratic education. Too much speculation and little empirical research was available to answer basic questions on democracy, authoritarianism, multiculturalism, and education on a truly international scale. Much has been written on worldwide democratization in the 1990s. Still too few empirical studies reported popular attitudes of people living in countries of the world.

To this end, we designed an international investigation using a standard questionnaire. Initially, we did not expect to receive contributions from 44 countries with almost 10 000 respondents. The success of our admittedly pilot approach has enabled us to present results and test hypotheses on a truly international scale. Such findings are rare in political socialization, education, empirical political science, or political psychology research.

The Project Design

The main concepts were operationalized in a comprehensive questionnaire (see Appendix). It included 77 opinion and attitudinal statements, background questions, ratings, and self-ratings. We kept this questionnaire relatively short to improve chances for cooperation and to make translations easier. However, this method limited the more complete operationalization of some concepts. We kept all questionnaires exactly the same. Thereby, we could fairly compare across groups, cultures, countries, and continents. The questionnaire included six main themes: 1) general political and social factors, 2) political education, 3) authoritarian and democratic attitudes, 4) ratings of political leaders, 5) personal background questions, and 6) political self-ratings.

To prevent response set, about half the items were worded using a liberal and the other half a conservative direction throughout the questionnaire. This also improved cooperation of both students and colleagues since both liberals and conservatives were able to recognize their ideology as part of the content. In this way, we avoided political one-sidedness in sample selection.

General Social and Political Themes

The questionnaire started with items related to general political themes (democracy, multiculturalism, equality, militarism and patriotism). Included were items such as: 'Democracy is by far the best form of government for our country and people' (#1), 'it should be allowed to use the army to maintain law and order' (#7), 'when it comes to things that count most, all races, religious groups, and nationalities are pretty much alike and equal' (#19), and 'our political institutions are the best in the world' (#10). Most items used had all been part of previous (sometimes large-scale) surveys on pro-democracy, anti-militarism, nondogmatism, anti-chauvinism, and pro-equality.

One part included themes related to tendencies in teaching or education. The content of the items expressed both liberal and progressive themes, as well as authoritarian and nationalist ones. An example of a liberal item was: 'Our schools ought to teach us more about promoting individual freedom, popular participation, keeping the peace, and achieving economic equality and justice for all (#22). By contrast, a conservative item was: 'Our schools already teach us too much about other lands, peoples, cultures and races' (#23). Some items related to the content of education and to teaching goals, while others related more to the style of teaching and methods used.

In the next part, we used items from a short standard scale of authoritarianism (Middendorp, 1978; Middendorp, 1991; Meloen and Middendorp, 1991; Eisinga and Scheepers, 1989). This scale was extensively pretested. It proved to be reliable and unidimensional in several national random samples in the Netherlands. The items were taken from the original Adorno et al. (1950) F scale. To guard against response set, these items were randomly alternated with items from a scale of pro-democratic attitudes (Roe, 1975).

In another part of the survey, we listed 14 well-known international political leaders. Respondents rated them on a 9-point scale, from 'most disliked' to 'most admired' persons. Both liberals and conservatives, dictators and reformers, and militarists and pacifists were included: Ronald Reagan,

Mao Tse Tung, Franklin D. Roosevelt, Mikhail Gorbachev, Dwight D. Eisenhower, Karl Marx, Martin Luther King, Adolf Hitler, John F. Kennedy, Joseph Stalin, Nelson Mandela, Napoleon Bonaparte, Saddam Hussein, and Mahatma Gandhi. As the project expanded, there was a need for additional heroes (or villains) in certain countries. Thus, in Poland only we added Lech Walesa and Pope John Paul to the standard questionnaire; in Russia only, we included Vladimir Zhirinovsky and Boris Yeltsin.

We asked a limited number of personal background questions such as birth year and gender. Several questions delved into parental background: 1) being raised mainly on a farm, in a rural town, suburb, city, or large city, 2) having parents of working, lower middle, higher middle or upper class origin, 3) a father who had completed primary, secondary/high school, or college/university. One question related to mass media attention. The respondent was asked from which medium he/she obtained most public information among radio, television (TV), newspaper, word-of-mouth, or magazines.

In the last part of the survey, ten bi-polar political self-ratings assessed the respondents' political self-image on a 7-point scale. Respondents were asked to rate themselves on being political versus nonpolitical, liberal versus conservative, right-wing versus left-wing, anti-authoritarian versus authoritarian, internationalist versus isolationist, militarist versus pacifist, equalitarian versus elitist, multiculturalist versus nationalist, cosmopolitan versus provincial. A religious self-rating (religious versus not religious) was also included, but no labels of religions were used because denominations would be too different for many so countries, while the concept of religion is a universal one. In several countries (such as Italy, Belgium, the Netherlands, and Greece), questions about political party loyalty were added.

International Survey

Through an international network of colleagues, we distributed the questionnaire to many English and non-English speaking samples. The English version was used for those who spoke English as a primary (US and Canada) or secondary (but often, national) language as in India, Hong Kong, and Kenya. For most of the other samples, the questionnaire was translated into the local national language. The English version served as a model for all translations.

The translators were generally colleagues with a university education and a good understanding of English, all of them native speakers in their own language: French, German, Spanish, Italian Swedish, Finnish, Estonian, Lithuanian, Russian, Polish, Hungarian, Greek, Chinese, Japanese, Arabic, and Hindi. Additionally, both authors checked the translations thoroughly with all the means available. Most errors were corrected when we sent the translated questionnaires back and forth for an interactive review. Therefore, we believe these translations were quite adequate for our purposes.

Figure 2.1. Survey on democracy, authoritarianism, and multiculturalism in 44 countries (1991-97)

After the translation was considered satisfactory, colleagues were asked to find appropriate samples for the distribution of the questionnaire. Mainly university students were sampled, but there were some secondary school students and older adult, part-time students in evening or extension classes. To avoid homogeneous student samples (Meloen, 1983, 1993), our colleagues were asked to find groups as varied as possible, especially in their supposed SES, ethnicity, liberalism, and conservatism. This resulted in considerable differentiation among our samples.

Initially, samples were requested of 100 to 200 respondents; many of our samples are this size. In some instances, we received many more, up to 900 (Russia) and 1200 (US). We aimed to include at least 50 respondents from each country, but failed to collect such numbers in four countries (countries such as China, Taiwan, and Hong Kong; however, they share the same Chinese culture and together make a Chinese sample of about 100) for a variety of reasons. Also, despite much effort and repeated reminders, we were unable to secure an adequate number of UK respondents, just as the IEA study had experienced in the early 1970s.

Table 2.1. Number of respondents by country and region

World Region	Country	By Country	By 8 Regions	By 12 Regions
North America	Canada	104	1376	1376
	USA	1272		
West Europe (North)	Finland	256	2582	1509
	Sweden	99		
	Germany	280		
	UK	38		
	Netherlands	447		
	Belgium	418		
	Austria	93		
West Europe (South)	France	86		1073
	Spain	546		
	Portugal	98		
	Italy	123		
	Greece	220		
East Europe	Estonia	302	1608	1608
	Lithuania	100		
	Poland	600		
	Hungary	169		
	Croatia	195		
	Serbia	200		
CIS-Russia	Russia	908	1393	1393
	Ukraine	210		
	Belarus	275		
Latin America	Mexico	216	910	910
	Costa Rica	87		
	Martinique	104		
	Colombia	100		
	Venezuela	108		
	Chile	195		
	Argentina	100		
Africa	Kenya	101	400	400
	Uganda	96		
	Nigeria	88		
	South Africa	115		
Asia (Middle East)	Kuwait	61	1322	600
	Turkey	539		
Asia (South)	India	289		289
Asia (Central)	PR China	17		17
Asia (East)	Japan	100		416
	Philippines	238		
	Taiwan	30		
	Hong Kong	48		
Oceania	Australia	61	122	122
	New Zealand	61		
Total World Regions		*9713*	*9713*	*9713*

In most cases, our international cooperation was quite successful (see Table 2.1, Figure 2.1). Many colleagues were interested and cooperated enthusiastically. But in PR China, it was almost impossible to obtain cooperation from communist authorities. We heard that hundreds of questionnaires were completed, but only a few were returned to us. Apparently, 'democracy' and 'authority' aroused too much suspicion there.

Although the samples do not constitute randomness in the various populations, we think the groups are well enough varied and heterogeneous in background and attitudes to allow some preliminary analyses of the consistency and interrelations among the main concepts and variables. Obviously, 100 respondents cannot represent an entire country. However, we pooled the 10 000 respondents into eight (sometimes 12) world regions. Thus, obtained differences may be somewhat more indicative of realities in these regions.

This project was an entirely unsupported initiative. To satisfy strict statistical conventions, we consider this study a rather extensive pilot project. We hope this will eventually lead to a more representative study in the future. Less representative samples (like even smaller focus groups) can provide a basis for explorative studies which may open up new research fields.

The Sample

The survey data were collected between 1991 and 1997. We continued collecting samples over this entire period since contacting people was time-intensive. We wanted to include as many non-Western samples as possible to avoid a Western bias in the results. But in non-Western countries, questionnaires are unfamiliar and experience in administering them is often lacking (especially in Belarus and Russia). Therefore, it sometimes took years before we received the completed questionnaires.

Our final sample included 9713 respondents from 44 countries. Respondents' ages ranged from 13 to over 65, although the majority was between 18 and 27 (university student ages). A few samples of younger high school students were included, as well as some groups of part-time students, who tended to be much older, many over 35 years of age. Both sexes were equally represented, with slightly more females (53 per cent) than males (47 per cent).

There was also a reasonable variation in the types of studies and professional interests of the respondents. Most (56 per cent) came from unspecified general studies programs, but there were also psychology (12 per cent) and political science (11 per cent) students since most of our contacts were from the social sciences. Also included were some technical or vocational (6 per cent), secondary school (8 per cent) and older part-time (7 per cent) students.

Respondents rated their parents' SES relatively high, mainly as upper middle class (48 per cent). The lower 'working' classes were consistently under-represented (17 per cent). This was common for most university samples in these 44 countries. The remaining students were from the lower middle (29 per cent) and upper (7 per cent) classes. Most students had college/university-educated parents (52 per cent). Fewer students had fathers with just high school (or secondary) education (31 per cent); respondents whose fathers only had primary education were a minority (17 per cent). These data confirm that our students were mainly from the better educated and upper middle classes of the surveyed societies. Although not surprising, this consistency of university background over the 44 countries is noteworthy.

Past research (especially in the 1960s and 1970s) on students often produced a dominance of left-wingers. By contrast, our 1990s sample shows about equal left- (28 per cent) and right-wing (31 per cent) preferences; therefore, political interest is more balanced. More remarkably (probably more in line with the political scene of the 1990s), the largest group (41 per cent) has no left- or right-wing leanings especially among the very young, women, and those from former communist countries.

The samples came from large and small countries. Countries with fewer than ten million inhabitants had 15 per cent of the respondents; from larger countries, the percentages were: 23 per cent (10-20 million), 19 per cent (20-50 million), 17 per cent (50-100 million), and 27 per cent (over 100 million). Most respondents came from countries where Christianity (especially Roman Catholicism) is (or was) historically dominant. This is not so remarkable since the Judeo-Christian heritage is a key part of Western culture. Some non-Western religions (Islam and Hinduism) are also represented (see Table 2.2).

Table 2.2. Dominant religions in respondents' countries (N = 44)

Religion	Respondents	Percentage
Christian Protestant	2724	28
Christian Roman Catholic	3761	39
Christian Orthodox	2144	22
Buddhist, Shinto, Confucian	195	2
Islam	600	6
Hindu	289	3
Total	9713	100

Using Huntington's (1996) nine world civilization categories, 61 per cent of our respondents live in Western civilizations, 8 per cent in Latin American, 4 per cent in African, 6 per cent in Islamic, 1 per cent in Sinic, 3 per cent in Hindu, 16 per cent in orthodox (Christian), and 1 per cent in Japanese. In terms of Western and non-Western civilizations, our sample has a rather high percentage of non-Western respondents (39 per cent). As many international surveys are often limited to Western countries, our survey better represents non-Westerners who are too often ignored in Western research on democratic and related political, cultural, and social attitudes.

The questionnaires were coded using the same format during this six year period. We rigorously checked and tested the files for any coding errors. To make sense of the results and to test our hypotheses, we applied data reduction methods (mainly factor analysis and reliability analysis).

The Project Concepts

The main variables of this survey resulted from previous investigations, theoretical assumptions, and new empirical analyses. For the constructed scales, we will present factor-analytic and reliability results, both the Cronbach alpha and an alpha-30 estimate. This is the estimated reliability if the scale contained 30 items with the mean inter-item correlation of the original scale. The alpha-30 categories are: 'very strong' (1.00 to .95), 'strong' (.95 to .90), 'moderately strong' (.90 to .85), 'weak' (.85 to .80), and 'very weak' (less than .80). Original scales with reliabilities lower than .60 qualify as 'potential scales' which need improvement.

Main Issues

Most statements in the questionnaire (see Appendix) were related to democratic and authoritarian issues, political repression and militarism, multiculturalism and racism, and equalitarianism and social hierarchy. Factor analysis showed six factors that were named psychological authoritarianism, political repression, militarism, multiculturalism, democratic attitudes, and attitudes about a democratic political system (see Table 2.3).

Psychological Authoritarianism

The first variable was called psychological authoritarianism (see Table 2.4), since it included most of the Adorno et al. items, widely used in previous international surveys (Meloen 1983, 1991a; Middendorp 1991). It is based mainly on psychological research over several decades (Meloen 1991a). Short and unidimensional, it was one of the better performing scales in the survey (Cronbach alpha of .76), and can be classified as 'strong' (alpha-30 of .92).

Table 2.3. Factor-analysis survey of democracy and authoritarianism

Factor	1 Psychological Authoritarian Attitudes	2 Political Repression	3 Democratic Attitudes	4 Multicul- turalism	5 Militarism	6 Democratic System Attitudes
IT37	.57					
IT46	.57					
IT38	.55					
IT35	.54					
IT44	.52					
IT15	.47				.37	
IT14	.44					
IT40	.41	.37				
IT20		.52				
IT11		.49				
IT32		.48				
IT9	.35	.46				
IT8		.44				
IT2		.43				
IT12		.41				
IT34						
IT43			.70			
IT36			.63			
IT45			.57			
IT39			.52			
IT42			.51			
IT33				.55		
IT13				.54		
IT3				.50		
IT19				.49		
IT18				.47		
IT31				.42		
IT47				.40		
IT17				.36		
IT21						
IT6					.57	
IT5					.51	
IT7					.48	
IT41						
IT10						.69
IT16						.62
IT1						.51

Notes: Rotated factor matrix; six factors, Kaiser normalization; explained variance 37.3%; only loadings >.35 shown

Table 2.4. Authoritarian attitudes: psychological authoritarianism (AUTH8)

1. IT14   Freedom of speech does not justify someone's teaching foreign or disloyal ideas in our schools.
2. IT15   Patriotism and loyalty to our established ways of life are the most important requirements for good citizenship.
3. IT35   Young people sometimes get rebellious ideas, but as they grow up, they ought to get over them and settle down.
4. IT37   Most of our social problems would be solved if we could somehow get rid of the immoral, crooked, and feebleminded people.
5. IT38   What this country needs most, more than laws and political programs, are a few courageous, tireless, devoted leaders in whom the people can put their faith.
6. IT40   A person who has bad manners, habits, and breeding can hardly expect to get along with decent people.
7. IT44   Sex crimes (such as rape and attacks on children) deserve more than mere imprisonment; such criminals ought to be publicly whipped or worse.
8. IT46   If people would talk less and work more, everybody would be better off.

Notes: 8 items; number of respondents = 8710; 7 point scale; alpha = .76; mean inter-item correlation = .28; alpha-30 = .92 or a strong scale.

Political Repression

The items in this scale (see Table 2.5) reflect authoritarian tendencies similar to the previous scale. However, the difference is that statements in the political repression scale emphasize psychological issues less and stress political measures of repression. Abolishing minority rights, outlawing political parties, and intentionally using force make this scale both more severe and political in nature. Other themes here reflect rather cynical and elitist views, often associated with the 'tough' nature of the political measures, which are both violent and aggressive. This scale alpha of .66 is somewhat less internally consistent than the former and is classified as a moderately strong scale.

Militarism

The content of this factor is quite clearly related to core military issues: military budgets, using the military against civilians, and the use of force in general (see Table 2.6). This scale is too short to produce higher reliability levels, but the co-variance of the items in the factor analysis procedure appears to be very consistent. Therefore, we include this scale here without any hesitation. The scale could be improved in an expanded international survey. It classifies as a potentially moderately strong scale.

Table 2.5. Authoritarian attitudes: political repression (REPRES7)

1. IT2   The majority should abolish minority rights if they choose to do so.
2. IT8   Most people don't know what is good for them.
3. IT9   It may be necessary to outlaw or ban certain political parties/groups who are likely to cause public disorder or trouble.
4. IT11   Regardless of what some people say, there are certain races, nationalities, or religions that just will not properly mix with our way of life.
5. IT12   Our true and traditional way of life is disappearing so fast that we may have to use force to save it.
6. IT20   We certainly owe respect to higher classes of people in our society, especially when the honor and positions they have come from birth, family, traditions, and custom.
7. IT32   People can be divided into two distinct classes: the weak and the strong.

Notes: 7 items; number of respondents = 8683; 7 point scale; alpha = .66; mean inter-item correlation = .21; alpha-30 = .89 or a moderately strong scale

Table 2.6. Authoritarian attitudes: militarism (MIL3)

1. IT5   If our government has to economize, cutting the military budget should be a high priority. (reversed item).
2. IT6   The best way to prevent war is to make sure that one is at least as powerful as one's possible opponent.
3. IT7   It should be allowed to use the army to maintain law and order.

Notes: 3 items; number of respondents = 9041; 7 point scale; alpha = .42; mean inter-item correlation = .19; alpha-30 = .88 or a potentially moderately strong scale

Multiculturalism

This factor included several items related to multiculturalism and anti-racism (see Table 2.7). Although not all items refer specifically to multiculturalism, multicultural equalitarianism is an important common denominator in this scale. It produced a moderate reliability level (alpha of .62) and classifies as a moderately strong scale. It showed consistent results in analyses performed across various test populations.

Democratic Attitudes

This scale was designed after Roe's (1975) model. The highest loading items were used for this short scale (see Table 2.8). Democratic attitudes are considered here mainly as those favoring practical political decentralization, reducing the power of political elites, and popular decision making. In fact, these are more fundamental principles of democracy than voting rights or a parliament. These aspects of formal institutionalized democracy appear to be a separate factor. This democratic decentralization attitude regularly appeared and existed independently in our analyses. Although this scale shows only modest reliability (alpha of .62), it still classifies as a strong scale.

Table 2.7. Multiculturalism (MCULT8)

1. IT3   It will do us all a lot of good if people of all races, nationalities, religions, and classes attend private or government-run schools together everywhere in our country.
2. IT13 People who hate our way of life should have a chance to be heard in public.
3. IT17 Although it may be true about fine race horses, there are not any breeds of people who are naturally better than others.
4. IT18 There should be laws against marriage between persons of different races (reversed).
5. IT19 When it comes to things that count most, all races, religious groups, and nationalities are pretty much alike and equal.
6. IT31 It is a moral duty to care about the needy.
7. IT33 One should be concerned with the wishes of the minorities in our society at all times.
8. IT47 Every individual has a right for self-determination.

Notes: 8 items; number of respondents = 8732; 7 point scale; alpha = .62; mean inter-item correlation = .17; alpha-30 =.86 or a moderately strong scale

Table 2.8. Democratic attitudes (DEMOAT5)

1. IT36 Our society can only make further social progress if the power is no longer shared among a small elite.
2. IT39 Political power should be decentralized as much as possible.
3. IT42 Although there are differences between people there is no reason to grant more influence to some than to others.
4. IT43 It is a pity that politics are made by small groups of influential people.
5. IT45 The people should be directly involved when decisions are made that concern all.

Notes: 5 items; number of respondents = 9213; 7 point scale; alpha = .62; mean inter-item correlation = .25; alpha-30 = .91 or a strong scale

Attitudes toward a Democratic System

This concept was only marginally represented in our survey (see Table 2.9). Yet these three items co-varied strongly in all our analyses and appeared to be independent of other democratic attitudinal clusters. This warranted its inclusion as a separate factor. The content clearly supports democracy as a political system and evaluates its political institutions. Democratic government is valued positively, but its institutions are critically weighed since most respondents tend to disagree that they are 'the best' in the world (except for American students who are taught in and out of school that 'we are the greatest'). The third item seems to express acceptance of this democratic deficit being rather 'common' in most democracies. 'The institutions may not be the best, but there is no better political system', it seems to suggest, as well as 'this way, we are not worse off than other democracies'. The strongest item is the first one, which is clear in its content; it states a positive orientation toward the democratic system. This scale is also too short to show high reliability. For this reason, we could as well use the main issue represented by the item (IT1 or DEMO1) on democracy as being the best form of government. However, a longer scale would likely perform better since this still classifies as a potentially moderately strong scale in the alpha-30 analysis.

Table 2.9. Attitude toward democratic system (DEMO3)

1. IT1   Democracy by far is the best form of government for our country and people.
2. IT10   Our political institutions are the best in the world.
3. IT16   Our way of life is about as good as any other.

Notes: 3 items; number of respondents = 9024; 7 point scale; alpha = .45; mean inter-item correlation = .21; alpha-30 = .89 or a potentially moderately strong scale

Evaluation of Political Leaders

A political leaning can be inferred more indirectly from the ratings of well-known political figures (see Table 2.10). A number of dictators, political reformers, and US presidents were included in this survey. Three factors emerged from our factor analysis, neatly clustering around each type of leader as expected. Interestingly enough, the dictators included both left- and right-wingers, while the reformers were not only very popular among students, but also came from very different political scenarios (apartheid, southern US racism, Indian colonialism, and Soviet communism). Their common nonviolent efforts were well recognized. We excluded the ratings of Karl Marx (not really a politician), and Napoleon Bonaparte (too far back in history and a more problematic figure). The US presidents surprisingly loaded on one factor, even though some were conservative Republicans (Reagan and Eisenhower) and others more liberal Democrats (Kennedy and Roosevelt). The reason for this grouping was not clear to us and we were uncertain about them as a group (perhaps this is an expression of a general pro- or anti-Americanism). They were moderately popular, somewhat less so than the real reformers, but still very positively rated cross-nationally.

Table 2.10. Factor analysis of political leaders' ratings

Code Variable	Factor 1 Reformers	Factor 2 US Presidents	Factor 3 Dictators
MANDELA	.78		
KING	.76		
GANDHI	.74		
GORBACHEV	.49		
EISENHOWER		.76	
ROOSEVELT		.74	
REAGAN		.70	
KENNEDY		.62	
STALIN			.76
HUSSEIN			.68
MAO			.67
HITLER			.66

Notes: rotated factor matrix; 3 factors; Kaiser normalization; explained variance 52.9%; only loadings >.35 shown

Evaluation of Dictators

The dictators were obviously rated extremely negatively, especially Adolph Hitler (see Table 2.11). Joseph Stalin, Mao Tse Tung, and Saddam Hussein also were evaluated very harshly. It is hard to believe there still are supporters for these political criminals, but although their numbers are low, they still exist. The scale separates those favoring dictatorial tendencies from those without such leanings. The dictator scale was consistent internally (alpha of .64) and qualified as a strong unidimensional scale.

Table 2.11. Evaluations of dictators (DICTATOR)

1. MAO   Mao Tse Tung
2. STALIN   Joseph Stalin
3. HITLER   Adolph Hitler
4. HUSSEIN Saddam Hussein

Notes: 4 items; number of respondents = 8506; 9 point rating scale; alpha = .64; mean inter-item correlation = .31; alpha-30 = .93 or a strong scale

Evaluation of Reformers

The ratings of political reformers were also one-dimensional (see Table 2.12). Mohandas 'Mahatma' Gandhi, Nelson Mandela, and Martin Luther King were extremely popular. Mikhail Gorbachev was not very popular for our Russian samples, but elsewhere was still positively valued. The reformer scale was quite reliable for a very short scale (alpha of .68) and classifies as another strong scale.

Table 2.12. Evaluation of reformers (REFORMER)

1. GORBACHEV   Mikhail Gorbachev
2. KING   Martin Luther King
3. MANDELA   Nelson Mandela
4. GANDHI   Mohandas 'Mahatma' Gandhi

Notes: 4 items; number of respondents = 8511; 9 point rating scale; alpha = .68; mean inter-item correlation = .36; alpha-30 = .94 or a strong scale

Political Self-Ratings

More revealing than indirect preferences for political leaders or political issues, may be political self-ratings (see Table 2.13). We included several. Somewhat to our surprise, not all loaded on one factor, although unidimensionality was often assumed. There appear to be at least two coherent empirically derived factors.

Table 2.13. Factor analysis of political self ratings

		Factor 1 *Self-Right-Wing*	Factor 2 *Self-Multiculturalist*
Self-Militarist	SMILIT	.69	
Self-Authoritarian	SAUTH	.62	
Self-Right-Wing	SRIGHTW	.60	
Self-Elitist	SELITE	.57	
Self-Conservative	SCONS	.44	-.35
Self-Cosmopolitan	SCOSMO		.77
Self-Internationalist	SINTER		.76
Self-Multiculturalist	SMCULT		.64

Notes: rotated factor matrix; 2 factors; Kaiser normalization; explained variance 45.0%; only loadings >.35 shown

Self-Rating as Right-Wing

The combination of rating oneself right-wing, militarist, authoritarian, conservative, and elitist lead to a 'self-right-wing' factor (see Table 2.14). Most such tendencies seem to converge as expected. This combination of preferences probably can be interpreted as general authoritarianism if we use a 'broad' definition. The self-right-wing scale was not highly reliable, but it is a potentially moderately strong scale. Unfortunately, it will be hard to find additional items since so much of the political spectrum is already included.

Table 2.14. Self-rating as right-wing (SRIGHT5)

1. SCONS   self-rating conservative vs liberal
2. SRIGHTW   self-rating right-wing vs left-wing
3. SAUTH   self-rating authoritarian vs anti-authoritarian
4. SMILIT   self-rating militarist vs pacifist
5. SELITE   self-rating elitist vs equalitarian

Notes: 5 items; number of respondents = 8395; 7 point rating scale; alpha = .58; mean inter-item correlation = .22; alpha-30 = .89 or a potentially moderately strong scale

Self-Rating as Multicultural

Surprisingly, three self-ratings clustered on considering oneself international-ist, cosmopolitan, and multicultural (see Table 2.15). This factor may include broad areas of world-mindedness. In the past, such a factor was often identi-fied as part of a general left-/right-wing political schema or cognitive map. Despite including only three items, the scale is relatively reliable (alpha of .60 and a high inter-item correlation of .34). It could qualify as a strong scale, provided similar items could be found to add to the measure.

Table 2.15. Self-rating as multicultural (SMCULT3)

1. SINTER   self-rating internationalist vs isolationist
2. SMCULT   self-rating multiculturalist vs nationalist
3. SCOSMO   self-rating cosmopolitan vs provincial

Notes: 3 items; number of respondents = 8694; 7 point rating scale; alpha = .60; mean inter-item correlation = .34; alpha-30 = .94 or a strong scale

Democratic, Authoritarian, and Multicultural Attitudes

One may wonder whether our scales adequately sample theoretical fields of democratic, authoritarian and multicultural attitudes. Since we want to assess their relationship to certain educational tendencies, we must answer this question. We conducted a factor analysis to extract the main underlying fac-tors (see Table 2.16). This did not entirely lead us to all our expected factors.

A second factor, authoritarian attitudes, was clearly a separate element, including psychological authoritarianism, political repression, militarism, and support for dictators. This sinister combination needs little comment from us. But the first factor included both democratic attitudes and multiculturalism. The difference between the first and third factor seems to be that this latter factor includes support for the formal democratic political system. The first factor, by contrast, refers to a broader spectrum of attitudes (multiculturalism and decentralization of power, support for democracy, and multiracial reformers) more basic to democracy. Since both self-definitions of multiculturalism and multicultural attitudes appear in the first factor, it was called the democratic multiculturalism factor. One may argue multiculturalism is a necessary prerequisite for a pluralistic democracy since most anti-democratic governments routinely oppress political, ethnic, national, or religious minorities.

Table 2.16. Democratic, authoritarian, and multicultural attitudes

		Factor 1 Democratic Multiculturalism	Factor 2 General Authoritarianism	Factor 3 Pro-demo- cratic system
Democratic Attitudes	DEMOAT5	.77		
Multiculturalism	MCULT8	.69		
Self-Right-Wing	SRIGHT5	-.68		
Support Reformers	REFORMER	.58	.43	
Self-Multicultural	SMCULT3	.47		
Authoritarian Attitudes	AUTH8		.86	
Political Repression	REPRES7		.66	
Militarism	MIL3		.56	
Support Dictators	DICTATOR		.42	
Pro-Democratic System	DEMO3			.84

Notes: rotated factor matrix; 3 factors; Kaiser normalization; explained variance 56.8%; only loadings >.40 shown

General Authoritarianism

Psychological authoritarianism, political repression, and militarism appear to be part of one larger factor. In many analyses, the separate attitudinal items for these variables were part of the first principal component (PC), too. Apparently, the items can best be considered part of a 'second order' factor of general authoritarianism. Authoritarianism concepts that have been used (Adorno et al., 1950; Rokeach, 1960; Altemeyer, 1988, 1996) indicate that many political issues relate to authoritarianism (Middendorp 1978, 1991). For this reason, a general authoritarianism scale (AUTH20) was constructed, including 20 items from this first (PC) factor. This new scale showed a remarkable level of internal consistency (Cronbach alpha of .83). It is classified as a moderately strong scale.

Democratic Multiculturalism

Our multiculturalism factor included both multicultural and democratic attitudes. We explored the option that it could be considered another 'second order' attitudinal scale. This was not impossible since our democratic multiculturalism scale (MCDEMO13) showed reasonable reliability (alpha of .71); it was also a moderately strong scale.

For reasons of interpretation, we will show separately both the results of the first order variables (psychological authoritarianism, political repression, militarism, democratic attitudes, multiculturalism) and the second order ones (general authoritarianism and democratic multiculturalism). The less well operationalized variable (democratic system) appeared independent in both our first and second order factor analysis. Therefore, this variable will be included, but separately from those first mentioned.

Political Attitudes toward Education

A separate and important issue in this survey concerns attitudes toward certain types of education. The items were taken from previous OECD/CERI surveys (Farnen, 1994b, pp. 86-102; Wagner, 1990, pp.1-13). They were phrased both in a liberal and conservative-nationalist direction. The included items appeared to be part of two separate factors (see Table 2.17). The liberal items all loaded on the liberal education attitudinal factor and, conversely, nationalist items on the nationalist one. We may assume that the two hypothesized factors are appropriately depicted here.

Table 2.17. Factor analysis of political attitudes toward education

	FACTOR 1 Nationalist Education Orientation	FACTOR 2 Liberal Education Orientation
IT29	.68	
IT25	.68	
IT23	.67	
IT27	.51	
IT24		.67
IT22		.65
IT28		.53
IT30		.50
IT26		.50

Notes: rotated factor matrix; 2 factors; Kaiser normalization; explained variance 38.5%; only loadings >.35 shown

Liberal Attitudes toward Policy Positions on Education

The issues in this scale involve teaching peace and freedom, respect for minority groups, and eliminating nationalistic themes from education (see Table 2.18). These can clearly be identified as liberal positions. Less clear, but still often associated with this ideological stance, are methods of teaching that help students become more active and critical toward the world around them. The scale is not highly reliable, but it showed enough coherence in our factor analysis. It should be improved since it seems to include more than one clear issue. Presently, it qualifies as potentially moderately strong scale.

Table 2.18. Liberal education attitudes (EDLIB5)

1. IT22 Our schools ought to teach us more about promoting individual freedom, popular participation, keeping the peace, and achieving economic equality and justice for all.
2. IT24 Our schools ought to teach us more about the United Nations, comparative government, and keeping the peace through international organizations and peacekeeping alliances.
3. IT26 With respect to members of minority groups, parents of minority children should become partners with the schools by helping to determine school curricula and policies and by becoming more directly involved in the schools (e.g., by teaching a course).
4. IT28 Concerning teaching and testing methods in our schools, process is more important than content so that students are active, involved, and critical learners and so that assessment of results is based on less formal means, including student self-assessment.
5. IT30 Concerning history, social study, and civic education, we should eliminate isolationist, provincial, and nationalistic themes from the curriculum so that students can learn more about international topics (such as the UN, EEC, PLO, OAU, CSCE, GCC, and OPEC).

Notes: 5 items; number of respondents = 8945; 7 point scale; alpha = .49; mean inter-item correlation = .17; alpha-30 = .85 or a potentially moderately strong scale

Table 2.19. Nationalistic education attitudes (EDNAT4)

1. IT23 Our schools already teach too much about other lands, peoples, cultures, and races.
2. IT25 With respect to minority languages and cultures, our schools ought to prohibit such languages for individual learning, classroom instruction, and separate school subjects.
3. IT27 Concerning teaching and testing methods in the schools, students should be grouped by ability, should learn basic facts, and should take competitive subject examinations so everybody knows where they stand in a course and teachers can be held accountable.
4. IT29 Concerning history, social studies, and civic education, teaching about other countries' history, government, cultures and peoples is far less important than teaching about patriotism, our nation's glorious history, and our outstanding military achievements.

Notes: 4 items; number of respondents = 8998; 7 point scale; alpha = .53; mean inter-item correlation = .22; alpha-30 = .89 or a potentially moderately strong scale

Nationalist Attitudes toward Policy Positions on Education

In this scale, the issues range from xenophobic tendencies to glorification of nationalism and militarism (see Table 2.19). Such issues can best be understood in terms of conceptualizing a very negative type of narrow and mean-spirited nationalism. Hard-boiled teaching methods may not be directly related, but much of this was associated with rather traditional and conservative teaching methods. This scale is also not highly reliable, but it seems to perform somewhat better than its liberal counterpart. It classifies as a potentially moderately strong scale. It should be improved in any follow-up survey.

Translation Test

One might assume that translated questionnaires perform less well than those in the original language. This could result from factors such as minor errors or translating too literally instead of translating the functional meaning of an item. Much has been written about this phenomenon in cross-cultural studies, so we were aware of it from the start (Meloen and Veenman, 1990).

We cross-checked for gross translation errors. After data collection, we computed reliabilities for the main variables in the English and translated questionnaires. In case of errors or misunderstandings, translated ones should perform less well and their reliabilities be substantially lower. We tested this for the two main 'second order' factors: general authoritarianism and democratic multiculturalism scales (see Table 2.20). In general, there were three categories: English speakers answering the original English questionnaire, partly English speakers (as the second national or personal language) answering the English version, and non-English speakers answering a translated questionnaire in their own language. The last group was divided into those who spoke Western European (not English) languages (German, Swedish, French, Spanish) and other languages (Russian, Hindi, Japanese, Arabic).

Results show (Table 2.20) hardly any differences in obtained reliabilities between the English original and translated questionnaires. Both general authoritarianism (alphas around .80) and multiculturalism (alphas around .70) do not weaken or collapse. Apparently, they were measured equally well with the original English questionnaire and the translations. Surprisingly, a translation tends to show slightly better results if it is in the respondent's own language, rather than if partly English-speaking respondents answered an English language questionnaire. This was the case in India and Kenya where English is one of the national languages, but it also happened in Portugal in English university classes. In all, no substantial differences between alphas appeared. Our translation efforts seem to have only minor effects, if any.

Table 2.20 Reliabilities across translated questionnaires

Questionnaire Language	Language of Respondents	General Authoritarianism		Democratic Multiculturalism	
		Respondents	Alpha	Respondents	Alpha
1. English original	English	1417	.83	1462	.70
2. English original	Partly English	1256	.78	1284	.69
3. Translated total	Non-English total	5741	.83	5556	.71
Translated					
3a.West Euro	West Euro	2303	.82	2480	.70
3b.Non-West Euro	Non-West Euro	3253	.80	3261	.70
Totals		*8229*	*.83*	*8487*	*.71*

Notes: non-English total = non-English West European + non-English non-West European; general authoritarianism = AUTH20; democratic multiculturalism = MCDEMO13

CONCLUSIONS

Between 1991 and 1997, we collected data from 44 countries from nearly 10 000 students on democratic attitudes, authoritarianism, multiculturalism, liberal and nationalist tendencies in education, support for dictators and reformers, political self-ratings, and social background. We evaluated their attitudes in light of the international drive toward democratization. Statistical analysis supported the existence of the main concepts of attitudes toward democracy, authoritarianism, and multiculturalism. General and psychological authoritarianism, dictator and reformer ratings, and both multicultural attitudes and composite self-ratings on multiculturalism were strong variables. Moderately performing ones were democratic attitudes, general multiculturalism, and political repression. Attitudes about the democratic system, militarism, self-rating as right-wing, and liberal and nationalist education could be improved in a future more definitive test internationally on national samples. A test showed that translations had little effect on results. Therefore, our translations seem to have been quite adequate for the stated purposes.

3 Political and Educational Systems in 44 Countries

INTRODUCTION

This chapter reviews key features of the 44 countries we surveyed. Descriptions of political and educational systems give a general context. Major political/educational features appear in Tables 3.1 and 3.2 and Figure 3.1. Key sources for this summary are Hunter (*Statesman's Yearbook*, 1994-5), *Europa Yearbook* (1995), Kurian (ed.) (*World Education Encyclopedia*, 1988), and Banks et al. (*Political Handbook of the World*, 1995, 1997). Defense costs from the worldwide web's CIA Fact Book (*odci.gov/cia/publications/factbook/country-frame.html*) report reveal that in 1996, $750 billion (one-third by the US; 2 per cent of the gross world product) was spent on arms. For political/educational analysis, we used *Freedom in the World* (Freedom House, 1995, 1996, 1998) reports on civil rights/liberties; *Prospects of Democracy* (Vanhanen, 1997); *Encyclopedia of Human Rights* (Lawson, 1996); and *Political Parties of the World* (Day, German, and Campbell, 1996).

Figure 3.1. Freedom ratings of 44 targeted countries. Source: Freedom House (1996).

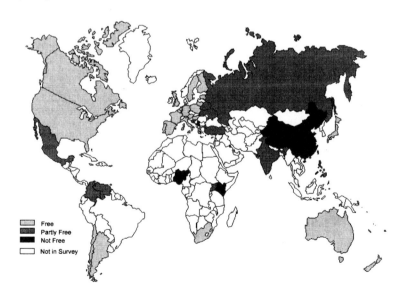

Free
Partly Free
Not Free
Not in Survey

Table 3.1. Major political/educational features of 44 surveyed countries

Country	Years School Required	% Literate	Education $ over Military $	Democracy Rating Freedom House 1995-96	Vanhanen
Argentina	7	95	yes	partly free	yes
Australia	10	99	yes	yes	yes
Austria	9	98	yes	yes	yes
Belgium	8	99	yes	yes	yes
Belorussia	11	98	no	not free	no
Canada	10	99	yes	yes	yes
Chile	8	90	yes	yes	yes
PR China	0	75	yes	not free	developing
Colombia	6	91	yes	partly free	yes
Costa Rica	9	93	yes	yes	yes
Croatia	9	90	no	partly free	yes
Estonia	9	99	yes	yes	yes
Finland	9	99	yes	yes	yes
France	10	99	yes	yes	yes
Germany	10	98	yes	yes	yes
Greece	9	93	no	yes	yes
Hong Kong	9	77	yes	partly free	not rated
Hungary	10	98	yes	yes	yes
India	5	36	no	partly free	not fully
Italy	8	93	yes	yes	yes
Japan	9	99	yes	yes	yes
Kenya	0	69	no	not free	no
Kuwait	8	73	no	partly free	yes
Lithuania	10	98	yes	yes	yes
Martinique	10	93	yes	yes	yes
Mexico	6	74	yes	partly free	yes
Netherlands	10	99	yes	yes	yes
New Zealand	10	99	yes	yes	yes
Nigeria	6	51	yes	not free	no
Philippines	6	95	yes	partly free	yes
Poland	8	98	yes	yes	yes
Portugal	6	85	yes	yes	yes
Russia	10	98	yes	partly free	no
Serbia	8	98	no	not free	no
South Africa	10	76	yes	yes	yes
Spain	10	97	yes	yes	yes
Sweden	9	99	yes	yes	yes
Taiwan	6	94	yes	partly free	yes
Turkey	8	91	no	partly free	yes
Uganda	0	62	yes	partly free	no
Ukraine	9	98	yes	partly free	no
UK	11	99	yes	yes	yes
US	10	98	yes	yes	yes
Venezuela	6	86	yes	partly free	yes

EIGHT WORLD REGIONS

North American Region

This region is represented in our survey by Canada and the US. **Canada**, a democracy, was politically connected to the UK until 1982. The population is diverse (40 per cent British; 27 per cent French; 20 per cent European; 1.5 per cent Amerind; 11.5 per cent Asian/other); 20 per cent are foreign born; two-thirds speak English, one-quarter French, and 13 per cent another language; 47 per cent are Roman Catholic and 41 per cent Protestants. Concentrated in the east, most of the population lives within 100 miles of the US border. Provincial legislators are responsible for the educational system. There is a system for state, public, federal, and private religious schools (with some state support). Approximately 40 per cent of the school enrollment is in denominational schools, mostly in Quebec. Canada has a free press, employs progressive educational methods, and spends about $1000 (US) per capita on public education. The educational system meets the needs of those with handicaps, native peoples, ethnic, and linguistic minorities.

The **United States of America** (US), a democratic federal republic, enjoys regional, ethnic, religious, economic, political, and cultural diversity. Three government branches (president, congress, and supreme court) have separate and concurrent powers. The free print and electronic media are mainly profit-oriented. Declining public participation in elections is a democratic deficit. Education is financed and managed by states and municipalities. Minority students (native Americans, blacks, and Hispanics) receive less educational benefits than whites and Asians. Schools serve linguistic minorities; improve educational quality; implement new science, mathematics, and technology programs; and provide programs for special, bilingual, and talented students. Students were exposed to many civics, government, and social science courses, but recent trends favor American history and geography. These increase nationalistic orientations and depend on rote memorization of facts instead of decision making, problem solving, and critical thinking skills.

In North America, Canada and the US are developed democracies with educational systems designed to serve all, including ethnic, linguistic, and cultural minorities. The school systems of both countries undergird the democratic process and further its aims.

Latin American Region

The Latin American countries in our survey are Argentina, Chile, Colombia, Costa Rica, Martinique, Mexico, and Venezuela.

Argentina is a federal (provincial) constitutional republic with a congress, president, and federal judicial system. It is a democracy, but has been repeatedly subjected to authoritarian and/or military rule. Women are denied equal rights; nationalistic factions dominate the political parties. Argentina has territorial claims against the UK and Chile. The suppressed press and active domestic terrorist groups limit the quality of democracy. Schools are supported with national and provincial funds. They suffer high drop-out rates; only 44 per cent of the secondary age group is in school. Most secondary students are enrolled in technical education; textbook production is highly centralized; there is no teacher shortage; parochial education plays an increasing role; and recent curriculum reforms downplay academic subjects.

Chile, a democracy, formerly had Marxist and military-dictatorial governments. Right- and left-wing terrorist groups are still active. TV is state-controlled; however, newspapers, radio stations, and cinemas are unregulated. Education is both public and private (mainly Roman Catholic), class-based, politically dominated, either democratic, Marxist, fascist/corporate, or nationalistic. Over 60 per cent of school-aged children are under tuition. The education system strives to produce a good worker, citizen, and 'patriot'. The Ministry of Education administers the system; textbook production is centralized. Although decentralization and privatization efforts have increased, most support for education is still centralized.

Colombia is a partly free, transitional democracy. Voter registration and turnout rates are relatively low. The competitive multiparty system includes a former guerilla organization (M-19), communist, socialist, women's, and workers parties. Violent rebel and clandestine groups are very active. While the radio and press are privately owned and free, the TV system is state-run. Schooling is under national control, direction, and funding. Primary schools are oversubscribed; secondary schools enroll about half of the eligible age group; universities are expanding. Education is class- and urban-based; nearly half the secondary enrollments are in Catholic parochial schools.

Costa Rica, a democracy, has 'police', but no 'official' army. There is a state ministry for 'worship'. National funds support local school councils. In its OAS role, Costa Rica has opposed dictatorships; been allied with other liberal, democratic regimes; and provided Latin American peace brokers. It has two major and 12 minor political parties. News media are uncensored, but the government supervises radio and TV. Discrimination in education is forbidden. History and geography help develop civic competence and love of country; recognize citizenship duties, rights, and liberties; respect human dignity; and promote democratic values.

French Martinique is a democratic, French possession. France pays for defense and appoints a prefect to work with popularly elected general and regional councils. Martinique sends representatives to the French assembly. The spirit of right-wing nationalistic, independence, or socialist equality runs high. Martinique is subject to high unemployment, frequent riots and strikes, and dependence on sugar cane and banana exports. Most elections feature high nonvoting rates (75-85 per cent). There is a colonial judicial system. Radio and TV broadcasting is licensed; mass media are free and uncensored.

Mexico is a partly free, transitional democracy of 31 states (each with its own constitution, governor, and legislature) and a federal district with an appointed governor. The political scene features assassinations, violence, graft, corruption, and drug deals. News media are free, but government-regulated. Mexican ideology governed education, focusing on religious, nationalistic, and socialist themes. Education used history, geography, and biographies of heroes to teach patriotism, unity, participation, and revolutionary ideology.

Venezuela is a partly free, transitional democracy. Voting is legally compulsory, but unenforced. Coups, assassinations, dictatorships, corruption, and economic crises are common. News media are 'free', but censorship prevails in emergencies. Self-supervised radio and TV are federally controlled. Schools (controlled by the Central Ministry of Education) use rote memorization and are examination-based, dogmatic, and authoritarian. High attrition and drop-out rates (50 and 75 per cent in secondary and primary schools, respectively) prevail. For 40 years, Venezuela has attempted to mount a democratic 'revolution by education', but has not succeeded.

In Latin America, Argentina, Costa Rica, Chile, Argentina, and Martinique are increasingly democratic and less authoritarian. They spend much of the national treasure on education. Colombia, Mexico, and Venezuela are more elitist, violent, corrupt; less democratic; and likely to limit press freedom and civil rights. School systems are elitist, centralized, undemocratic; they are one-party and often parochial-school dominated or dependent.

Western European (North) Region

Seven European Union countries represent this region: Austria, Belgium, Finland, Germany, the Netherlands, Sweden, and the UK.

Austria is a democracy with nine provinces, including Vienna. All telecommunications, radio, and TV are state-controlled and licensed, but operate freely. Media privatization is underway. The federal ministry of education controls and supervises schooling. Schooling lasts six days per week and is free, as are state-supplied textbooks.

Belgium is a democracy. Mandatory voting (with fines) is in effect. The judicial system is based on the French model. The seven larger and seven smaller political parties are ethnic-based, including French, Dutch, bilingual, and German-speaking groups plus the Flemish Bloc (VB). The ethnic/party-based press is not censored. The government supports three (French, Dutch, and German) radio-TV systems. VB militants victimize many city-dwelling Moroccans and Turks. Anti-immigrant political groups are getting stronger. The national budget supports public, Catholic parochial, and ethnic schools. The 75 per cent Catholic population is composed of Walloon (33 per cent), Flemish (55 per cent), and mixed/other (12 per cent). The education of foreign/migrant children (20-34 per cent of the urban school population) is a major responsibility. There are many textbook choices, just as there are different foreign language radio, TV, and print media. The primary school curriculum stresses religion, ethics, environment, geography, history; secondary schools offer social education, psychology, economics, and mass media courses.

Finland, historically dominated by Sweden and Russia, perpetuates past political conflicts. The major three socialist and eight nonsocialist parties form coalitions, leaving six minor parties out of power. Finns fear Russian nationalists and seek new ties with the West through EU and NATO associate membership. Its press is free and unencumbered. Schooling is bilingual when needed. Instruction is provided in religion, environmental studies, history, social studies, civics, citizenship, and geography, but technical and agricultural training dominates. A newer upper-secondary school curriculum allows electives. The education system is controlled via a ministerial bureaucracy at the provincial/municipal level along with elected local school boards which include teachers. The state reimburses municipalities at 75-85 per cent of the basic costs of schooling.

Germany (FRG) is a democracy. The 16 states and lower house select the president; the lower house designates the prime minister. About 20 per cent of federal and state legislators are female. The judicial structure includes federal constitutional, supreme, and inferior courts. Civil rights/liberties can be abridged during national emergencies; certain political parties can be outlawed if they endanger 'the basic libertarian democratic order'. There are six major and several minor political parties and extremist groups, including four violence-prone neo-Nazi groups. Germany has had Europe's highest immigration rates. The press is free, except to those who misuse it to destroy the democratic system. Conglomerates dominate the print media, but radio and TV stations are more competitive. While Germany tightened restrictions for asylum seekers, it loosened requirements for citizenship for non-Germans. Although part of the national budget supports education, most funding comes from the 16 *Länder* and municipalities. The *Länder* control education, resulting in variations in curricula, structure, and organization. School attendance is 100 per cent at primary and 94 per cent at secondary levels. Former GDR schools now conform with the Western system and values.

The parliament of **the Netherlands** is chosen democratically through universal suffrage. The free, open news media are partly religion-based. The four major and five minor political parties form coalitions. About 6 per cent of the population immigrated from Morocco, Spain, Turkey, Yugoslavia, Surinam, Antilles, and Molucca; also, there are Sinti/Roma residents. Municipalities supervise public schools; school boards administer publicly funded religious schools (70 per cent of all schools). The educational system is devoted to increasing students' knowledge about international and Dutch institutions, democracy, and responsibilities. Schools emphasize equal educational opportunity; however, some find the system elitist, at best. Despite the attention schools give to political topics, prejudice toward and ignorance of neighboring countries remains as well as a lack of interest in politics and knowledge about the EU, male-female differences, and TV news dependence.

Sweden, a democracy, recently was governed by conservative and labor party coalitions, with nine other bourgeois, socialist, or ecological parties plus three other minor leftist groups. The press is party-linked and privately owned; radio and TV (except for one private channel) is government-dominated. Sweden provides Lapps and recent immigrants with bilingual education, mother tongue, Swedish as a second language, and English instruction. Only 2 per cent of schools are private and publicly supported. Textbooks are government-approved, privately written and produced, and can be selected by each school district. Schooling is decentralized; parliament sets overall school policy; county and local boards of education play an increasingly important role. Sweden led the way in special, vocational, international, and curriculum reforms; it continues to be an educational leader in the West. Women comprise almost 50 per cent of the work force, are about 30 per cent of national and local officials, and are one-third of cabinet officials.

The **United Kingdom** (UK) is governed by a democratic parliamentary regime. Freedom of the press is limited by self-censorship; radio/TV broadcasting is provided by the BBC and independent commercial companies, subject to government control, yet independent in programming. Through the British Commonwealth, the UK has ties with its former colonies. Women have 10 per cent membership in the House of Commons, serve in cabinet posts, and served as speaker/prime minister of the Commons. The majority of English are white, but in the 1970s, Commonwealth immigrants from Africa, Pakistan, Bangladesh, the West Indies, India, and elsewhere created unanticipated economic and social effects, including racial tensions. Both public and private schools are managed by local education authorities (LEAs) of county and city governments. Both types of schools receive public funds, must pray, teach religion, but excuse recusants for 'conscience'. The UK has demanding school examinations. The private, grammar, comprehensive school battle is drawn along class, party, and ideological lines. The Conservative government introduced a core curriculum of basic studies and traditional subject matter, bypassed partisan LEAs, and politicized educational policy. Improving schools to benefit ethnic/racial minorities and adding politics and citizenship courses were new initiatives in the 1990s.

These northwest European nations are free and democratic. Each is committed to education in general and civic education in particular; each handles minority politics democratically. The relative strength of native right-wing and neo-Nazi groups and parties (forbidden, but operating in FRG, Belgium, and the UK) is a matter for social differentiation. These countries have high literacy rates, high percentages of youth in school, long life expectancies, and stable political regimes. Both FRG and the Netherlands have fully developed, active civic education programs. Sweden is a world model for dealing with civics, multicultural education, and gender/ethnicity incorporation.

Western European (South) Region

The southern region of the European Union includes France, Greece, Italy, Spain, and Portugal.

France is a democracy. Neither the National Assembly nor the judicial system rival the president's actual or potential political power. Press freedom is guaranteed; radio and TV is a mixture of state-owned and -regulated and commercial private stations. Newspapers are left-, right-, or religious-oriented; they cannot criticize the president or a politician's private life. The school system has a state-supported private (mainly Roman Catholic) component for 17 per cent of children. French schools were recently decentralized and became more flexible. Political topics (history, ethics, and geography) are taught in primary school. The system tends to be both nationalistic in goals and elitist in philosophy. Democratizing the system would require more local autonomy, professional involvement, and parent-teacher-student cooperation.

Greece is a democracy. Frequent territorial disputes have heightened the military's role. The ideologically partisan news media were censored, with restrictions lifted in 1993; radio and TV are mainly state-owned and -operated, but private commercial stations operate with or without licenses. Persistent educational problems include an overpoliticized system which resists efforts at decentralization and local control, overdependence on restrictive examinations, low-paid teachers, overemphasis on classical subjects and non-vocational training, and elite versus mass divisions. While Greek education seems to promote humanism, morality, religion, national consciousness, and democracy, only the subjects taught in schools for elites (not the masses) further these objectives. Greece neglects the needs of female students; women are over-represented among the illiterate population.

Italy is a recently reformed democracy. An alliance of five parties leads Italy. There are 12 parties in direct opposition plus three national and three regional parties. Only 10 per cent of women hold public office. Newspapers are party-linked, centrist, and regional; three state TV stations compete with private radio and TV stations. Italian education, controlled by the ministry of public instruction, tends to be formal, traditional, and classical. Plans to reform the system include abolishing lyceums, raising school leaving age to 15, introducing technical studies, abolishing some exams, and introducing five streams of study, including a history, philosophy, and social science track.

Portugal is a democracy. The judicial system is based on the French model. There are at least 17 minor opposition parties. The press is free: the radio and TV system is partially state-owned and competes with two private, independent TV stations and three privately owned radio stations. The Portuguese curriculum includes civic education. Dropout rates go from 30 percent in grade 7 to 80 per cent by grade 12, causing a serious elitist crisis. The educational system is highly centralized.

Spain is a democracy. The country is 99 per cent Catholic. The 1978 constitution disavowed fascism, disestablished Catholicism, and guaranteed basic freedoms. Political alliances prevented the growth of a two-party system. There are many regional political parties (representing nationalist and ethnic groups) plus feminist, green, and two minor fascist ones. Journalists must have a university degree, the press is free and uncensored, and radio and TV are both state and privately owned. There are large-scale battles over increasing national aid to private schools and increasing public control. Spain provides civic education in grades 6 to 8, emphasizing social studies, civics, ethics, geography, current civilizations, current events, and moral education.

The South West European countries are democracies, but the degree of democratic tradition varies. France experienced imperialism, dictatorships, Vichy collaboration in WWII, and colonialism. Italy had a fascist past, a north/south split, and a history of political corruption, tax evasion, and instability. Greece, Spain, and Portugal experienced militarism and/or fascism. They tend to be harsh with minorities (Basque separatists) and have a close relationship with the Catholic Church. Private elite education and formal classical instruction with harsh examination systems do not promote school-based democracy. Civic education courses do little to offset these undemocratic tendencies.

East European Region

This is a less homogeneous region. In the cold war, communism dominated Croatia, Estonia, Hungary, Lithuania, Poland, and Serbia.

Croatia, a semi-fascist, authoritarian state, was ruled by Franjo Tudjman (head of the Croatian Democratic Union, HDZ) until his death in December 1999. Other political parties existed but were ineffective. In February 2000, Stipe Mesic was elected president, promising to integrate Croatia into the heart of democratic Europe. Women play no role in the governing party. The only female cabinet minister in the early 1990s was in charge of education. The constitution extols democracy, social justice, human rights, lawfulness, and a competitive party system. Croatia waged wars with Serbia since gaining independence from Yugoslavia. Serb residents were guaranteed autonomy in 1991, but this has not happened except for a self-proclaimed 'Republic of Serbian Krajina'. There are six regional papers; the radio and TV stations are run by Croatian Radio-Television. There are both public and private schools.

Estonia is a democracy. Estonians have not treated resident Russians kindly, considering them a hindrance to full independence and national sovereignty. A border dispute with Russia was settled in 1997. Estonia's goals include securing statehood, a market economy, environmental health, civil society, and European integration. Political parties focus on independence; the elected leader is from the four-party 'pro-patria' coalition. Other parties are radical, conservative, or moderate based on market, environmental, or national principles. Women play a minor role in public life. Newspapers are linked to cities, politics, or ethnic groups. Radio and TV are both state and privately run. The education system is traditionally organized. The language of instruction is either Estonian (mainly) or Russian.

Hungary is a democracy. Women do not play a significant role in national politics. Hungary has six major competitive political parties (out of a total of 18). Party differences involve ethnic nationalist issues and media privatization. Minorities are represented in the parliament. Hungary has a large Romany community (with a 'Gypsy' council) and many other ethnic groups. There is press freedom, but the state Hungarian radio and TV monopoly has been challenged in the courts, parliament, and the press throughout the 1990s. A centralized ministry controls education. Reforms include increasing diversity and decentralization, developing cognitive and decision-making skills, and forming social values. The curriculum includes history, political economy, civics, geography, economics, law, and political 'ideology'.

Lithuania is a democracy. Two major and many minor political parties are based on ideology or ethnicity. The population is 81 per cent Lithuanian, 9 per cent Russian, 7 per cent Polish, 1.5 per cent Belorussian, and 1 per cent Ukrainian. Lithuania had trouble with Belarus and Russia over boundaries, troops, pardoning former Nazis, energy policy, and citizenship rights. News media (some of which are bilingual) are not censored. The language of instruction is Lithuanian, but may include Russian, Polish, or Yiddish. The educational system allows private schooling.

Poland is a democracy with over 100 political parties. Seven major party groups (including alliances) won seats. The groups are mainly divided along left-right, religious, occupational, or ethnic lines. The press is free and robust; radio and TV is privatized. Women play a minor role in politics. The education system, centralized in a Warsaw ministry, provides courses in geography, history, civic education, 'defense', history, social science, occupational safety, health, law, and economics. A mid-1990s statement on civic education was so generalized and abstract that it satisfied all leaders, but provided no guidance for teachers or parents. Private schooling, especially church-related, has also returned to Poland with a vengeance.

Serbia/(former) Yugoslavia is a fascist, authoritarian state. The constitution set up a 'democratic' republic, encouraged competitive elections, and withdrew autonomy from Kosovo (resulting in ethnic conflict with Albanians) and Vojvodina. The ruling 'socialist' party under Slobodan Milošvić is descended from the former Communist Party. Some of the many parties represent ethnic groups. Although opponents won elections, corrupt judges who overturned their victories were, in turn, sanctioned by international organizations. The population includes Serbs (62.3 per cent), Albanians (16.6 per cent), Montenegrins (5 per cent), Hungarians (3.3 per cent), Yugoslavs (3.3 per cent), and Muslims (3.1 per cent). There is some self-government at the Serbian and Montenegrin republic and local levels, except in Kosovo. News media are linked to ethnic minorities; radio and TV (including private and cable stations) are state-controlled, censored, or closed. Education is organized at the republic level. Albanian schools in Kosovo have been closed since 1990. These children attend unofficial classes run by the illegal 'Republic of Kosovo'. Serbia spends 72 per cent of its federal budget on their military, leaving little for education. The country is under UN sanctions and was suspended from most international organizations.

In Eastern Europe, Estonia, Hungary, Lithuania, and Poland were classified free and democratic (Freedom House, Vanhanen); Croatia partly free (Freedom House), yet democratic (Vanhanen); Serbia not free (Freedom House), but democratic (Vanhanen). Croatia and Serbia have dictatorial leaders, engage in warlike behavior, and terrorize local populations. They are both 'not free' and undemocratic (Farnen and German, 1997, 1998). Serbia, especially, has become an authoritarian, bellicose society, sponsoring 'ethnic cleansing' in Bosnia and supporting a virtual tyranny over Kosovo. In both countries, the educational systems do little to reinforce democracy, teaching nationalism, militarism, provincialism, and right-wing, fascist ideology. Hungary, Poland, Estonia, and Lithuania reformed their political systems, but find it hard to reform their economies. They suffer with their authoritarian-favoring religious traditions (Catholicism and Orthodoxy); minority populations bedevil Estonia and Lithuania (resident Russians) plus Hungary (Roma).

Poland and Hungary are the most progressive, signified by their involvement with NATO and the EU. In the 1990s, Hungary reverted toward authoritarian leadership and exhibits anti-Semitism (without many Jews) and nationalism. In Poland, Hungary, and the Baltic republics, their failed tradition of communist education still influences current practices.

CIS-Russian Region

The Commonwealth of Independent States (CIS) region is represented in our survey by Belorussia, Russia, and Ukraine.

Belorussia (Republic of Belarus) is a neo-communist authoritarian political system dominated by Communist and Agrarian political parties. Their 1996 constitution (adopted by referendum) gave overwhelming power to the president, but the international community refused to recognize the legitimacy of this undemocratic, dictatorial action. The six provinces hold local elections. In the early 1990s, the government introduced education in the Belorussian language and emphasized non-Soviet or non-Russian history and literature, but this reform only reached 35 per cent of all pupils by 1995.

The **Russian Federation** is a partly free transitional democracy. Russians are 83 per cent of the population in a state with 100 nationalities. Since 1994, there are 28 parties and 9 unrecognized political groups based on economic, ideological, nationalistic, gender, ecological, and religious beliefs. Women play a minor role in politics and government, but 24 (of 450) Duma seats are held by members of the Women of Russia Party. The press is free, with many communist-era holdovers. There is a private broadcasting service and cable TV, but the Russian Radio and TV Service nearly monopolizes news collection and dissemination. Although most instruction is in Russian, ten other languages are used in high schools. Private schools emerged in the 1990s. The revised curriculum ended politically directed courses in scientific socialism/Marxism-Leninism, began a new approach to Soviet and Russian history teaching, and lifted the ban on formerly censored books.

Ukraine is a partly free transitional democracy. The population includes 73 per cent Ukrainians, 22 per cent Russians, 5 per cent Jews, and many other minorities. There are 26 nationalist, centrist, and leftist groups plus 20 minor and regional parties. The press is uncensored, but newspapers are linked to government or party organizations. The state-controlled radio and TV system broadcasts in Russian and Ukrainian. The Ukrainian educational system tried to reverse the 'Russification' process begun in the 1980s when half the students were taught in each language. When Ukrainian became the official language, this changed the nature of school offerings because all students could study in this language as well as Russian, Hungarian, and Polish. Other educational and curricular changes included greater emphasis on Ukrainian history and literature and a new opportunity to attend private schools.

In CIS-Russia, Belorussia, Russia, and Ukraine are former USSR-dominated communist states. Belorussia has followed the Russian line since 1989; Ukraine tried a different tack. All three have huge economic problems and recurrent political crises. In Russia, old communists and new fascists rally against Yeltsin's quasi-democratic forces. There are disputes between Russia and Ukraine over the Crimea, arguments between Belorussia and the international diplomatic community in Minsk, and disagreements between Belorussia and Russia over common markets, political unification, debts, and energy credits. Economic woes delayed reforming educational systems, which tend to be nationalistic and self-serving in a barren effort to rebuild national egos.

African Region

In Africa, we included Kenya, Nigeria, South Africa, and Uganda.

Kenya is not a democracy. Kenya's official language is English; Swahili is its national language, with several others from its 25 ethnic groups. Kenya's history is filled with violence, human rights abuses, corruption, martial law, and one-party rule. President H.E. Moi terrorized political opponents, rigged elections, stifled free speech, enforced undemocratic economic reforms, and rejected criticism of his authoritarian dictatorship. The constitution increases centralization and destroys tribal, party, and governmental checks and balances. Political parties fill the civil service, bribe voters, and violate human rights. Parties are banned and legitimized, accused of treason or sedition, and operate from exile or clandestine headquarters. The censored press cannot criticize the government or black nationalism. Journalists were detained, expelled, or threatened. There is one state radio and TV broadcasting corporation. Western media mogul Rupert Murdoch and CNN set up a commercial partnership with the dictator's party. The education ministry controls finances, public and private schools, and examinations. The educational system is devoted to meeting the manpower development model and independence from colonialism. It is elitist, discriminates against women, encourages rote learning, and is undemocratic. Kenya needs basic, general, vocational, and interdisciplinary educational programs.

Nigeria is not democratic; it has had a military government since 1983. It has no secret elections and has an appointed (not elected) cabinet. The military appoints the judiciary. Nigeria is beset with coups, plots, counterplots, religious and ethnic frictions, corruption, and international crises. Three newspapers were banned in 1994; the government has controlled radio and TV since 1975. There were signs in 1998 that the military might free political prisoners and begin peaceful elections and civilian rule. Although Nigeria has a high birth rate, few attend school. National and regional departments of education cooperate. Despite its size and oil revenues, Nigeria does not adequately fund education. Schooling is elitist; ethnic rivalries, political instability, anti-foreign/Western prejudices, and nationalization of private education combine to decrease the quality of education. The emphasis on examinations produces rote learning and unthinking students.

South Africa is a new democracy. Until 1991, it practiced apartheid. Of the three major political parties, Nelson Mandela's ANC is dominant. In 1990, races included 70 per cent Bantu, 16 per cent whites, 11 per cent 'coloreds', and 3 per cent Asians. South Africa makes few provisions for women in national politics. It still has severe problems with the white minority, internal tribal conflict, land redistribution, and general public policy-making. The press was censored, journalists detained, and newspapers closed during the years of white rule. The South Africa Broadcasting Corporation controls radio and TV stations which air programs in several national and native languages. Under the old regime, schooling was centralized, separatist, urban-based, linguistically divided, and racist-inspired. Teachers' associations were race-based. The education community is committed to full citizenship rights and equal participation for all (liberals) or the status quo (conservatives).

Uganda is a partly free, transitional democracy. Its president and prime minister serve by force of arms and a dubious (but internationally approved) electoral victory (74 per cent of the popular vote). It has been ruled by many military dictators, including 'President for Life' Colonel Idi Amin. The present military regime has banned all political party activity (supposedly, until a 1999 national referendum). Women cannot participate in the movements, armies, and alliances which substitute for political parties. The press is not free; it is censored and under threat. Radio and TV are government-controlled. Most schools receive government support, yet all schools charge fees. Examinations are highly competitive. The curriculum is formal, elitist, and unrelated to important social needs.

Nigeria, Uganda and Kenya have nondemocratic military dictatorships; South Africa has democratic potential. The prospects for democracy there remain dim since there are also tribal disputes, long-standing economic hardships, and recurrent political crises. The old colonial infrastructure has been seriously impaired. Kenya spends so much on defense (two third of the national budget), that it has little left for education and national development.

Middle East Asian Region

In the Middle East Asian region, we surveyed Kuwait and Turkey.

Kuwait, although partly free, is no democracy. Its sheik (ruling as emir) appoints a prime minister who chairs his cabinet. Elections staff the national legislative assembly (which the emir may dissolve). The 1992 elections marked a return to Islamic law, but some political pluralism was evident. The existing movements, groups, and alliances are considered 'tendencies'; they 'sputtered out' by the mid-1990s, leaving the Islamic fundamentalist and pro-democracy movements in doubt. The radio and TV systems are government-controlled. The press has been variously free and censored in the 1990s, with no criticism of the emir allowed. Neither women nor soldiers can vote; only 15 per cent of the population is enfranchised. The right to an education is a public liberty. Since extending compulsory education to women and guest workers' (75 per cent of the total workforce) children are controversial pro-posals, their implementation faltered. The education ministry is responsible for all public and private (mostly Arab and foreign national) schools. Kuwait is stratified and segregated and depends on foreign-born teachers to staff its elitist and undemocratic schools.

Turkey is a partly free, transitional democracy. Its political party system is rife with factions, divisive ideology, and intense partisanship. The Turkish constitutional court outlawed Communist, Workers, and Kurdish parties. Extremist groups hold liberationist ideas. Of the 12 parties represented in the assembly, two are dominant. The press is relatively free, but certain ideas (separatism, fundamentalism, and communism) are forbidden. Radio and TV systems are free. The highly centralized, authoritarian school system discriminates against female students. Public and private schools serve the small minority, not the masses. There is an urban/rural imbalance. There is no established social science tradition. The examinations system is overburdened.

In the Middle East, both Turkey and Kuwait spend more on defense than on education. Though allied with the West, they are only a half-way democracy (Turkey) and an enlightened monarchy (Kuwait), so that either royal despotism or a new military junta lurk not far away. Both educational systems are centralized, anti-female, elitist, undemocratic, and conformist.

South Asia Region

The south Asian subcontinent is dominated by India. **India** is not a democracy. It has many political parties (including the Congress Alliance and other leftist, socialist, communist, Marxist, and Hindu groups) and suffers intense internal (Hindu fundamentalists, Sikhs seeking autonomy, Muslims wanting religious freedom) and external (military, border, or ethnic strife with Pakistan, China, Sri Lanka) problems. India has a large Muslim minority (11 per cent) in addition to predominant Hinduism (83 per cent) and other religious groups. Over 1600 languages and dialects are spoken in India. Caste discrimination is illegal, but practiced widely. Females play a minor political role and are traditionally discriminated against. India has 36 000 newspapers (city or regionally based) and magazines in 98 languages and dialects. The English language press is dominant politically. The information and broadcasting ministry supervises radio and TV; foreign cable and satellite TV are being legitimized. Central and federal governments control education. Instructors use local, Hindi, and English languages. Primary school enrollment averages 66 per cent, but over 70 per cent (mostly girls and low caste persons) drop out before grade 8. Examinations and stiff grading systems stifle problem solving, creativity, and interactions with teachers and fellow students.

In south Asia, India is a huge, overpopulated, inhumane, and divided society rife with ethnic, religious, class, caste, and other social divisions. Schooling and defense budgets are roughly equal. The educational system is elitist, discriminates against Muslims and women, and does not serve the people, most of whom are illiterate. Internal and external violence threatens the existence of a chimerical democratic government which is distorted in the Western press with misleading terms such as 'the world's largest democracy'.

Central Asian Region

The central Asian region is dominated by China. **China** is not a democracy, but a totalitarian, communist people's republic. The Chinese inveigh against 'bourgeois liberalization', 'imperialism', 'revisionism', and other loaded terms. China is a one-party state with eight minor parties. Press, radio, and TV are under strict government control. Despite its strong anti-intellectual strain and lack of compulsory schooling, China targets education for 'ideological awakening'. The central ministry of education controls the system, including examinations (locally administered and supervised) and textbooks. Schools are heavily politicized. Students are examined on Marxist-Leninist-Maoist ideology. Bilingual education is allowed for students whose native language is not Mandarin. The Han ethnic group is 94 per cent of the population, but there are 55 other national minorities. Overseas Chinese may attend China's schools and universities. China wants to create students who are both 'red' and 'expert' for a developing socialist country.

In this central Asian region, China claims that economic democracy (equality) precedes political democracy (individual and social). The 1989 Tiananmen Square massacre of thousands of student demonstrators after declaring martial law shows the state's totalitarian nature, along with other human rights abuses, China's seizing of Tibet, border wars with India and Vietnam, hostile gestures toward Taiwan, sales of arms abroad, and threats of bellicose nuclear and missile development policies. Using the school system to ensure party loyalty and ideological indoctrination is the classic communist line to ensure proletarian dictatorship under central party hegemony.

East Asian Region

The east Asian region includes Hong Kong, Japan, the Philippines, and Taiwan.

Hong Kong, prior to 1997, was a British Crown Colony. Then, it reverted to Chinese communist control with the promise that free market capitalism and electoral democracy would continue for 50 years. But Chinese and Hong Kong leaders debate which of the pre-reversion democratic institutions would remain and which would yield to PRC centralized political control. Hong Kong's business elite either immigrated with their British passports or agreed to abide by Chinese dictates. With its 98 per cent Chinese population, transition has been peaceful and unstoppable. Hong Kong retains some (though daily decreasing) vestiges of democratic government, while its freewheeling economy thrives as a 'special administrative region'. The pre-1997 school system provided instruction in Chinese and English. The state-supported educational system administered English, Anglo-Chinese, and Chinese schools. The entire school system was diverse, pluralistic, complex, and enclaved, defying a standard description. Hong Kong prepared for PRC takeover by introducing Mandarin Chinese instruction in schools. It is doubtful that the school system can escape future political manipulation since the PRC will surely insist on total 'sinoization' of education along communist lines.

Japan is a democracy which retains its own nuances and processes (such as a constitutional monarchy with a sovereign emperor without divine rights). The dominant Liberal Democratic Party rules either alone or with Social Democratic and ex-LDP splinter party coalitions. Real political power resides in the Diet's lower chamber. Opposition parties include right-wing, socialist, reformer, clean government, communist, progressive, salarymen, welfare, peace, pensioner, youth, trade unionist, Marxist, and revolutionary groups. News media are privately owned and free. Radio and TV systems (public and private) are financed with subscription fees or advertising. The school system is becoming more centralized; the ministry approves all textbooks. Women are given short shrift in Japanese education, politics, and business. Teachers are 70 per cent unionized and politically (left-wing) active. The bureaucratized system relies on harsh examinations and private out-of-school tutors. Public schools promote conformity, dullness, and mediocrity.

Taiwan (ROC) is a partly free, transitional democracy. It was ruled by Chiang Kai-Shek's party (Kuomintang) since 1949, declaring martial law and a permanent 'state of emergency' on the island. Two million mainland exiles and their descendants dominated 13 million native residents. No advocacy of democracy was allowed under threat of deportation, imprisonment, or execution for anti-KMT ('treasonable') activities. Since 1986, the KMT loosened its hold on Taiwan, abolishing martial law, changing its position on sovereignty over the mainland, accepting a new 'one China' policy, allowing opposition political parties, abolishing the sedition law, and setting up a new national assembly and political system with a directly elected president and vice president. The 1992 elections resulted in multiparty representation with the KMT (in the majority), the Democratic Progressive Party, independents, and others. The first native Taiwanese became premier in 1993. Central (15 per cent), provincial (25 per cent), and municipal/county (35 per cent) governments share education costs. The elementary and middle school curriculum relies on social studies subjects such as civics, ethics, history, and geography. Senior high schools also teach civics, three principles (nationalism, democracy, and work life) of the people, history, geography, and military training. The system emphasizes examinations, rote memorization, firm discipline, and official moral and political values and success. Females are less important in both schooling and politics.

The Philippines is a partly free, transitional democracy. Local government is extensive. Politics is dominated by National and Liberal parties. Many legitimate opposition parties exist beside illegal, militarily active groups. Women play no important political role. There are multiple radio and TV stations and newspapers. The elementary school system is mainly public; the secondary is private. Women are adequately represented in school enrollments. Muslim schools are in the southern part of the country. Drop-out rates are declining. The education ministry supervises all schools. Municipal, provincial, city, and national governments support education. Primary school pupils study character education, civics, geography, and history; secondary students have social studies and civic education, with youth development and citizen army training. Schools desperately need democratic reform.

These east Asian states are led by Japan (most democratic) followed by Taiwan (more recently democratized), the Philippines (gradually democratized after Marcos' dictatorship), and Hong Kong (lost much political freedom after becoming part of the PRC). All spend more on education than defense. Freedom will increase, but probably not much in Hong Kong.

Oceania Region

The Oceania region is represented by Australia and New Zealand.

Australia, a democracy, dominates its aboriginal minority and encouraged the in-migration of up to 200 000 people per year while maintaining a 'whites-only' policy for them. The governor general links Australia to the Commonwealth of Nations and the British sovereign. A complete mass communications system keeps the electorate fully informed of national and world news. Voting at age 18 is compulsory. The population is 95 per cent Caucasian, 4 per cent Asian, and 1 per cent aborigine or other. The educational system is state-run. There is a large private and parochial school system; 25 per cent of students at times attend independent schools.

New Zealand is a democracy. Official languages are English and Maori. Education, telecommunications, and mass media systems are excellent. Maori language schooling is supported. Per capita education expenses are lower than in some English-speaking countries; budgetary and deficit reduction is emphasized; many see schooling as an expensive social entitlement. The educational system is homogeneous, centralized, and increases one's 'cultural capital' for personal/social improvement. Educational self-criticism focused on the examinations system, adequacy of schools for minorities, over-selectivity in higher education, and adequacy of school-work relationships.

In Oceania, Australia and New Zealand are stable democracies with evidence of pluralism (although Australia had a racist immigration policy), multiple school types, mixed media, and political party competition. Both spend far more on education than on defense. Their school systems are highly respected and perform admirably, including student exposure to formal political education and political socialization processes.

CONCLUSIONS: REGIONAL PATTERNS

The preceding descriptions and statistics on government, education, and defense expenditures reveal some patterns. Countries which spend much on defense (Kenya, Uganda, Taiwan, India, Nigeria, and Serbia) are not democratized and usually spend relatively little on education (partly because their economies cannot support both guns and butter). Countries with high per capita expenditures on education are usually democracies (Sweden, the Netherlands, Canada, US, FRG, and Belgium) and usually have a strong system of democratic civic education (especially true in the Netherlands, Sweden, and FRG).

Another characteristic of undemocratic, authoritarian countries is the high level of violence, conflict, and bellicosity associated with their civilian- and military-linked regimes. They fight with neighbors over borders or ethnic nationality issues and repeatedly quell riots and rebellions at home (China, India, Serbia, Kenya, Uganda, and Nigeria). Their political systems produce authoritarian-type educational systems to maintain conventionalism, submission, and state-sanctioned aggression when the regime in power orders it.

Table 3.2. Major political/educational features of 44 surveyed countries

Country	Type of System	Multicultural Divisions	Comments
Argentina	federal republic with president and 2-house congress	mainly Spanish-speaking and Roman Catholic; English, Italian, German, French minorities	political competition mainly among military, middle class, and Peronists
Australia	federal system, bicameral parliament, prime minister, governor general	Catholics, Anglicans, other denominations; minority (Asian and native) population 5%	racist immigration policies, domination over native peoples
Austria	federal republic; president; bicameral legislature; 2-party dominant	mostly German and Roman Catholic; Slovene, Croatian, Hungarian, and Polish minorities	divisive, localized politics; provincial power; fragmented political parties
Belgium	parliamentary monarchy, bicameral legislature; ethnic political party system	entire system is ethnically based; anti-immigrant feelings run high	Flemish Bloc very active and anti-immigrant; polity is split along policy lines
Byelorussia	republic; bicameral parliament, president, prime minister; 2-party, communist-style rule	most are Orthodox and Belorussian; minorities are Russians, Poles, Ukrainians, and Jews	closely linked to Russia, despite recent attempts to nationalize it while fostering independence
Canada	2-party dominant parliamentary with prime minister; federal system	ethnic rivalry threatens nation if French minority secedes	immigrant-country; racial, ethnic, religious, and regional divisions
Chile	Competitive parties; 2-house congress and president	Spanish main language; mixed population; 5% Indian minority	mixed past of Marxist, military, and democratic rule
Peoples' Republic of China	totalitarian communist party selects officials, electorate assents	Han ethnic group dominates; Mandarin is official language; 55 other Chinese nationalities	ruled by Mao-style communism for 50 years with few changes
Colombia	republic; president; 2-house congress; competitive parties	mainly Spanish and Roman Catholic; Indian tribes in isolated areas	long history of drug wars, rebellion, and military rule
Costa Rica	2-party dominant; president; unicameral legislature	Catholic official religion; 80% white, 17% mixed, 2% black, 1% Indians	'banana republic' under US economic domination

Country	Type of System	Multicultural Divisions	Comments
Croatia	bicameral parliamentary republic; president and prime minister; dictatorial rule without party opposition until 1999	predominantly Croatian; large Serb, Muslim, and other minority groups; mainly Roman Catholic, then Orthodox, also Muslims and others	ethnic rivalries and national feelings run high and are exploited by fascist dictator and his party
Estonia	parliamentary republic; prime minister and president; competitive party system	Estonian is official language; mostly Lutherans, some Orthodox; ethnicities: Estonian, Russian, Ukrainian, Belorussian, Finnish	nationalism and independence are rallying cries for major parties
Finland	republic, unicameral system, prime minister, president, competitive party system	Finnish and Swedish are official languages; most people are Lutheran/Evangelical	Greek Orthodox and Lapps/Saami minorities; parties split on economic lines
France	republic, bicameral parliament, president premier; 2-party rule	primarily Roman Catholic, but diverse; small percentage are immigrants or noncitizens	the few non-French are hated by FN Party
Germany	federal, bicameral, 2-party dominant system, prime minister and president	Catholics, Lutherans, Muslims; immigrants, guest workers, asylum seekers, Serbs, Danes	party divisions along religious, class, environmental, and regional lines
Greece	republic; parliament, prime minister, ceremonial president; competitive party system, Socialists and Conservatives	religion Greek Orthodox; Muslim minority; no interference with state church permitted; ethnic disputes with Albania and Macedonia	constant conflicts with Turkey and other neighbors over border, ethnic, and property issues
(PRC) Hong Kong	before 1997, UK colony with basic democratic institutions; now PRC rule; local politics uncertain	mostly Chinese from Canton; schools now teach Mandarin Chinese and Marxism/Maoism	free markets and democracy are to last 50 years, but this may not happen
Hungary	republic; unicameral national assembly, president, and prime minister; competitive party system	concerned about Hungarian minorities in neighboring countries; major minority is Romany; Roman Catholicism is major religion	1989 constitution guarantees human rights and party pluralism
India	federal republic; bicameral parliament, president, and prime minister; 1-party rule	enormous linguistic, ethnic, religious, and other differences, such as caste discrimination	intense external and internal strife over ethnic, religious, and border issues

Country	Type of System	Multicultural Divisions	Comments
Italy	republic; bicameral parliament, president, premier; competitive party system	nearly universally Roman Catholic; no major immigrant or minority groups	Fascist Party is forbidden; political alliances changed often in the 1990s
Japan	parliamentary democracy; bicameral legislature and prime minister; 2-party dominant, competitive elections	religions include Buddhism, Shintoism, and Christianity; national pride runs high; discrimination against certain groups/women is rife	women especially unequal and discriminated against as are non-Japanese, such as Koreans
Kenya	republic; unicameral legislature; president is a virtual dictator	multilingual and multiethnic with religion split among Protestants, Catholics, and others	has 50 tribes and 25 ethnic groups plus Asians and Europeans; repeated conflicts with neighbors
Kuwait	monarchy run by sheik ruling as emir with advisory national assembly, but no political parties	only 15% can vote; remaining residents are foreigners and guest workers	has returned to Islamic fundamentalist law since 1992; women are second class citizens
Lithuania	parliamentary republic; president and prime minister; competitive party system	mostly Lithuanian; Russian, Polish, Belorussian, and Ukrainian minorities; other languages used in schools	had several previous conflicts with neighbors, but they are now resolved
French Martinique	French overseas possession; competitively elected local government	mostly African Americans and Roman Catholics	divisions are rightwing/nationalistic, independence, and socialist egalitarian
Mexico	federal republic, president; bicameral congress, one-party dominant	Spanish and Roman Catholicism predominant; Indian and Protestant minorities	recent party competition; system has violence, drugs, rebellions, and corruption
Netherlands	constitutional monarchy, bicameral parliament; prime minister; coalitions	society is pillarized among Catholics, Protestants, and others (Muslims and Jews)	school system pillarized; 70% enrolled in private/state-funded schools
New Zealand	two-party dominant, parliamentary system; prime minister	official languages are English and Maori; supports political representation and education of Maori minority	still has Commonwealth links; has more progressive minority relations than Australia
Nigeria	federal republic under military rule since 1983	large Christian and Islamic groups; four different languages	many wars with neighbors; typical military-fascist state

Country	Type of System	Multicultural Divisions	Comments
Philippines	republic; bicameral legislature and president; two-party dominant electoral system	mainly Roman Catholic; Islam is tolerated and accommodated; Muslim schools and local autonomy allowed	politics is violent, corrupt, and unstable; women are mistreated, but 'protected' against abortion
Poland	parliamentary republic; bicameral legislature, president, prime minister; competitive parties	mainly Roman Catholic; parties divided on religious, ethnic, and other lines	nationalism, economics, ethnicity, and religion/anti-Semitism are basis for political parties
Portugal	republic, unicameral legislature, prime minister, president; two-party competitive system	predominantly Roman Catholic; religious schools are state-supported	no major ethnic or national minorities are politically involved
Russia	republic; bicameral parliament, prime minister, and strong president; Communist-dominated multiparty system	Russians predominate out of 100 nationalities; Russian is official language, but others are allowed locally	electorate undemocratic, authoritarian; support Zhirinovsky's extreme nationalist party; religious, ethnic, ideological parties
Serbia	federal republic; bicameral legislature, prime minister, and president; ruled by dictator with Communist Party backing	Serbian, Albanian, and other ethnic groups, including Muslims; mainly Orthodox; Muslim, Christian minorities; Serbs at war with Albanians in Kosovo	present government is unreformed communist variety guilty of past unrestrained genocide
South Africa	republic; bicameral legislature and president; one-party dominant	11 languages used; predominantly Christian, Hindu, and Islamic religions	racial, ethnic, and tribal divisions although Bantus are the majority
Spain	parliamentary monarchy; bicameral legislature, prime minister; very competitive party system	official Spanish and four regional languages; regional parties for national and ethnic groups; illegal fascist parties	many regional divisions; most serious is Basque nationalists in the northern regions
Sweden	constitutional monarchy; unicameral legislature; prime minister; 2-party dominant system	mainly Lutherans; some Catholics, religious minorities from Greek, Turkish, and Yugoslavian immigrants and guest workers	large Lapp minority in north; gender equality is predominant; private education is very small

Country	Type of System	Multicultural Divisions	Comments
Taiwan	republic; national assembly, president, and prime minister; competitive elections since 1992	long-standing rivalry between native Taiwanese and mainland exiles diminished in 1990s	KMT ruled for 50 years until democratization began in 1990s
Turkey	republic; unicameral parliament, president, prime minister; two-party domination	Turkish is primary language and Islam main religion; Kurdish and other minorities	Turkish courts outlawed the Kurdish parties; Islamic fundamentalism is rife
Uganda	republic under military rule	5 official languages; Christianity and Islam are major religions	authoritarian state under long-term military rule
Ukraine	republic; unicameral parliament, prime minister, president; parties competitive, fragmented	Ukrainians predominate, but minorities are Russians, Jews, Roma, and other ethnic groups	problems with Russia over the Crimea, treatment of Russian minority, and use of Russian in schools
United Kingdom	constitutional monarchy; bicameral parliament; prime minister; two-party dominant system	mainly English-speaking, some minority languages; two religions; Commonwealth resident minorities 8% of population; active racist and neo-Nazi groups	political parties divided along partisan policy lines as well as racial and SES divisions
United States of America	federal republic; two-party dominant, presidential system; two-house legislature	immigrant-receiving; ethnic, racial, religious diversity; main groups are whites, blacks, Hispanics, and Asians	checks and balances, separation of powers, and federal/state divisions often cause gridlock
Venezuela	federal republic; president; bicameral congress; competitive parties with two dominant	mainly Spanish-speaking and Roman Catholic; Indian tribes/dialects in interior	highly politicized, divided nation; violence, graft, and militarism prevalent

4 International and Cross-National Research Findings on Democracy

INTRODUCTION

In this chapter and the next two, we review some of the research results on democracy, authoritarianism, and democratic political education, three major topics in this project. These themes are introduced to explain and interpret our empirical findings reported later on. (For a more elaborate discussion, see Farnen, 1996, pp. 55-69 and Dekker, 1996, pp. 386-400.)

DEMOCRACY

There are at least two prominent Western views of democracy, the 'strong' or participatory and the 'weak' or elitist representative viewpoint. These views have different theories about citizen's rights, duties, and roles. The strong viewpoint includes direct, mass, classical, normative, and communitarian features; the 'weak' emphasizes indirect, elite, modern, empirical, and liberal/republican aspects. They stress citizens' participatory and decision-making or problem-solving roles that we see as key democratic elements.

'Strong' Democracy

Participatory democrats believe that politics is omnipresent and happens whenever conflict can be resolved, public decisions are made, and power and authority come into play (that is, during elections, at home or work, in school, or in the community). Citizens share power equally as well as decision-making responsibility. Systemic instability occurs whenever elitism, authoritarianism, prejudice, alienation, and private or public bureaucratization stifle free thought and action. Democracy is seen as an ideal, but also as a real choice and a process allowing for individual, shared group, and leadership behavior.

'Strong' democrats are also social democrats; are group-oriented; and believe the individual is autonomous, rational, social, educable, and can do good or evil. Community norms and habits, compromise, fairness, and common sense reinforce social solidarity. The public benefits when community well-being and individual rights are balanced. Citizens are 'civic officials' in a democracy. It is their job to improve self and community decision-making and citizenship competencies. Leadership is chosen on the basis of personal philosophy, loyalty, merit, elections, issue stands, and group representation.

Government must be regularly recreated and reinvented. Shared decision-making vitiates the need for violence or revolts since serious disputes may be peacefully resolved via compromises. Citizen involvement reduces alienation while increasing efficacy. New conceptions of the public good develop through group discourse while informing citizen-participants so they become as expert in policy matters as their leaders. 'Strong' democracy means more than voting in elections; it also means fulfilling an obligation for participatory self-governance, including assuming the burdens of civic engagement plus watching over the behaviors of elected officials. 'Strong' democrats hold that citizens need more knowledge, more education, better decision-making skills, and a greater role in public problem-solving and public policy formation.

'Weak' Democracy

'Weak' democracy holds that the official public sphere alone is the province of politics, whereby elites are chosen by voters to represent the citizenry. Worthy citizens can join the elite of wealth, talent, and power. Elites can secure stability and avoid anarchy; they do not trust the uninformed, alien-ated, and inactive masses, so citizen efficacy is irrelevant. They agree on basic education for all and a minimalist citizen role in choosing leaders or even joining the leadership cadre, if qualified. The emphasis is on freedom and individualism, even though their view of human nature is the darkest sort: irrational, banal, self-interested, and evil. Laws and written contracts and courts must control the potentially rebellious people; the threat is a tyrannous state which may curtail elite rights. Citizen involvement has to be narrowly limited to voting to safeguard 'freedom', autonomy, and citizen obedience. Chosen leaders have the prior approval of the power elites of education, po-sition, wealth, and family. Not all can understand the true public philosophy.

Democracy becomes a competitive political process, where the unin-formed reluctantly vote for governors from different sets of elites. Popular control of the official elite is very limited and no policy alternatives are supplied from the ground up. Elites see political equality as restricted to vot-ing and fear a revolt of the masses against elite government would threaten social stability. The people are considered too stupid to understand political issues. The public is best left to sports, TV, entertainment, and consuming.

Alternative Views

Vanhanen (1997, pp. 28-42) summarizes alternative views (such as the Free-dom House one) of democracy before arriving at his own. From those included, the principal factors stressed are significant political (party) competition, increased public participation, and the presence of civil rights and liberties. Democracy is also a system which is the opposite of authoritarianism or autocracy with its self-chosen ruler who has unlimited power. These definitions can be refined to include key elements such as polyarchies, popular sovereignty and constitutionalism, political equality, pluralism, and specific economic and social features such as a literate and educated citizenry and a developed, modern, urban, nonagriculturally dependent population.

Just as there are varieties of authoritarianism, such as its totalitarian (Russian, Cuban, or Chinese communist and Nazi fascist) style of complete state societal control, so there are different brands of democracy which supposedly or allegedly exist. These brands include Western liberal, radical (direct), socialist (economic egalitarian), and consociational (veto-groups and concurrent majorities) democracies. It is also possible to restrict democracy to specific decision-making methods so free and equal citizens have ultimate power in the political process (for example, in regular, honest, and free competitive, universal elections of popularly responsible governmental officials).

While some scholars (from a Marxist or third world perspective) claim there are no worldwide definitions of democracy, their argument has theoretical and connotative but not empirical/factual or denotative proof. Marxist scholars who stressed the need for economic over political equality and civil rights/liberties have now been largely discredited, at least in their Leninist-Maoist modes. Social democracy (emphasizing economic, political, and legal justice, equity, and equality) is still very much alive in the Western tradition, despite the triumph of free market capitalism. It is the Asian (sometimes applied to Africa and Latin America) variety of guided democracy that is, perhaps, the most misguided. While social, liberal, and consociational democracy are practically synonymous terms, socialist democracy has failed its democratic test; Asian guided democracy is not so much democratic as an apologia for the status quo. Asians, it is claimed, prefer good government over human rights and democracy. In practice, these 'guided democracies' practice pre-trial detention, press censorship, harsh penalties for minor crimes, and property seizures. Lacking a strong democratic civic tradition, these countries willingly accept coups, violate human rights, and target centralized control to reduce crime and reform the economy. When the economy stays depressed, citizens have neither economic nor political freedom or security They deny individualism, civil rights/liberties, and self-determination. Asian religious traditions emphasize communitarianism, consensus, obedience, security, law observance, and social harmony over private virtues or public values. While there are alternative native movements in Asia to institute 'reciprocated toleration', diversity, pluralism, and basic democratic change, these reforms are only at the elementary level, far short of meeting the more worldwide requirements of democracy mentioned previously (Kausikan, 1993; Makiya, 1994).

Consociational Democracy

Synonyms for this term include multiethnic democracy, power sharing, cross-cutting cleavages, vote pooling, and majority control theory. Ethnic groups were once based on linguistic groups, but in the modern era, the communal group based on religious and other cultural differences set them apart, often in a hostile way. Such divisions threaten democratic unity and consensus. Alternatives to democracy use cruel conflict resolution methods such as assimilation of 'the other', partition, expulsion, 'ethnic cleansing', and genocide as in Bosnia and Kosovo. Ethnicity theories claim it is either a primordial given (instrumentally taken or learned) or constructed at a critical period in the group's life.

Nation builders have to assume ethnicity is malleable and adaptable and would yield to the force of modernization. But the experiences of Russia, Spain, Canada, the US, Belgium, and Switzerland show that these two forces have a separate life. The military past has given way to multiculturalism and affirmative action in the US as well as differentiating between native and recent immigrant groups in their willingness to assimilate or conform. To meet such challenges, political scientists have asked how to accommodate ethnicity in a democracy if such differences cannot be eliminated.

Cross-cutting cleavages as a spur to democracy assume that the more and diverse groups to which a person belongs, the more tolerant and moderate (contrasted with intolerant and hostile) a person is likely to be. Also, when a political party must appeal to a variety of voters, this increases moderate pluralism; but a two-party system is also less likely than a multiparty system to promote factionalism. Federalism also adds regional cleavages to the mix as long as the regional and ethnic boundaries vary, which is not the case in Canada and India. Critics of the cross-cutting theory claim that ethnic groups will still seek representation, even in two-party dominant systems. They also believe an emphasis on moderation could increase with minority party representation. In practice, federalism has not worked to cross-cut ethnic divisions in India, Canada, Nigeria, Belgium, or Switzerland.

Vote pooling is a variant of the cross-cutting cleavage approach. It has been tried with vote distribution and alternative votes in Nigeria and Sri Lanka. The Nigerian system required a candidate not only to obtain more votes than his/her opponents nationwide, but also to get at least 25 per cent of the other votes in two-thirds of 19 states. This system rewards moderation in candidate appeals. Critics of this theory charge that the system discourages compromise and coalition building, that it may not produce a winner, that it could discourage one's own group support, that incentives for moderation are not real, and that this system is already in effect in two-person run-off elections.

Another substitute for power sharing is control theory. It is an alternative to civil war and seeks civil peace and political stability in ethnically divided societies. This system is not a model for a democracy since it is undemocratic or under a majority dictatorship (as existed in Northern Ireland from the 1920s to 1960s). The excluded minority of Catholics in this case are clearly victims of a tyrannous majority with both 'peace' and 'democracy' imposed on them. The only real utility of control theory is that it can serve as a useful polar extreme or model to power sharing or consociational democracy.

Consociational democracy applies to those societies which are split into religious, ethnic, racial, linguistic, or regional divisions. These countries have grand coalitions which guarantee local autonomy with cooperative decision-making by representatives of all important groups regarding what is good for the whole polity and separate autonomy for each subunit on other matters. The government functions on the principle of proportionality regarding political representation, civil service posts, budgeting, and a minority veto on issues vital to minority interests or the over-representation of minorities in the government. This system has worked well in the past in Western Europe, particularly in Switzerland, Belgium, Austria, and the Netherlands. It has been only partially successful in Asia (Malaysia) and Africa. To be success-ful, this format requires no absolute majority segment, relative economic equality, a restricted population size, membership segments of roughly equal size, a countrywide spirit of larger loyalties, and a tradition of consensual politics. One prominent criticism of proportional representation is that it encourages multiparty coalitions, making government less effective, but specific examples of such systems in the Netherlands or Switzerland indicate there is no democratic deficit at all (Lijphart, 1993 and 1995).

Social Democracy

Social democracy, unlike communism, does not require nationalizing pro-ductive means. Socialist governments have power without doing so to eradi-cate poverty, stimulate investments, increase labor mobility, provide welfare, and maintain income levels. The model for this 'functional socialism' or socio-political-economic system is Sweden and its UK mentor J. M. Keynes. He rationalized private ownership with democratic economic regulation of investment, crime, and taxation with the presence of strong labor unions. In the 1980s, social democratic governments lost power (but regained it in the 1990s) in Scandinavia, Germany, and the UK for a variety of reasons, the most basic of which is these governments' inability to maintain full employment, investment levels, prosperity, and union cooperation. However, the socialist critique of capitalism is still based on charges that the market system is undemocratic, unequal, selfish, and restricts opportunity. The US market economy is stagnant in key sectors, with real wages constant in the last decade and a shrinking middle and growing underclass at the bottom 40 per cent of the society. Citizens do not vote; yet if the voting rate is lowest, the prison population is the world's highest. Nevertheless, its free market capitalism is extolled regardless of its inefficiencies, chimerical stock prices, imperfect markets, and inhumanity to so many of its citizens. The socialist criticism of the US system is that such widespread disparities should not be allowed to exist since the people are sovereign; they can reallocate economic resources in a more equitable fashion using the democratic state as an intermediary. To achieve collective sovereignty and the rights of all to participate in public decision-making, democratic socialism advocates increased access to politics and to higher education with the aim to promote citizens' material security and chances for equal opportunity (Przeworski, 1993).

DEMOCRATIC TRANSITIONS

Transitions from an authoritarian to a democratic regime in the last decades can be explained as the result of resolving ideological, political, and social conflicts. Democratic institution building and consolidation were sparked by various factors such as the death of a dictator, a military defeat, a new international economic opportunity, or the emergence of a new generation of political leaders desiring a fresh start. These same factors applied to Spain, Greece, and Portugal in the 1970s as well as to Latin America in the 1980s when new civil constitutional regimes appeared. However fragile they seemed, these regime types have broad-based, if not deep, public support.

Latin American democracies have a number of hurdles to overcome before democracy can be consolidated. These include the debt crisis, rigid class structures, lack of pluralism, and a fragmented civil society. The same situation in Central and Eastern Europe requires facing up to old boundary disputes, making the transition from a command to a market system, and implementing rapid changes in society, politics, and economics which normally require at least a generation to complete. Only in Hungary, Poland, the Czech Republic, and (recently) Slovakia was a democratic compromise struck between the old and new regimes. Moreover, the earlier experiences of Latin America in institution building were studied and Central and Eastern Europe emulated South Europe in their joint desire to join Western European economic institutions even if they had to pay the same high price as previous democratization attempts required.

In Central and Eastern Europe, the transitions occurring in the 1989-91 period were the product of a bunched or contagion effect as the USSR divested itself of its empire and colonies. These efforts were encouraged from Moscow and resulted in peaceful anti-communist revolutions to destroy state monopolies on power, to increase freedom, and to produce a pluralist political community and, eventually, a democratic civic culture. Since the West also cut off post-cold war military aid to African one-party dictatorial states, this produced a simultaneous incentive toward free competitive elections and freedom of speech for opposition groups there. Even South Africa (bastion of apartheid) enfranchised its black citizens, dismantled the old government, and turned power over to its opponents. Some of the former white-dominated states have better prospects for democratization than do others in sub-Sahara Africa because of infrastructure, educational, administrative, and legal system precedents. So while transitions have happened and three-decade-old military regimes have been toppled, the day of the dictator in Africa is not at an end and little democratic 'contagion effect' is possible there (Whitehind, 1993).

The Role of the Military

The military has played a different role in various regimes in the transition to democracy. In Latin America in the 1960s and 1970s, a succession of military coups mixed with civilian rule did not prepare the way for modernization, but rather set back both human rights and material well-being/economic development. The situation varied as in Argentina, Colombia, Chile, Brazil, Nicaragua, and Uruguay the armed forces sided with the right, but in another case with the left (Peru).

In Eastern Europe, the military were part of the power structure under Soviet hegemony, but their loyalty to the old state could not be guaranteed during the 1989-91 transition to democracy period unlike those earlier years when troops were used to quell riots in Berlin, Prague, and Budapest. In Poland, the military actually assisted in the transition period. But, after a brief romance with Solidarity (which recently experienced a political revival as well), the Polish people returned the old, but reformed, communists to power. In Romania, the military assisted the old communist/security forces coalition to remove the dictator and to establish a new government. In Russia, the armed forces were in the background throughout the transition period. Some military participated in the August 1991 coup attempt while others are still active in Russian politics.

In Asia and Africa, we see that India has not allowed its military to play a leading political role, despite its border disputes and the international rebukes it received about its active nuclear and missile development policies.

China is governed by a totalitarian type of civilian control of the military. The military in the Middle East has played various roles over the years as part of the power elite, as director of crowd control, or as foil to the mosque and the bazaar with its religious fundamentalism seen as a threat to the secular state as in Algeria. By contrast, military rule in Africa has been long-term, widespread, and endemic. Military and civilian regimes there succeed one another with different ethnic groups dominant, different religious groups in power, different ideologies espoused, and national populism as a single constant.

As many regimes democratized, some precipitating event (a lost war, popular revolt, or military coup) opened up the system. Then, moderation, planning, compromise, and positioning at the center become important as do political parties, especially those backed by workers, trade unions, key interest groups, and economic elites. Social forces often consolidate democratic gains, letting the military retire from politics for awhile (DiTella, 1995).

CONCLUSIONS

This chapter discussed 'strong' and 'weak' democratic theory as well as consociational and social democratic theory. We also explored the concept of militarism as well as transitions from military/communist/authoritarian regimes to democratic government, a process now underway in Latin America, Africa, Asia, and Central and Eastern Europe. We also explored the idea of 'guided democracy' and the Asian variants of secure or good versus democratic government. This discussion will be useful for interpreting the results of our research/survey into democratic and authoritarian regime types as well as their accompanying educational systems which we discuss later under such topics as political socialization and civic education.

5 International and Cross-National Research Findings on Authoritarianism: Regimes and Individuals

INTRODUCTION

Authoritarianism exists in bureaucratic, military, or technocratic governments. These regimes are undemocratic, self-chosen, and elite-ruled; do not respond to the popular will; and engineer popular consent and base their power on monopolizing the means and use of force. Totalitarianism is an extreme form of authoritarianism (in Cuba, China, Serbia, and Croatia). Under totalitarianism, nothing is free from state control. Communications, unions, schools, parties, and property use are controlled via a security apparatus to ensure engineered consent. Opposition groups are driven underground; national patriotism stifles dissent. Authoritarian regimes do not respect democratic principles of freedom, equality, human rights, or popular participation.

FASCIST/TOTALITARIAN TENDENCIES IN WEST AND EAST

Surveys in Europe and the US indicate that political currents of change exist. Increasingly, citizens are willing to trade freedom for security, losing interest in politics, and demonstrating intolerance of 'others'. Fundamentalist religion, God, and prayer are making a comeback. Censorship is widely endorsed, ethnic minority groups and gays are treated with suspicion, political efficacy is waning, and democracy is supported only in abstract (versus concrete) instances. A general belief in personal satisfaction reached record high levels.

In Western Europe, only small parties reflect extremist views with leaders who espouse fascist ideology. These are Belgium's Flemish Block, the Netherlands' Center Party (renamed Center Democrats), France's National Front, and Germany's Republicans. The US, UK, and Canada also have such parties. But in the Russian Duma, Zhirnovsky's Liberal Democratic Party (a misnomer since it is neither liberal nor democratic) is the third largest party. These groups are not only white supremacists, but also anti-Roma, anti-immigrant, militarist, gun-wielding super patriots, and extremely violent in their hatred of liberal democracy. Their members strongly endorse social conventions (religious fundamentalism, the nuclear family, and anti-homosexuality), willingly submit to the dominant authority of their leader and party, and act aggressively toward those they see as inferiors (VanDyke, 1988, pp. 120-57).

In Eastern Europe, stereotypes against one's neighbors abound; anti-Semitism has returned. Border disputes exist, patriotism levels everywhere are elevated, and hatred of Sinti/Roma is universally high. Survey results in Russia, Ukraine, and Lithuania indicate that levels of democratic and governmental support vary as do those for a new dictatorship. People have lost faith in democracy and democratic government and long for the old regime's security. Authoritarianism in one form or another has a good chance of making a comeback in Eastern Europe, as it already has in Serbia and Croatia (Farnen, 1996, pp. 73-8; *Times Mirror*, 1991, pp. 27-43; *Times Mirror*, 16 September 1991; *Times Mirror*, 27 January 1993). Surveys of ten Eastern European countries indicate that Slovaks prejudiced against Jews, 'Gypsies', and Hungarians were also quite nationalistic and militaristic, opposed civil rights, preferred continuing state ownership of communist property, and were anti-capitalistic (Bútorová et al., 1993, pp. 23-7).

Bulgarians still seek a strong dictator, but Czechs and Hungarians are quite far along in their democratic transition. Slovaks, much like Czechs, do not favor dictatorial rule, although former Prime Minister Mečíar once filled this bill. Neither Romania nor Slovakia want a return to the past; both are optimistic about the future. Croatians support their parliament and detest Belgrade. Belorussians seek a strong man to rule and join Ukraine in preferring the old system; both are pessimistic and anti-democratic. The average level of democrats in these ten countries combined was 32 per cent, while reactionaries represented 23 per cent. The most democratic were the Czechs, Romanians, and Slovenes; the least democratic were the Hungarians, Belorussians, and Ukrainians. Overall, 25 per cent would approve suspension of parliament and 42 per cent preferred strong-man rule. Threats from internal and external sources were widely believed (Rose and Haerpfer, 1993, pp. 72-82).

A 1991-96 longitudinal survey of Central/Eastern European elites reveals a checkered pattern of democratic development in 12 countries (Farnen and German, 1996; 1997, pp. 1-10; 1998, pp. 1-24). Toleration mean scores dropped in the region from 1991-96, but increases were found in Poland, Croatia, Slovenia, and Russia. Romania, Bulgaria, Lithuania, Hungary, and Latvia (rated least tolerant). The extent of civil rights education expanded from 1993-96 overall, particularly in the Czech Republic, (Eastern) Germany, Hungary, Latvia, and Poland. Regarding nationalism, overall levels in the region are not very high, but several countries (Croatia, the Czech Republic, Latvia, Poland, Serbia, Slovakia, and Slovenia) are among the highest in the region.

Generally, it is not possible to say with any confidence that these countries are truly democratic, but the Czech Republic, (Eastern) Germany, and Slovenia are already the most democratized; Hungary, Latvia, Poland, Lithuania, Slovakia, and Romania are next in line; at the end are Croatia, Albania, Bulgaria, and Serbia.

AUTHORITARIANISM: SYSTEMIC LEVEL

In contrast to totalitarian regimes, authoritarian political systems permit some forms of opposition (such as in fascist Spain from monarchists or in communist Poland from the Catholic Church and Solidarity). Citizens' freedoms are limited, opposition movements are repressed, and military (rather than civil) courts try cases harshly when they involve strikes, party, or propaganda activities. Torture, disappearances, detention, and assassination are not uncommon. Totalitarian regimes (such as Mao's China, Hitler's Germany, Castro's Cuba, or Stalin's Russia) are more repressive. But both types of regimes crush human rights and lack international legitimacy. Examples of post-1945 military authoritarian regimes are Franco's Spain, Peron's Argentina, Nasser's Egypt, and Pinochet's Chile. Strictly military regimes (in Argentina, Peru, and Uruguay in the 1970s and 1980s) ruled without civilians and parties. Such regimes may set up a more temporary or caretaker government (such as in Greece in the 1970s) until they achieve their objectives (such as removing fundamentalists or leftists). Some form of authoritarian or totalitarian rule has governed much of the world in the 20th century, only giving way to more democratic regimes over the last 20 years.

Post-Stalinist communist regimes in Eastern Europe were modified from totalitarian to authoritarian after losing their ideological links to communism and liberalizing their societies. These regimes became more pluralistic and allowed for more bureaucratic autonomy and the growth of privatization and civil society features with a diminution in party rule and ideological fervor.

A more elaborate type of authoritarian rule espouses the organic state or corporatism, which represents syndicalist interest groups (trade unions) and meets their demands in a sort of 'organic democracy' (Spain, Portugal, Brazil, Mexico, and Argentina). These regimes are actually pseudo democracies since political parties do not exist and the leadership cannot easily be replaced. Many of the post-colonial regimes in Africa also set up nominally unified or single-party democracies installing some form of African socialism. After this, authoritarian dictatorships were established based on personal tyrannies (Uganda and Zaire). Although some of these regimes allowed liberalization of religion, work, press, and travel, they seldom wanted democracy to replace them. By contrast, in Eastern Europe (Bulgaria, Poland, Hungary, and Lithuania), some of the former authoritarian party elite won free elections in the post-communist period, marching to victory under the banner of a reformed party or a new social democratic standard (Linz, 1995).

A study of 1960s to 1980s authoritarian rule in Brazil, Chile, Argentina, and Uruguay gave rise to the concept of bureaucratic authoritarianism in Latin America. Technocratic leaders modernized economies in Brazil, Argentina, Chile, and Uruguay and harshly repressed labor and opposition groups. The political and economic environment was based on inequality, state protectionism, economic nationalism, and neutralization of the labor movement. Bureaucrats postponed redistribution, sparked economic growth, increased competitiveness, controlled labor, and sought international partners. This type of authoritarianism differed from traditional and populist models which promoted political mobilization of the people. Attempts to apply this model to Eastern Europe, the Middle East, and East or Southeast Asia were unsuccessful, but the growth of an authoritarian bureaucracy may help explain the rise of authoritarian regimes. In Latin America in the 1990s, a pattern of alternating between competitive and authoritarian regimes emerged. Advocating economic nationalism, mishandling the debt crisis, and lessening the military's role were affected by a worldwide democratization trend. As a result, some influenced countries (Brazil and Chile) experienced marked and lasting economic progress. South American people learned a new respect for building electoral democracy on the ashes of these draconian military bureaucracies, some of which terrorized their own peoples (Collier, 1993).

AUTHORITARIANISM: INDIVIDUAL LEVEL

Right-Wing Authoritarianism

On right-wing authoritarianism (RWA) in North America, Altemeyer (1981, 1988, 1996) expressed a grim view of authoritarianism's potential and democracy's lack of an effective response. He concluded that citizens do not cherish their freedoms enough to resist tyranny at home or from abroad, that they do not resist authority, and that the Nazi past in Germany can become the fascist present in North America (Altemeyer, 1981, p. 6; 1988, p. 276; 1996, p. 5). His research indicated that Canadian legislators' party affiliation and ideological stance could be predicted along a left/right continuum. His long-term study of Canadian students and their parents regarding party affiliations also shows the relevance of authoritarianism as a major factor in conservative party support. He found independent support among Canadian students for Milgram's (1974) bogus punishment scenario: US learning experiments when subjects were told to administer a 'very severe shock' to uncooperative learners and dutifully did so (Altemeyer, 1988, pp. 239-68). These findings lend credence to Meloen, van der Linden, and de Witte's (1994, pp. 72-99) study of Belgian high school students who demonstrated a behavioral connection between authoritarianism, racist party sympathy, and voter support for anti-minority, ethnocentric, and national in-group sentiments in Flanders.

After decades of research, Altemeyer summarized the main features of authoritarians (1996, pp. 1-45, 112-3, 144-5, 165-6, 214-306). He found that high RWAs tend to be persons who would destroy human rights guarantees; would allow those who attack minorities or corrupt governmental officials to go free; are prejudiced against racial, religious, national, immigrant, linguistic, and other ethnic minorities; believe strongly in the group, patriotism, nationalism, militarism, and loyalty; are poor reasoners, thinkers, inferers, and hold contradictory views without realizing it; are poor critical thinkers and rely on incomplete evidence for self-support; are easy victims for propaganda; use a double standard in thinking; are major instigators of intergroup conflict and racism; are ethnocentric, prejudiced, dogmatic, and zealots; and are major supporters of right-wing parties in the US and Canada. Low RWAs oppose abuse of power; oppose vigilante activity; let the punishment fit the crime; are consistent, careful thinkers; face up to personality defects; are open-minded, undogmatic, independent, peace-loving, and less prejudiced.

Authoritarians exhibit a specific type of psychology. They are not adept at weighing evidence, critical thinking, drawing independent conclusions, and squaring the conclusions they reach with the rest of their cognitive schema or maps. Since the authoritarian disposition is to accept wholesale the beliefs of others in terms of submitting to authority and accepting the conventional wisdom, they have little skill for problem solving or decision making. They also carry contradictory pictures in their heads. They may reject suspect ideas from 'dangerous' sources, but they also place faith over reason and accept flimsy evidence if it supports their preselected viewpoints. They also may be quite vulnerable to a communication that is manipulative and merely reinforces their present beliefs, whether true or not; they are very gullible, inflate themselves, and blame others for their personal defects. Their views are often inconsistent. They are blind when it comes to self-awareness and knowing oneself and they endorse contradictory ideas and principles. They are neither fair nor principled since they deny a double standard, which they clearly use, or other facts of self-disclosure (self-esteem deficiencies or degree of prejudice). They are also self-righteous, if not self-fulfilling.

Prejudice and ethnocentrism are highly correlated with RWA in Canada, the US, Russia, and South Africa. RWAs are highly prejudiced against homosexuals and AIDS victims, while approving gay bashing, despite the illegality of such beatings. RWA men are more aggressive toward women in terms of their potential for assault. RWAs are mean-spirited toward student peers in trouble, the homeless, atheists, welfare recipients, 'radicals', and disruptive environmentalists. Both Canadian/US students and their parents were very punitive in their harsh treatment of alleged criminals. High RWA scorers supported authorities over war victims and gays, demonstrators, child molesters, hippies, and peasants as objects of officially sanctioned violence.

High RWAs in Canada and the US espouse traditional religious beliefs and Christian orthodoxy. North American, English, and Russian RWAs also endorsed traditional sex roles, conformed to group norms (Canada) and traditional practices (England), and the conventional philosophy (Russia: equality; the US: *laissez faire* individualism). US students who scored higher on a conservatism scale (with items supporting militarism and loyalty tests and opposing socialized medicine and limits on the FBI) also were high-scoring RWAs along with accepting conventionalism and societal rules. Authoritarianism positively correlated with Canadian students' authority values, punitiveness, sexual constraint, traditionalism, and sense of propriety. The religiously dogmatic and fundamentalists are supremely prejudiced, intolerant, and aggressively authoritarian, whether Christian, Hindu, Jew, or Muslim. Those who are religious, but not fundamentalist, can be less preju-diced, more inclusive, more spiritually soul-searching, and less authoritarian. Unchanging dogmatism correlated with authoritarianism, fundamentalism, and ideational fanaticism.

In politics, RWA's are clearly right-wingers and support such political parties in (English-speaking) Canadian studies, especially among the politi-cally interested. In the US, support of low RWAs for Democrats and high RWAs for Republicans was another consistent tendency. This pattern of party support was also found among Australian adults, Israeli (both Jewish and Palestinian) students, and adults in the former USSR and Russia (the latter also supported nationalism and expressed dislike for democracy). Alte-meyer's study of Canadian MPs and American state lawmakers indicates that elected officials of given political parties are more RWA (Conservatives, Reform, and Republican parties) than their opponents (Liberals, NDP, and Democrats). The Conservative/Republican parties are also economically conservative, anti-equality, more ethnocentric, prejudiced (as are their follow-ers), dogmatic, anti-gay, radical, and zealots. High RWA scores positively correlated with nationalism, anti-abortion and anti-freedom views, anti-gun control, and pro-capital punishment. Regional differences are apparent in the US, with northern states' politicians being less authoritarian than southern ones. It is also clear that the conservative forces of high RWAs have more than their fair share of politicians in both countries. These proto-fascist high-RWA attitudes and personality features can best be labeled conservative or reactionary while their opposite low RWAs can be called liberal or progres-sive. Altemeyer's (1996, p. 289) research in the early 1990s found that 26 per cent of US state legislators surveyed agreed that once the governmental authorities identified the 'dangerous elements' in the society, 'every patriotic citizen' should help to 'stamp out the rot that is poisoning our country'.

Knowledge of authoritarianism may provide keys to prevent it. Accord-ing to Altemeyer, one's level of authoritarianism is determined during adoles-cence, depending on exposure to key life experiences (social learning theory). These experiences come from parents and religious training, physical punishment, learning manners, and treatment by authorities, but also from experiences with gays, dissent, patriotism, nontraditionalism, experimentation, breaking rules, distrusting parents, and harbored feelings of rebellion and unconventionalism. High RWAs are taught early to obey and to fear strangers.

Parents and media (TV) also produce models for social conventional behavior. Low-scoring RWAs come from untraditional egalitarian families, their parents are better-educated, children are taught independence, no physical punishment is used, authority is questioned, equality and cooperation are stressed, and religious practice is casual. Fear of other people is not learned; the family discusses human diversity and social injustice questions. The low-RWA child is more broadly experienced and widely traveled; he/she is more experimental, autonomous, and independent. Truth is discovered, decision making is learned, and problems are solved in a creative way.

Altemeyer maintains that countering authoritarianism is possible. High RWAs want to change to 'average' (not to low) scores. Anti-discrimination laws will be obeyed and contact between high RWAs and average people may change RWA prejudice levels. The more secular, nonreligious, and better educated the person, the greater the exposure to diversity, the lower RWA level which can be expected. Mass media which promote televised crime, violence, and the 'mean and scary' world syndrome need to be offset through citizens and opposition groups who can promote better fare. Churches need to reform the fundamentalists in their congregation regarding ethnocentrism, self-righteousness, racism, prejudice, and mean-spiritedness. Peaceful confrontation between groups without the rabble-rousing of RWA leaders can promote conflict reduction and compromise. Hate-mongering needs to be balanced with counterpropaganda and truth. High RWAs in or seeking public office (such as Jesse Helms, Strom Thurman, Pat Buchanan, Ollie North, Dick Armey, Trent Lott, or Newt Gingrich) need to be exposed for being proto-fascists, rather than the populist democrats and egalitarians they pretend to be. The lessons to be learned involve tolerance, gratitude, and generosity of spirit, equality, and humanity. In this respect, schools have a role to play. One syndicated columnist independently reached this conclusion when he identified Buchanan's 'nativism, authoritarianism, ethnic, and class resentment' as well as his populist passion for 'America first' (Krauthammer, 1992).

The Authoritarian Personality (TAP)

Key features of this related psychological concept identified in *The Authoritarian Personality* by Adorno, Frenkel-Brunswik, Levinson, and Sanford (1950) were rigid support for middle class values; automatic acceptance of authority; aggression displayed toward 'inferiors', minorities, or the 'tender-minded'; exaggerated sense of power, paranoia, and tough-mindedness; cynical toward others; projective tendencies; and a moralistic obsession with sex. At the personal level, authoritarians want power over people. They expect subservience from others. Friendship and love are lacking from their relationships. They are overly concerned with status, hierarchy, and authority. Women are disdained and seen as inferior objects, ready for exploitation. They are elitist in their views of education. They cultivate surprise/suspense, then demand homage (without praise), and play the tyrant, boss, father, or god roles on the job where they reward friends and punish enemies. They are humorless and serious; they cannot brook bad news, criticism, or challenges to their hardened views. Power manipulation and Machiavellian maneuvers/alliances are frequently used. They hold stereotypes, lack ethical norms, are prejudiced, and drive to dominate others. They are dogmatic, exclusive, blame others, and defend their egos through exploitation (Martin, 1989, pp. 43-5; Goldstein and Blackman, 1978, pp. 15-61).

The original TAP construct evolved during and after WWII, when fears of fascism were heightened. Adorno et al. (1950) based their research on American respondents and their answers to questions about ethnocentrism, anti-Semitism, conservatism, and anti-democratic/pro-fascist (F-scale) attitudes. Since the Korean War broke out around that time, Americans shifted their fears from the black- or brown-shirted menace to the red variety. Nevertheless, this project was heralded as the flagship of the social science intellectual fleet, which was the basis for over 3000 publications since 1950. But the exigencies of the ensuing cold war consigned TAP to the drydocks of empirical research. One of the reasons was an exaggerated torrent of criticism based on methodological and ideological questions. These critiques focused on 'yea saying' or acquiescence and the alleged existence of a 'left-wing authoritarianism', a bigfoot-like creature who lurked somewhere in the M-I complex woods to scare the public into spending big dollars on prosecuting the cold war against the evil empire and its allies. A host of alternative research designs (such as Eysenck's T-factor, Rokeach's Dogmatism scale) were brought forward to challenge TAP's alleged ideological bias.

However, when field tested in Italy, the US, and the Netherlands, Rokeach's Dogmatism scale produced results similar to the F-scale, including identification of right-wing extremist party members in these countries (Meloen, 1994a, 1991a), while alternative scales (Altemeyer, Lederer) also produced highly correlated results (Meloen, van der Linden, and de Witte, 1996). Additionally, Meloen (1983, 1993) found in a 24-country review of over 30 years of F-scale research that F scores showed high levels of authoritarianism among English fascists in the early 1950s and late 1960s as compared with only average levels for students at the more recent time. A group of US 'super patriots' had high scores as contrasted with a group of US art students tested concurrently. In South Africa, high scores were reported for Afrikaner students in 1970 and 1980 as contrasted with average scores for English-speaking students in 1980. A group of former SS and Wehrmacht members were tested 20 years after WWII's end. Whereas the former SS displayed very high scores and still preferred a strong leader (dictatorship), the regular army veterans scored lower and preferred democracy or monarchy (Meloen 1983, 1993). Additional results were found for the extreme-right in Belgium and Italy (see chapter 7). Such results indicated that this personality construct had continuing relevance and reliably and validly measured pro-fascist and anti-democratic attitudes (Meloen, 1993; Meloen and Middendorp, 1991).

Political Cognitions

Much TAP research was conducted on 'captive' school and college students because of low cost and high accessibility. Therefore, it remains unclear if authoritarianism qualifies as an ideology of the general public, as a personality dimension, or as a syndrome or cognitive map/schema to manage personal information. Altemeyer (1981, 1988, 1996) maintains that the F-scale measures beliefs rather than personality traits and can be modified by education. Cognitive political studies emphasize the structure rather than the content of beliefs and uses developmental (Piaget, Kohlberg), social learning (Bandura), or adaptive theories (Ward, 1986).

Sidanius' work on nature/nurture interactions and sociopolitical ideology in cross-national contexts strongly supports TAP theory and undergirds 'context theory' (cultural-historical, time-space continuum). His measures of conservatism, racism, sexual repression, and authoritarianism were somewhat related to cognitive complexity and flexibility. This showed that TAP is relevant to the political domain. Sociopolitical dimensions, such as racism and authoritarian aggression, are related to cognitive complexity/behavior albeit political-economic conservatism and religiosity are not (Sidanius, 1978, 1984, 1985; Sidanius et al., 1983; Sidanius and Ekehammar, 1976).

The cognitive component of authoritarianism can be linked to 'integrative complexity' (information processing), sophistication, and its effect on political thinking and conduct. Authoritarians are rigid thinkers, use simplified categories, use polarizations and stereotypes, and have an intolerance of ambiguity. Integrative complexity was applied to the content of speeches by 35 US senators from 1981 to 1985. Isolationists had lower integrative complexity scores than internationalists. Conservative senators had lower levels of integrative complexity than moderates or liberals, based on their voting records and policy statements.

Times of threat and crisis may also have an impact on integrative complexity as they do on authoritarianism for leaders and followers. When leaders interact internationally, the cognitive processing method operates as a personality trait, a rhetorical strategy, or a coping mechanism to guide personal performance and policy making (Pervin, 1990, pp. 672-5).

Ward (1986) supports the direction of this research, but raises questions. In contrast to TAP and extremism research, context theory holds that left and right extremists exhibit greater cognitive complexity and skills, flexibility, and more tolerance of ambiguity than moderates. Extremists develop beliefs in an active, independent, self-driven manner, rather than based on social conformity. Most people are political moderates because they lack social-political interests and passively adopt others' views. Extremists also seem to have higher levels of political interest, competence, deviance, and unpopularity for their views. Yet, their personalities demonstrate 'field independence, high ego strength, and high stress tolerance'. Compared with moderates, extremists have much higher cognitive complexity levels. Some research on radicals, rioters, and terrorists support context theory in demonstrating such qualities.

One study attempted to synthesize authoritarianism, ideology, and cognitive-developmental research among 700 older adolescents in Germany (Lind, Sandberger, and Bargel, 1982). The results showed links among ego strength, content of democratic orientations (egalitarianism, humanism, democratization, and participation), and the structure of one's moral judgements. Education was important in developing a democratic personality.

Dogmatism is a cognitive aspect of personality, while tendermindedness is a moral or religious one, along with authoritarianism. It defines good and evil based on superiority and authority. Conservatism, militarism, and nationalism are ideological guides to social organization. Compulsion runs the gamut of the personality in a continuum from one extreme benefitting all (radicalism, democracy, openmindedness, nonconformism, pacifism, compassion) to the other bettering the few (conservatism, authoritarianism, dogmatism, conventional religiosity, militarism, and compulsion) (Eckhardt, 1991).

Left-Wing Authoritarianism

Winter (1996) discussed left-wing authoritarianism and the Shils' (1954) critique of TAP. Knutson (1974) surveyed California party activists using F-scale scores as a base or criterion measure. Left-wing party members scored appreciably lower than center or moderate party members on authoritarianism, intolerance for ambiguity, and threat orientation. They were roughly equal to the moderates in dogmatism, but lower than right-wingers, scored the same on 'faith in people' as moderates, but lower than right-wing party members (Winter, 1996, pp. 239-41). So while some regimes may claim to be leftist and democratic, political characteristics of systems may not be used to estimate individual personality characteristics. We cannot safely conclude that leftists are as authoritarian as rightists have already been shown to be.

Altemeyer (1988, 1996) maintains that left-wing militant authoritarianism means dedication to the violent overthrow of established authority, aggression toward such authorities or those who support them, and adherence to revolutionary conventionalism. He developed a special scale to flush out these elusive features and discovered that this creation of Shils is a figment of the master's own imagination which exists theoretically, but not, at the moment, empirically. The idea that there is a leftist authoritarianism of revolutionary conspirators who preach political correctness and practice censorship is purely a leftover intellectual remnant of the cold war.

The only truth to this concept is that stale, old-style, unreformed communists, many still living and ruling in Eastern Europe (Russia, Serbia, Hungary, Slovakia, Poland, and the Czech Republic), are extreme left-wing, and closely resemble right-wing authoritarianism as the McFarland et al. (1990, 1993) studies verified. More moderate social democrats do not fill the bill for being RWAs as much as their conservative opponents (who are more likely to be RWAs) would like them to be. Soviet communists were more similar to Western fascist-type authoritarians than to Western left-wing social democrats who are often nonauthoritarian, free-speech advocates, dissenters, civil rights proponents, with unconventional and unsubmissive behavioral characteristics (McFarland et al., 1990, pp. 5-7). Previously, Soviet capitalists, dissenters, and democrats were called 'reactionary', 'decadent', or 'right-wing' by the power elite. But they were more akin to their pro-democratic and anti-fascist left-wing and social liberal brethren in the West. Thus, we conclude that authoritarians support existing power structures and would use force to defend such regimes (Winter, 1996, pp. 241-7; Meloen, 1991a, 1994a).

CROSS-NATIONAL TRENDS

The US and Canada

McFarland and Adelson (1996, pp. 1-57) examined the correlates of prejudice such as authoritarianism, social dominance orientation (SDO), anomie, intelligence, collective self-esteem or just-world beliefs, social desirability, hostility-aggressiveness, personal value sets, and the demographic correlates of gender, SES, hardship, age, urbanism, and education. In Kentucky and Tennessee, they sampled 297 adults and 478 students. The results showed authoritarianism and SDO independently best predicted all four types of prejudice plus latent prejudice among both age groups. Of the demographic variables, only gender was a good predictor of latent prejudice.

Some specific findings about patriotism are also of interest since it correlated positively with need for structure, personal/collective self-esteem, traditionalism, conformity, and security. Authoritarianism is correlated with need for structure, collective self-esteem, traditionalism, conformity, security, and presenting oneself in a favorable light, but not with maintaining a favorable self-image of/for oneself for both samples. SDO correlated negatively and significantly with universalism and attributional complexity, need for cognition, and nonformation of stereotypes; authoritarianism was unrelated to both. SDO appears to be unrelated to education and intelligence levels, but is associated with hostile aggression (physical and verbal, anger, hostility) and psychoticism (antisocial or criminal tendencies, sexual aggression, anti-immigrant/guest worker prejudice).

The study also showed that authoritarianism was not simply a product of a lack of education or intelligence. Moreover, SDO is even less related to these two independent variables. Both of the primary dependent variables (authoritarianism and SDO) in this association have original relationships to socialization practices and social learning experiences so that clinical interviews might help to partially unravel these precursors.

Ray (1976) tried unsuccessfully to replace TAP with his 'directiveness' concept, despite its disutility. Forbes tried to advance Ray's cause although his work is largely discredited today. Forbes explained everything in terms of laissez-faire, free enterprisers, and marketization, following Milton Friedman and Ludwig von Mises. Forbes took on the critical theory of the Frankfurt School with the vengeance of a free-market buccaneer trying to drive out the competition and set up his own corporate monopoly. The aspersions Forbes cast on TAP social science methodology and theory were mainly anecdotal and from far right field. He claimed that ethnocentrism and authoritarianism are unrelated because different nationalisms have their unique concepts and different psychologies. Forbes criticized the Berkeley School for not accepting Plato's typology which already included a timocratic regime ideal type. He claimed that the F scale was useless for Canadian nationalism based on the lack of big 'in-group' or 'out-group' differences there. He called authoritarianism and ethnocentrism 'bogus concepts' and accused the Berkeley group of harboring provincialism, demonstrating ethnocentrism, and exhibiting their own 'false consciousness' in their 'pseudo-objective' research (Forbes, 1985, pp. 4-15, 56-64, and 142-69).

In a path and meta-analysis study (Hamilton and Mineo, 1996, p. 49), a communications persuasibility model showed anxiety increased dogmatism, which increased authoritarianism, which then increased ethnocentrism. Ethnocentrism increased right opinionation (bolstered conservatism and intolerance of liberalism); dogmatism increased left opinionation (strengthened liberalism and intolerance of conservatism). Pre-message attitudes result from a receiver's direct experience or authorities. Post-message attitudes stem from evaluating the source and messages. One's belief system provides the interface between message and source evaluation, which dynamically interact. Fear appeals can impact personal anxiety about self, regardless of source credibility. For the authoritarian receiver, the source's reputation will greatly influence post-message evaluations which then will affect attitudinal changes. For nonauthoritarians, message evaluations will influence post-message evaluations of the source and attitudinal changes (Hamilton and Mineo, 1996).

Examining the relationship between social issues and RWA among 357 Kansas State University students, a recent study showed that RWA is associated with prejudice toward AIDS victims, negative views of human rights, and anti-environmental and drug user stances. Religious RWAs are no longer politically inactive or apathetic, so they may now engage in alternative or nontraditional forms of activity such as changing lifestyles, favoring community organization, buying a benefit concert ticket, or contributing to a voluntary organization. The social issues concerned the Middle East/Persian Gulf crisis, the US budget deficit, abortion, environmental issues, homelessness, education, constitutional rights, violence against women, campaign costs, political action committees, and health care. For all but three issues (environment, homelessness, and anti-female violence), traditional means for political action were used. High authoritarians also tended to use these nontraditional forms of political activity more than low authoritarians. High authoritarians were more likely to be involved in the Persian Gulf War and abortion issues; low authoritarians were more likely to use nontraditional political avenues for their environmental activities. All students viewed these issues as both important and emotionally significant. Educated authoritarians may feel more politically efficacious than those with less education (Hastings, 1996).

The Netherlands

In a Dutch research project, national random samples (Meloen and Middendorp, 1991) were used between 1970 and 1985. It included a short F-scale plus dogmatism, conservatism, socialism, and liberalism scales. The F-scale predicted political activity levels and anti-authoritarianism correlated well with postmaterialism. Dutch authoritarians are less interested in politics or political information and distrust politicians, democracy, and free speech. They embrace nationalistic symbols, sanction moralistic-conservative ideas, and envision a bygone era when a strong leader could reform today's 'degenerated society'. Politics is men's work. They oppose aid to the third world and environmentalism and admire the elite and private property. They object to equal opportunity policy, believe themselves to be 'traditional', 'anti-social-ist', 'right-wing', and 'conservative' in self-designations. They use TV for en-tertainment, but not much other mass media. Their strict moralistic and harsh disciplinarian childrearing practices are often shared with parents, suggesting intergenerational transfer of punitiveness. They are anti-minority, pro-native white, and racist. Some contradictions and inconsistencies in policy sup-port/choices were also found. Their key concepts at issue were equality versus freedom. Party preferences were also predictable based on F scores, with the radical left lowest and conservatives (European 'liberal' individualists) and fundamentalist right-wingers highest on the measures.

Meloen and Middendorp (1991) concluded that relationships between scale scores and political/economic conditions remain mixed or unclear, but when combined with family factors (father's educational level and severity of parental punishment), the relative stability in authoritarianism over differ-ent birth cohorts supports the assertion (with which Altemeyer's research agrees) that childrearing may outweigh socioeconomic variables as causative antecedents for the development of the authoritarian personality syndrome.

In addition to father's education, the other more powerful explanatory variables over time included one's own level of education (negative) and the respondent's age (positive) along with self-ratings as left/right. Somewhat weaker associations were found between political interest and political knowl-edge (both negative) and time spent watching entertainment TV (positive) and higher authoritarianism levels. Anti-authoritarianism was positively associ-ated with preference for democratic childrearing practices and authoritarian-ism with anomie, nationalism, free enterprise, moralism, and traditional gen-der/family roles. Authoritarians were found to be anti-democratic, pro-censor-ship, opposed to third world developmental aid, anti-internationalist; intoler-ant of women, gays, criminals; and opposed to governmental intervention.

From other perspectives (van der Grift, de Vos, and Meloen, 1991, pp. 1-15), anti-Semitism levels in Dutch secondary schools (with 867 respon-dents) were examined. Economic, political, and cultural/religious types of anti-Semitism were all correlated with authoritarianism. Low or anti-authori-tarians paid attention to and had more knowledge about WWII events (such as the Nazi persecutions). Two in-school factors (a less authoritarian climate and exploring the Nazi past) would most likely help to reduce anti-Semitism levels as well as the appeal of a strong leader.

Hagendoorn (1993) identifies three models of authoritarianism: classic psychoanalytical, sociological (stressing family relations), and developmental (claiming authority attitudes are set during adolescence and can be changed by education). Unlike Altemeyer, he claims that none of them is a clear danger to democracy. Research conducted between 1982 and 1991 shows that parental harshness and lack of love toward the child does not necessarily produce authoritarian responses. Vollebergh (1991, 1996) concludes that one's views of human nature, family determinants, political culture, levels of education, and other socialization factors influence independent thinking and willingness to accept authority. Altemeyer's (1981, 1988, 1996) and Todd's (1985, 1987) research on family types, value modeling, and implicitly learned behavior indicates schooling may reinforce or modify previously learned behaviors in egalitarian, nuclear, communal, and authoritarian families.

Scheepers, Felling, and Peters (1992) tested models of relationships and found educational level negatively correlated with anomie and authoritarianism and anomie positively associated with ethnocentrism and authoritarianism. They also found the largest positive and significant correlations between authoritarianism and unfavorable out-group and favorable in-group attitudes. They concluded that when one's social environment produces anomie and ethnocentrism, authoritarianism both explains and mediates such effects.

Authoritarianism was also related to public policy options. Dekker and Ester (1992, 1993) used Dutch survey data from 1975-89 to associate one's level of authoritarianism with having stereotyped views about the unemployed. Political distrust, right-wing views, and racial/religious discrimination tendencies were positively associated with stereotyping; negative correlations were found for political freedom, protest, democratization, and tolerance.

Germany

Lederer (1982) reported on cross-national (US and FRG) analyses of adolescent authoritarianism between 1945 and 1978-79. She describes the climate of freedom in German schools in the 1970s when student obedience and teacher authority were both in question. She noted that anti-authoritarianism is not the same as participatory democracy. Later, Lederer (1993) described cross-national variations in authoritarianism in the US, Austria, and West and East Germany. Seven scales were combined into a new general authoritarianism measure (NGAS). The highest factor loadings in the US in 1966 were for parental loyalty and respect and in 1978 for obedience to authority, patriotism and loyalty, parental loyalty and children's conformity, and xenophobia. The FRG's 1979 highs were for general obedience, patriotism and loyalty, morality, parental obedience, moral standards, discipline, determination and strong will, corrupting youth, and leadership directiveness. Austria's 1980 highs were for disciplined obedience, parental obedience, moral standards, determination, and strong will. West German youth were more authoritarian than Americans in 1945; but by 1979, Germans were more democratic.

There were few differences among US, German, and Austrian students, but Austrians were somewhat more authoritarian. Austrian and American, but not German, students often indicated respect for state authority while rejecting foreigners. In all three countries, students gave high scores to 'disciplined obedience to authority'; East German youth were significantly more authoritarian and prejudiced. Their ethnocentrism levels were startlingly different.

Lederer attributed such changes in Germany to a new democratic educational philosophy and a different family structure than in the past. Both trends were against obedience, order, and authoritarianism at home and in school up to the early 1970s. Childhood socialization patterns were liberalized, strict parental rule was relaxed, there was less corporal punishment, and stress was placed on 'self-reliance' and 'free will' rather than 'obedience' and 'submission' during the post-war period. Children increasingly played a more significant role in democratic family decision making. German political culture changed dramatically from a subject/parochial post-war typology to a democratic/participant-oriented system. Via personality and cultural interactions, the 'national character' blossomed in a new civil society and civic culture (Lederer, 1993).

Another analysis of these same trends in the US, Germany, and eight other countries confirmed these results (Torney, Oppenheim, and Farnen, 1975, pp. 220-3). This research project tested authoritarianism, tolerance, civil liberties, and support for equality/women's rights. It showed that when a country's support for the national government and civic interest were above the overall mean among 14-year-olds, democratic values scores were lower. This was also true for the US. The US exhibited the same pattern with the lowest democratic values scores and higher support/participation scores. By contrast, just as with the 14-year-old group, Germany had the highest democratic values score along with positive political interest/participation scores.

Oesterreich (1993, pp. 1-11) investigated East and West Berlin vocational and academic high school students' views in 1991 about nationalism, racism, dogmatism, authoritarianism, and ethnocentrism. East Berliners were much more negative in their attitudes toward foreigners. He attributes these differences to the competitive economic situation, the feeling of being second-class citizens, and Bonn's broken preunification promises. These findings are similar to Sniderman, Tetlock, and Peterson's (1993); they use social context theory and authoritarianism to explain US racism, still seeing authoritarianism as causing racial discrimination. This is especially true among uneducated, lower-SES, working-class respondents in their surveys who discriminated based on race. However, Oesterreich's authoritarianism measure is new, unfamiliar, untested, and may be invalid and unreliable.

Belgium

Lipset's (1959) thesis about democracy and working class authoritarianism was investigated by de Witte (1996) who asked whether Belgian unskilled blue collar workers are bourgeois or authoritarian. He concluded that the working and middle classes only partly hold the same views and values since the middle class cherishes (individual) freedom and the working class equality and collectivity. The working class is more conservative than the middle class *vis á vis* traditional values and norms regarding family, childrearing, and work. But on the socioeconomic level, the working class is more progressive, lamenting their social positions, lack of social mobility, and need for unions and the government to ensure social progress and change.

Another study (Meloen, van der Linden, and de Witte 1994, 1996) researched 900 Flemish high school students and found that the Adorno et al. (1950), Lederer (1983), and Altemeyer (1988) authoritarianism scales equally well predicted anti-minority feelings, ethnocentrism, national in-group preferences, anti-Semitism, anti-feminism, pro-apartheid attitudes, trust in authorities, and pro-racist party sympathies and voting preferences.

They developed a model whereby parental education, school type, and religious identifications were the best predictors of authoritarianism. Anti-minority ethnocentrism and national in-group favoritism predicted voting preferences for a Flemish anti-immigrant political party. Xenophobia, ethnocentrism, anti-minority feelings, and intense nationalism formed the core of authoritarianism and its product, political racism. The overall results lent credence to the Adorno et al. personality structure, the Lederer parental influence, and the Altemeyer social learning theories and models about the educational level of respondents and their parents.

Sweden

Sidanius et al. (1983) and Ekehammar et al. (1989) examined the relationship between social status and sociopolitical ideology in Sweden. Both their measures of ideology contain some TAP elements such as punitiveness (aggression) and political-economic conservatism, religion, racism, and general conservatism. Conservatism is a form of submission, religious deference is conventionalism, and racism is a form of aggression as well.

The Lipset thesis did not hold up in Sweden. Instead, the higher the SES, the higher were conservatism, capitalistic values, punitiveness, belief in social inequality, and racism scores. High SES persons were most opposed to economic equality, low SES most in its favor, and the middle class was mixed in its viewpoint, much as pluralistic interest group theory would have predicted.

In Sweden, the middle class is socially liberal while the upper and working classes (including adolescents) are more socially conservative.

The Ekehammar et al. (1989) study revisited the working class authoritarianism construct, testing Swedish, Australian, and American college and secondary school students aged 16 to 19 years. This study found that the higher the SES of a person, the more likely are that person's sociopolitical attitudes to be conservative. The lower economic conservatism of the working class as compared to the middle and upper classes was confirmed. The other part of the Lipsit thesis about higher noneconomic conservatism for the working class as compared with the other two classes was generally contradicted.

Sidanius (1984) compared political interest, information, and ideology with extremism, context theory, and parental educational levels in Sweden. Higher political interest and information skills were found among left and right extremists (compared with moderates). Higher educated parents had children with more heterogeneous ideologies. Sidanius et al. (1987) also compared Sweden and the US with respect to average levels of political sophistication. They found that Swedes had higher levels of ideological coherence, political interest, ideological variance, and strength in the interface between political party preference and political self-concept on one side versus ideological preferences and values on the other.

Russia

In his examination of the prospects for democracy in Russia, Popov (1995) assessed the strength of the authoritarian personality in the early 1990s. Authoritarian attitudes were present and equal to those in Ukraine and Belorussia. There was a higher level of authoritarianism in the Caucasus and Middle Asia and lower levels in the Baltic states. Russians supported parental discipline, strong leaders, willpower, hard work, and like values. They also had a long list of those who would be isolated from society, including homosexuals, drug addicts, prostitutes, AIDS victims, as well as murderers. One year earlier, 20-33 per cent said they would 'liquidate' some of these groups, so these later responses are really more humane (!) (Popov, 1995, pp. 122-7).

In a 1993 survey of Moscow adults, McFarland, Ageyev, and Djintcharadze (1996) found that authoritarianism thrives in the post-communist era. Authoritarianism was positively correlated with pro-communist and anti-capitalistic beliefs and negatively with support for democratic and capitalistic reform efforts, confirming 1989 and 1991 results. Authoritarianism predicted increased religiosity for those with a weaker communist faith as religion replaces communism. As in the US, Russian authoritarianism predicted negativism toward environmentalists and AIDS victims. Unlike American authoritarians, Russian RWAs blamed society (rather than the individual) for their poverty and homelessness, probably because of their conformity to Russian social norms (conventionalism). But other changes are underway because fewer low RWAs support Yeltsin, now that he seems less democratic.

While authoritarianism still predicts ethnocentrism and general prejudice in the West, Russia's levels are even higher. In Russia, authoritarianism is positively related to age, larger families and number of children fostered, lack of language proficiency and foreign travel (for women only), and negatively to size of one's home town, higher SES and white collar occupations, and higher income levels. Similar findings were evident regarding conservative organizational membership and both ethnic prejudice and anti-communism (in the West) and anti-capitalism (in the East). TAP/RWA cling together as a more unified personality construct in Russia than in the US or Canada.

Negative correlations between RWA and education still appear in the West, but this phenomenon mainly applies to Russian women. The contrast between the West's free exchange of ideas with the Soviets' emphasis on ideology, revealed truth, rote learning, and the autocratic classroom may partly explain this (McFarland et al., 1990, pp. 9-12; Simpson, 1972; Torney, Oppenheim, and Farnen, 1975).

Personal experiences were variously related to authoritarianism levels since opportunities for contact with gays or pornography were very limited. Yet, for Americans and Russians alike, positive evaluations of political protest and sexual freedom pointed to lower authoritarianism levels. Americans were less authoritarian than Russians in the extent to which they had unconventional sex, saw public power and authority misused, and criticized religion, strict family life, and restrictive cultural traditions. More important for Russians was a sense of rebellion toward political and parental restrictions. Here again, we underscore the importance of cultural context and understanding sources and manifestations of RWA/TAP.

McFarland et al. (1990, pp. 17-39) also found a 'mentality-experience split theory' which separates thought and action, so a wider gulf exists between personal experience and authoritarianism. There is also a common situation in Russia of decision-making delays and inaction, with intentions and activities having contradictory results. In the USSR, Poland, Hungary, and East Germany, individuals learned to play several different roles in everyday life, to operate on different political levels, and to speak different political languages in state, party, union, private group, church, educational, or family contexts. The skills needed were conformism on the job, democracy or paternalism at home, religious devotion in church, individualism in small group meetings, and a 'new socialist man' role in outward appearances. The individual had to have multiple political personalities to pull out of his/her intellectual closet, wearing whatever conceptual outfit a given occasion required. So one's cognitive style may be consistent or contradictory or consistently contradictory if one's survival requires cognitive dissonance to stay alive in the system (Farnen, 1990, pp. 87-93; Szabo, 1991).

(Former) Yugoslavia

Results similar to those found in the former USSR appeared in Siber's (1991) report which used judgement samples as the Yugoslavian population for a case study. Authoritarianism of the 'cognitive type' was formed via the political socialization process, encouraging both ethnocentrism and 'egal-itarian-statist' orientations. Authoritarianism is negatively associated with democratic self-management (compared with an uncritical attitude or adher-ence to an ideology) orientations and tolerance of others' ideologies, values, and political orientations. Positive intercorrelations appeared between authoritarianism and conformity, anomie, rigidity, anxiety, and aggressiveness. It was also related to educational level, social background, SES, and life course variables. The previous existence of an 'egalitarian mentality' with concurrent state support for everyone's 'equality in poverty' was another finding along with a reaffirmation of the authoritarian's willingness to accept any ideology which had the state authorities' approval. This environment provided fertile ground for political manipulation, conflict, aggression, and ethnic intolerance.

TRENDS IN AUTHORITARIANISM

Longitudinal Trends

In longitudinal authoritarianism research, fluctuations in time were found around mean levels. Using a 7-point scale, scores were produced averaging about 4.0, with a 'normal' range between 3.5 and 4.5 constituting the middle and scores below or above these numbers indicating lower or higher levels of authoritarianism. A meta analysis of 321 US samples and samples from 23 other countries of students and nonstudents (total of 47 016 respondents) in random and nonrandom samples between 1945 and 1980 produced a total US mean of 3.61, a student mean of 3.43, a nonstudent mean of 3.90, and a random sample mean of 3.96 (Meloen 1983, 1993). For European student and nonstudent groups from 1953 to 1977, the means for the former averaged 3.03 and 4.43 for the latter. US samples produced significantly higher F-scale scores in the South, rural, and interior regions as compared with urban, industrial, coastal, and non-South areas (Meloen, 1993, pp. 50-61).

Lederer (1993) noted a slight upward (but low-scoring) trend in the US between 1966 and 1978 and a downward one in the FRG between 1945 and 1978. Lederer and Kindervater's (1995, pp. 187-8) trend analysis examined the US, FRG, and East Germany from 1978-92, finding that youth had lower scores on basic authoritarianism and respect for state authority measures; the FRG decreased on general and basic scales, on respect for elder's authority and hostility to foreigners scales, and on Lederer's new general authoritarianism scale. By comparison, East German youth increased on three measures (general, respect for unspecific, and authoritarian family structure scales).

A downward trend, similar to the one in the FRG, was charted in the Netherlands from 1970 to 1985 (Meloen and Middendorp, 1991); a decrease in the US from 1954 to 1972 and an upward trend thereafter (1972-77) (Meloen, 1986, 1998); an upward trend in Canada from 1973 to 1987 (Altemeyer, 1988) and a slight decrease there since the early 1990s (Altemeyer, 1996). High and low score levels increased concurrently. Altemeyer (1988) noted the Canadian university population became more conservative and the number of left-wing low-scoring students shrank significantly. Some generational changes also occurred such as with the item that said 'a woman's place is wherever she wants it to be'. In 1973, the average student disagreed, but by 1982, the typical response was to agree strongly (Altemeyer, 1988, p. 26).

Meloen (1983, 1986, 1998) examined authoritarianism fluctuations, unemployment, and publications on homosexuality in the US during 1954-77. Fluctuations in authoritarianism were best explained in relation to concurrent sociopolitical events (level of militarism, social punitiveness, and religious orthodoxy) and economic factors (unemployment levels). Extending this analysis back to 1920, he estimated an increase in authoritarianism levels in the late 1940s and high levels in the 1950s, with a steady decrease in the Kennedy and Johnson eras. He computed a sequence of social authoritarianism, producing student authoritarianism and promoting authoritarian behavior. A national cycle of authoritarianism was postulated from the extreme of an overthrow of democracy to authoritarian actions and policies, stabilization of these giving rise to a new anti-authoritarian opposition, which initiated the democratic phase of the cycle again. Such cycles occurred frequently.

Our position on authoritarianism is the opposite of Molnar's (1995) extolling the virtues of authority, media censorship, corporal punishment in schools, and other archaic and Platonic public policy proposals. He slights authoritarian research and researchers using pejorative terms such as stereotyping, prejudice, and false categorization. His confusion about the words authority, authoritative, and authoritarianism is as upsetting as it is inexcusable.

Trends in Cohorts

Much of what we know about the ebb and flow of authoritarian measures over different age cohorts in the West comes from Dutch research. For example, Meloen and Middendorp (1991) found relative stability and slightly decreasing mean scores in 1970, 1975, and 1980 for the 1911-53 Dutch birth cohorts tested in three separate surveys. They also examined 1901-68 birth cohorts (using six sets of five-year cohorts and one large 1916-53 birth cohort in their 1970-80 research project). Then, cohort means dropped from 4.48 (1970) to 4.33 (1975) to 4.10 (1980), to 4.01 (1985). The 1901-15 cohorts were the most authoritarian groups (mean scores 4.75-5.06) as compared with younger (1954-68) cohorts who had lower (3.62-3.91) mean scores. The 1916-53 age cohorts showed the greatest resistance to the general trend of declining authoritarianism, decreasing over the ten years after 1970 from 4.40 to 4.27, less than all other decreases noted. These findings led them to label age and education as two 'constants' in this research along with left (liberal) versus right (conservative) self-ratings. Father's educational level was also important. They found no direct cause-effect relationship between economic circumstances (such as economic recession or unemployment levels and authoritarianism or extent of right-wing extremist activity in the country). Instead, they argued that a favorable political climate/culture encouraging expression of right-wing views may be more important than an economic crisis.

Lineage Relationships

Few scholars now (Hopf, 1993, is an exception) use psychoanalytical explanations (Altemeyer, 1988, pp. 62-6). Altemeyer (1988) discounted parental influence and advocated a social learning model (the growth of cognitions, the influence of imitation, cultural reinforcement, and so on). Authoritarian conventionalism and strict childrearing practices are often associated with intergenerational transfer of these same values. Hagendoorn (1993) reconceptualized and downplayed family influence while supporting the role which education/schools can play in reinforcing the democratic personality.

But Altemeyer found significant correlations between parents' and children's authoritarianism in Canada (average .40) which are as strong as that of respondents' educational levels and RWA scores (-.30 to -.40). The highest correlations with RWA were among parents who successfully focused on increasing their children's religious fundamentalism. Life cycle and resocialization patterns will likely have their effects in increased middle aged conservatism with appropriate mediated reinforcement, but personal (or, perhaps, mediated) contacts with 'aberrants' may temper authoritarianism's growth.

Meloen and Middendorp (1991, p. 58) found a relationship between experiences of being punished severely as a child and higher authoritarianism scores. These results were related to parental obedience, respect, children's obligations, loyalty, discipline, conformity, and rebelliousness. Meloen, van der Linden, and de Witte (1994, pp. 91-2) attributed parental influence to authoritarianism and right-wing voting preferences, father's educational level, religious identification, and parental choice of school (vocational or general).

Studies of Austrian and (eastern/western) German youth shed some light on interactions between childrearing and producing a social climate conducive to the growth or rejection of authoritarianism (Schmidt and Berger, 1993; Lederer, 1993). In Germany (1979, 1991) and Austria (1980, 1992), Lederer noted decreases in authoritarian family structure, reporting that Austrian 1980-82 changes may be attributed to more liberal family structure and heightened awareness of close Austrian links to the Nazi past. Schmidt and Berger's 1991-93 two-wave panel study of eastern and western German youth found connections among all youth and parental conformity norms. They showed the correspondence and stability between authoritarianism and right-wing self-placement as well as with anti-foreign/anti-immigrant behaviors/views. For this, they offered a social and situational explanation in the form of economic threats to low-education, -income, -status individuals and regarding governmentally approved sanctions against asylum seekers.

CONCLUSIONS

The changing nature of socialization and resocialization over a lifetime make it unlikely that individual authoritarianism is entirely permanent, unchanging, or completely parentally determined. Times favorable to authoritarianism may allow its more frequent public expression and appearance. Yet we need not assume these attitudinal or psychological structures are immune from learning or modification, just as the Western political culture and environment are evolving along new-age, global, postindustrial, and postmodern lines, something very different from a couple of generations ago.

6 International and Cross-National Research Findings on Political Socialization and Civic Education

INTRODUCTION

This chapter describes one model of democratic citizenship requirements and competencies in line with our previous 'strong'/'weak' democracy discussion. It surveys some major research findings about political socialization and education. These subjects relate to our conceptual focus on democracy, authority, nationalism, internationalism, multiculturalism, tolerance, and militarism.

POLITICAL SOCIALIZATION AND EDUCATION

Relevant books by theInternational Political Science Association Research Committee on political socialization and education include: *Reconceptualizing Politics, Socialization, and Education* (Farnen, 1993b), *Nationalism, Ethnicity, and Identity* (Farnen, 1994a), *Democracy, Socialization, and Conflicting Loyalties in East and West* (Farnen, Dekker, Meyenberg, and German, 1996), and *Politics, Sociology, and Economics of Education* (Farnen and Sünker, 1997). Other views on these topics can be found in *Integrating Political Science, Education and Public Policy* (Farnen, 1990).

NATIONALISM, RACISM, AND EDUCATION

Major findings concerning youth and nationalism from national and cross-national political socialization research have been summarized earlier (Farnen, 1996, pp. 82-105) as follows (date of report is in parentheses):

North America

American students' identity with their flag increased until grade 11. This included increased nationalism, only dropping in grade 12 (1963). In a US study of 2700 California children in grades 5 and 8, two-thirds of the respondents saw their common beliefs and values (not their language or residence) as the source of their common national identity. Symbolic growth (recognizing the flag) was mostly complete by the 8th grade. Most older children defend the US in ideological terms, yet one-quarter still depended on language and residence as defining factors (1971). Comparing US youth with others, Canadians (as with Italian adults) had greatest pride in their geography; Colombians prized Catholicism (1971). In the US, children's support for national heroes decreases with age; Congress and voting replace the president as symbols of government over time (becoming congruent with textbook, parent, teacher, and media perceptions); and only a small minority still choose the flag rather than public officials as representative of government (1969).

A US longitudinal panel study (1965, 1973, and 1982) of college-educated Vietnam protestors showed they mainly were Democrats; supported civil liberties, tolerance, integration; and were against school prayer, the military, police, and big business. They were more positive on women's rights, equality, minority aid, and minority equality. They were as a whole more in tune with social welfare liberalism, pro-democracy, anti-authoritarianism, anti-fascism, and were more nondogmatic in political orientation (1987).

' Jennings (1993, pp. 1-19) found educational level an important differentiating variable in terms of political salience, differences within and between age cohorts, and between parents and their offspring. From just after leaving high school, the college educated were stable in their political beliefs such as pro-civil liberties and toleration. College graduates reported their political views were challenged in school and differed appreciably from their parents. The more highly educated had higher political interest, efficacy, factual knowledge, sophistication, and participation at each point in the study. Social science and humanities majors tended to be more politically developed than education, business, or science majors. Their orientations were overall more liberal across the board on abortion, labor unions, and social security.

In contrast to African and Asian states (where strong family, village, provincial, tribal, or ethnolinguistic loyalties may retard nation-building), US socializing agents promote a national identity and loyalty of obedience, consent, and internalization of feeling. By adolescence, US youth succumbed to 'compulsory citizenship' which overshadows democratic principles of informed consent, voluntarism, and 'contingent obligation'. Even US minorities and recent immigrants are 'oversocialized' into superpatriotism (which is formed early, lasts long, and is seldom subject to re- or de-socialization) (1969).

West Europe

The 1990 European values study showed that the primary home-based socialization values in Western democracies included good manners, sense of responsibility, tolerance, and respect for others. These traditional values, with hard work and thrift, were grouped under 'conformity' values (contrasted with 'self-centered achievement' or modern values, including independence, imagination, determination, and perseverance). Denmark represented the latter and the US the former 'ideal types', reflecting what could be called democratic versus authoritarian social values. Further analysis using the world values study data set identified three cultural groups. There was the obedience/religious faith ('protestant ethic') cluster (US, Canada, Argentina, Mexico, Hungary) with independence or imagination not highly valued. The opposite group of independent and imaginative countries included Austria, Norway, Sweden, Brazil, and Chile, where obedience, religious faith, hard work, or thrift were at the opposite pole. The third cluster of tolerance countries included Portugal, Finland, and Poland with hard work, religious faith, obedience, and independence at the negative end of the continuum. Unique cases were Russia (hard work and thrift, positive; independence and imagination, negative) and Japan (unselfishness, positive; independence, negative).

Childhood studies in Europe found the reality of 'control, discipline, and management' actually replaced the values of educational freedom and democracy in schools. While schools are socially important, children's contribution to the production of knowledge is not recognized (Ovortrup, 1995, p. 9).

A 1993 study of 300 young Londoners indicated their views of race, patriotism, and national identity were primordial, instrumental, and racialized (being English was tantamount to being white). Such views were also differentiated by gender and race (Phoenix, 1995). Regarding their national symbols and identity, Scottish children were aware of and exhibited basic elements of ethnocentrism, prejudice, and chauvinism (1963).

A 1992-93 survey of Dutch 15-19 year olds sought an explanation for their severe anti-German attitudes. These Dutch students had the least sympathy for, the most negative attitudes toward, and the most disinterest about Germans as compared with other EC member, neighboring, and Western European states. They also lacked much knowledge about German politics and demographics. It was found that one's interaction or factual knowledge of Germany had no effect on one's rating of the FRG. The authors were forced to explain the phenomenon as an aspect of the Dutch political culture which has not forgotten or forgiven German behavior in WWII, a society-wide prejudice lasting until today (Dekker and Jansen, 1994).

One educational challenge in Finland is to help youth replace the destroyed past grand narratives (religion, communism, faith, certainty, universalism) with new ideologies based on factual and fictional information about the destruction of authority and tradition. Educators have to help youth avoid the 'skinhead' option of authoritarianism, nationalism, and paramilitarism as a false answer to a male identity crisis, requiring a new cultural solution to this problem which, itself, is nonaggressive (Länteenmaa, 1995).

Dekker and Ester (1993) used separate national samples in the Netherlands to assess 1975-91 political views. Youth attitudes generally mirror those
of the total Dutch society. The idea of youthful, urban, conservative, profes-
sionals ('yuppies') was a media creation since this group as a whole is liberal
left. With working class authoritarianism, education was more important than
SES in determining authoritarianism levels in the Netherlands. Controlling for
SES, authoritarianism also predicted racism. Education and mass media must
correct erroneous impressions of a conservative bias and higher racism among
the general public (which is both less racist and more liberal than most survey
respondents believed). Both nationalism and right-wing self-identification
increase with age, but on the average, they recently declined across all age
groups (Dekker and Ester, 1993). Vollebergh (1994, pp. 70-1) found that
increased educational level produced lower authoritarian levels in combination with improved educational standards and acquisition of higher social
status which accompanied increased higher education.

Oceania

A study of Australian children aged 5-16 (Connell, 1971) showed that national symbolism was regularly used by age 12, military and nationalist tradition (shared by parents) was strong, and a predominant popular ideology
based on nationalism, anti-communism, and external threats gripped the land.

New Zealanders display positive (apolitical), but Americans exhibit
negative (more political, ideological, power-projection-oriented, bellicose,
and hegemonic) patriotism. The degree of positive or negative patriotism
largely depends on a nation's militarism, history, and leadership role; threats
to its hegemony; or its place in the era's geopolitical realities. US patriotism
varied from the Revolutionary to the Persian Gulf wars since the duration, nature, size of threat, objectives, and enemies were different (Hirshberg, 1994).

East Europe

Völgyes (1993) describes the new authoritarianism in Eastern Europe as
accepting the continuing division of power between elites and the masses as
'legitimate'. Since communism left a vast gulf between the atomistic citizenry
at the lowest level and international communism at the highest level, there
was no intermediary unit as an object of loyalty to which the citizenry could
respond. Thus, 'neo-tribalism' (which expresses negativism toward all other
political objects, except the state) grows. These 'neo-tribalists' are character-
ized by aggression, zealotry, ethnic relativism, 'an ambivalent consciousness',

'schizophrenic allegiance', and concepts of 'good and evil' fiercely struggling between justice and both internal and external 'enemies'. These 'childhood diseases' produced ethnic rivalries, civil war, and risk of international conflict in Eastern Europe. The family still is the primary informal political socialization agent; school is the premier formal agency, along with the mass media.

Polish university students (Holly, 1994) indicated their relative social distance from distant and neighbor states with Germany being rationalized, Hungary effectively appreciated, and Canada sentimentally imagined.

Authoritarian personality characteristics in Hungary are linked to national exclusiveness, ethnocentrism, anti-Semitism, and lack of internationalist orientation. A strong sense of nationalism develops from grades 4 to 8. Youth's temporal sequencing went from parents and birthplace to language and group; to country awareness, jobs, and geography; finally to politics, social system, and group cohesion. History and geography curricula ignore ethnic minority questions, nationality issues and feelings, and reasoned patriotism since civic education is dull, faceless, ideological, and uninformative (Csepeli, 1989).

Dekker, Malova, and Theulings (1996) identified elite, organizational, ideological, and individual levels of nationalistic political attitudes. Nationalism was conceived of subjectively as belief in a nation, congruence between nation and state, support for realigned borders, use of national symbols, forced assimilation or deportation of oppositional ethnic national groups, distrust of external national groups, and rejection of international cooperation. They found about one-third of the Slovakian populace with clear nationalistic orientations at the highest individual level.

In a 1982 national sample of 10 to 14-year-olds in Hungary, a majority identified their own country as an idealized, near-perfect state. They had fully integrated national identity into their self-identification framework. Students from higher SES homes were more adept at answering questions as well as providing 'official' answers when requested. Young children were more ethnocentric and accepted official values, but older children were more critical of socialist, nationalist, and capitalistic values (Csepeli, 1994).

In 1992, a nationwide survey focused on Hungarian 10 to 17-year-olds' political socialization. Their political interest was low, the media and parents were primary sources of information, and very few would willingly play a leadership role in politics. Passivity was endemic. Students were willing to shelter Hungarian refugees from neighboring countries (which they were) or refugees from an Asian civil war (which they were not). Their human rights concerns were nonexistent. They were unwilling to protest discrimination against Sinti/Roma, Jews, or homosexuals, and especially against Transylvanian Hungarians, but not against Turks living in Bulgaria (Csepeli, 1994).

Hungarian children think (very) often about being Hungarian compared with their European identity. They are also proud to be both Hungarian and

European, with far fewer ashamed of either identity. Such identifications increase with age. In 1992, Hungarian children were more religious, prayed, attended Bible class, indicated a religious denomination, and approved of religious instruction in schools. More believed in God than in either the devil or communism (Csepeli, 1994).

One expert on Serbia says that former communist values have been replaced by authoritarian and nationalist ones, including religious revival, national patriotism, xenophobia, isolationism, intolerance, conformism, and authoritarianism. These values now comprise the content of political socialization and education in Serbia. The old communist elite used war to stay in power along with their monopoly of the state-owned TV service to produce 'patriotic ecstasy'. Authoritarianism among youth is widespread in the country and the most educated segment is the least authoritarian. Political schools were used through the 1980s to train political activists and party cadre/elites.

Since 1990, Serbian TV (the major news source for all age groups) used ethnicity to mount a media war against Kosovo. A 1990 youth survey of pro-social orientations found girls more altruistic than boys. Those youth who conformed to demands for submission to authority were the least pro-social. Parents, peers, and school were the principal agents of socialization. However, another survey at the same time showed that youth were quite participative, evidenced elements of democratic political culture, and exhibited very heterogeneous political values. Yet, in Serbia today, the new ideology of democracy and nationalism 'is just as collectivist and totalitarian as the old one' (Pantic, 1994, p. 381). The transformed communist elite are now hardened nationalists, intolerant revanchists, and xenophobic authoritarians. A 1993 sample of young Belgraders found a combination of the following value sets: religious (60 per cent), nonconformism (59 per cent), authoritarian (37 per cent), and 'openness to the world' (54 per cent). Two other 1993 surveys found a bell-shaped curve of Serbian supporters of fascism with more under age 29 least (14 per cent) in favor and confirmed the existence of mass xenophobia, but overwhelming opposition to ethnic cleansing (Pantic, 1994).

A Croatian scholar says the three pillars of socialization in Russia, Eastern Europe, the Balkans, and Croatia are 'orthodoxy, autocracy, and nationalism' where the nation state joins the church to produce conservative domination through the community. A 'convenient authoritarian structure [is] dominant in the population' (Siber , 1994, p. 363). Between 1965 and 1992, the Croatian population moved from near total approval to marry a person of another ethnicity to a small minority willing to do so.

A group of Polish researchers (Fratczak-Rudnicka et al., 1994) used a Dutch European Community survey form on a group of 175 Warsaw University and other higher educational institutions in Spring 1993. Results indicated that these students (aged 18-24) knew little about, but very much wanted to join, the EC. They also favored further European integration. However, they eliminated three groups as being non-European (namely, the US, Canadian, and 'Jewish' 'nations'). Also revealing were the facts that Polish students did not think the EC was much of a democratic institution. They did not favor women playing a greater role in politics, but they were in favor of having a minimum number of women as EC parliamentary candidates.

After being threatened and used as a tool in a political struggle, ethnic identity took on a new importance among 11-14 year old Croatians who were directly involved in the 1991 Serbo-Croatian war. The war process, itself, speeded up ethnic/national self-identification *vis á vis* the 'other' (Serbia) and created a long-lasting enemy image in the minds of these children based on feelings of fear, hatred, and loss (Povrzanovic, 1995).

A 1993 study of nationalist, racist, and anti-Sinti/Roma views in Hungary showed clear-cut attachment to national identity, distancing from the West, and anti-'gypsy' bias. Those who disagreed with some of these views were 'gypsy' students themselves (but they were equally nationalistic); boys were less nationalistic than girls, but more anti-gypsy; and younger students were more nationalistic, but less anti-gypsy. Those with more education tended to reject these views, but those in vocational schools and working were more anti-gypsy. Mother's education and urban residence also predicted less nationalism and less racism. Attitudes about using political violence were highly correlated with these primary variables. The less violent were higher SES students with Hungarian nationality and a better educated mother (Toth, 1995).

Africa

Kenyan and Tanzanian students who identified with their country and its leaders said that teachers and media were their key political educational sources. They accepted obedience and service roles of citizenship and showed increasing nationalism across the higher grades. Students were potentially disobedient despite the fact that they considered laws to be moral and did not want to conflict with the state. They also wanted to preserve their traditions and customs and found no problem in doing so (1967).

Asia

Types of nationalism across the world vary from state to state. For Chinese nationalism, one's primary loyalties are to family, province, linguistic or ethnic group, or to China and Chinese civilization, not to any nation-state (the PRC, itself). The essence of being Chinese is directly related to Chinese identity and loyalties. Despite the continuing division of China into Taiwan and other parts, China is still considered a prime number which has or will absorb Taipei, Hong Kong, Macau, and Formosa. Chineseness is based on a common sense of Chinese history, culture, and civilization. One's loyalties can leap from local to ethnic, popular, or civilization levels without intermediate steps at state (provincial) or nation-state levels (China as a place, history, and people with common religious traditions and a feudally organized polity).

In Japan, a neonationalism movement is underway, including reviving emperor worship. The goal is to preserve the outward signs of social harmony, conformity, consensus, and morality in Japanese schools and everyday life. New history textbooks in the 1980s advanced principles of loyalty, piety, 'racial purity' (the myth of a culturally superior, monocultural, and monoracial society), and reinforced extant structures of inequality. Japanese students now sing their anthem, salute their flag, and learn respect for the emperor as part of this conformity/harmony project (Fukurai and Alston, 1992).

ETHNICITY, MULTICULTURALISM, AND EDUCATION

National and cross-national research findings include the following results:
Research on childhood, youth, and schooling stresses negative (drugs, violence, TV, failure) rather than positive features (autonomy, individualism, family liberalism, sexual freedom). The public myth is of the deprived child in the deprived school or the deprived student studying with deprived teachers. The contradictions are between negotiated and command education, unplanned experience versus systematic education, autonomy outside versus subordination in school, self-control versus directedness, grouping by ability versus pluralism, holistic externality versus cognitive concentration, multicultural and ethnic pluralism versus a one-size-fits-all curriculum, and reforming communist teachers to teach Western democracy. Such tensions/conflicts/ambivalences require new strategies for humanizing the classroom, relaxed dress, vulgar language tolerance, self-regulation, negotiated discussions, consultations, pluralism, computerization, anti-violence, pro-activity, egalitarianism, equality, mainstreaming, and modernization. Other trends include personal development for democracy, tolerance, and pluralism; balancing classical education aims with external variety; and interrogating present in-school divisions by SES, gender, language, and personal needs (Lausitz, 1995).

A study of 8-15-year-olds in California concluded that the greatest deviations from democratic norms were among white students. Whites took pride in themselves *vis á vis* African Americans and subscribed to the notion that 'Negroes blame too many of their problems on whites' (Lawrence, 1970). Early socialization patterns help explain willingness to participate in urban riots. Attitudes about race, nation, and political personalities are formed early and last a lifetime (Sears and McConahay, 1970).

In a study of three groups of secondary school students in Georgia and California, higher SES respondents were less prejudiced than lower ones. Regardless of SES, African Americans had lower trust and higher dogmatism scores overall. The predominantly black Georgia school had higher dogmatism and lower tolerance scores as a whole (Simpson, 1971). In a grade 3-9 study in two northern cities, African Americans had lower patriotism, loyalty, and community support levels than whites when asked to evaluate statements such as 'sometimes, I'm not proud to be an American' (Greenburg, 1969).

There is considerable variation among US Latinos, including how they perceive the 'American dream' of unlimited progress, materialism, patriotism, and democracy. For instance, Puerto Ricans and Cubans (when compared with Mexican-Americans) want to return home sooner and think of themselves as Americans second, not first (Gann and Duigan, 1986). A study of three different Hispanic groups in three different states reported different results. Californian and New Mexican youth were more aware of their ethnic identities and separatist views, while Texan ones embraced liberal capitalism (perhaps because of previous exposure to a course on 'free enterprise' capitalism). Non-Texas students got their information on Chicano nationalism from outside the schools, speakers, and literature on this subject (Jankowski, 1986).

In the US, whites have distorted views of blacks; these impressions (whites and blacks earn as much money or have the same educational achievement levels) permeate the society from young to old citizens alike. Many whites believe there are twice as many African Americans living in the US as there actually are, so they want to limit their numbers. Half the white population believes racial integration is not important; half the black population thinks the opposite. There is a similar split regarding the existence of racism versus the realization of racial equality. For example, more than two-thirds of blacks say racism is 'a big problem' and discrimination is a leading cause of the present lot of African Americans, but only one-third of white Americans agree this is so (*Hartford Courant*, 8 October 1995).

US views on race and ethnicity are still quite flexible. Some views which whites have seem to be race-based (opposition to quotas, busing, and affirmative action), but are actually anti-government rather than racial attitudes. It may even be true (in contrast to other political socialization research) that these views can change if challenged and that they are not consistent, holistic, cognitively mapped, or ideological (Leo, 1994).

Brigham's (1993) study of college students at two racially different state universities in Tallahassee, Florida, found more frequent interracial contacts for blacks produced more positive racial attitudes for them than was the case for white students. While whites were positively affected, it was not at such a high level as for African American students. Sigelman and Welch (1993), using 1989 national survey data, found several positive (about 50 per cent) bi- or interracial attitudes remaining after reported contacts, especially among whites. Some of the effects of friendships and shared residence experiences result in reduced hostility and increased preference for racial integration. Ellison and Powers (1994) found interracial contacts early in life increase the chance that blacks will develop close friendships with whites. These friendships are among the strongest predictors of blacks' positive racial attitudes.

Two studies of national samples in the US found no evidence of decreasing tolerance of those age cohorts coming of age in the 1980s. The observed period effects from 1989 to 1990 are neither significant nor show any consistent decline in social liberalism (Steeh and Schuman, 1992). The second study (Danigelis and Cutler, 1991) used 18 national surveys from 1959 to 1985 (a meta-analysis). It found that the combined age cohorts over these years evidenced increased overall social liberalism in their attitudes. There were similar results for all four individual/separate age cohorts (more born from before 1910-38) in terms of both rates of liberalism for the youngest and oldest cohorts and the same levels of increased liberal racial attitudes among all four separate cohorts. The age-conservatism and age-rigidification hypotheses were not supported.

Watts (1996) described the influence of left and right ideology and its mutual impact on eastern and western Germans since the *Wende*. The left/right continuum absorbed earlier value conflicts concerning racism, xenophobia, foreigners, refugees, asylum seekers, and the *Volksdeutsch*. There are signs throughout Germany of the 'ethnicization' of ideology among older and younger Germans. Indicators of threat and social insecurity produce anomie which, in turn, is related to anti-foreigner and right-wing extremism. The targets of eastern German xenophobia are more directly related (compared with western Germans) to objects of direct economic threat and competition. It matters to all Germans whether the 'outsider' or 'foreigner' is seeking political asylum or is an ethnic German returning 'home' to the fatherland.

Educational nationalism moved in Britain from assimilationist, to integrationist, to cultural pluralist, and to resistance movements. The current 'white backlash' insists that recent immigrants adopt the dominant culture. The conservative national curriculum stresses Christian worship and British history, while discarding world studies, peace education, and political education. The UK pupils' view of minorities is based on myths and stereotypes learned at home, in the mass media, and in school. One study of school groups showed three-fourths of white students' essays exhibited antipathy, negativism, and xenophobia toward ethnic minorities; only one-quarter stressed acceptance, sympathy, or fairness. The latter were more clearly in accord with 'democratic notions of fair play, equal rights, tolerance, and a degree of fraternalism'. Hard evidence of educational nationalism in English schools offsets the impact of multiculturalism and anti-racist education (Tomlinson, 1993).

Studies of migrants to Western societies reveal internal discrepancies within ethnic groups. One study of Laotian immigrant leaders in the US (Hein, 1994) found that one-third primarily categorized themselves as migrants, whereas another third employed their minority status as the primary social orientation. Those who used the minority self-identification are actually more integrated or assimilated than are those who think of themselves as migrants when explaining their perception about reasons for their resultant or perceived inequality or experienced discrimination.

DOES POLITICAL EDUCATION MAKE A DIFFERENCE?

Certain kinds of schooling may have positive effects on democratic development and citizenship education, skills, and training. A democratic classroom climate is more likely to increase support for anti-authoritarianism and the inculcation of democratic values and increased political knowledge than are patriotic rituals, rote memorization, and passive student behaviors. These findings are based on a 10-nation cross-national survey of Western democratic systems and schools (Torney, Oppenheim, and Farnen, 1975, pp. 15-21).

Political information production is a result of school effects, SES and educational levels, and the home environment. Such knowledge alone does not promote participant orientations, citizen support, or active, loyal democrats. Socialization, cognitive studies, moral development, group processes, and informal reasoning findings and research can improve democratic schooling and group dynamics.

We know that teaching about democracy can make a difference, different kinds of political education have various beneficial outcomes, and critical thinking can be taught and learned. Community service programs can have an impact on students' political behaviors. They learn from textbooks, the politics curriculum, and the skills taught in school. Different SES schools and groups produce different kinds of civic education. US National Assessment of Educational Progress tests in 1976 found that those who studied politics in school scored better and that students enjoyed these classes. Minority deficiencies were noted in these surveys, indicating that US political education is not yet egalitarian since it mirrors the larger society. Results similar to the US findings were reported in the UK, Sweden, Papua New Guinea, and elsewhere. Other US studies showed marked differences in white, black, and Hispanic performance on civics tests. In the end, the results of political course exposure only amounted to 4 per cent net of any other influences. So it seems true cross-nationally that teaching politics can make a difference that teaching history, geography, and traditional subjects cannot duplicate. (For a more complete review of this research literature, see Farnen, 1996, pp. 87-97.)

Sears and Valentino (1997) refer to 'the dynamics of event-driven socialization', whereby their sample of adolescents (10-17 years old) was influenced during and after the 1980 presidential election in Wisconsin about their views on candidates and parties. They were socialized into politics during this political campaign so they learned things episodically (not incrementally) and the views thus generated often persisted into one's later years.

A survey (Ichilov, 1998, pp. 1-10) of citizenship education in a changing world summarized some interesting findings from Russia, Hungary, the US, Israel, Argentina, New Zealand, Africa, Hong Kong, Palestine, and the UK. For example, Russians are passive; Hungarians political spectators; Americans TV-dependent and politically uninformed. Hungarians are divided by ethnic rivalries and social and economic inequalities. Israel's reported civics curriculum revisions reflect broader social changes underway, just as Palestinians during the Intifada are more oriented to the street and peers than to family or school. American youth are very patriotic, anti-political, volunteeristic, and social-problem-oriented, but they are information-deprived and politically deficient. New Zealanders are apolitical nationalists and cosmopolitan internationalists who embrace world pluralism. Two African case studies illustrate the possibility of indigenous cultural conflict or compatibility with democratic institutions and human rights. In Hong Kong, the pre-1997 liberalization of the civics curriculum has been subject to PRC curtailment, but the opposite is true in Britain, where Ms. Thatcher's national curriculum of geography and history gave way to increased political subjects and public controversy in the classroom. These separate studies show the need for a basic reconceptualization of civic education along the lines of democratic participation, invoking civil courage against unjust authority, greater humanism and toleration, and a commitment to globalism, internationalism, and pluralism by furthering shared and socially constructed democratic values and morality.

CONCLUSIONS: CITIZENSHIP EDUCATION, STRENGTH, AND COMPETENCE

We continue our discussion of 'strong' and 'weak' democracy by concluding that the best cure for democracy's defects and deficiencies is not less, but more real democracy both in the school and its surrounding political environment. The representative or 'weak' democratic view says that only the elite need to be educated politically because the masses are hopeless. The elite perspective uses the mass media to promote consumerism, pro-governmental propaganda, and the modern equivalent of 'bread and circuses' (entertainment TV). The job of schooling in this system is to encourage nonpartisanship, produce system maintenance and support, and reproduce economic modes of production and the learning needed for success as a worker, not as a citizen. Civic education's job is to manufacture citizens who are obedient and law observant, who accept inequality and the hidden class-based curriculum to perform their role as passive citizens. The types of subjects 'weak' democratic educators foster are ancient history, the 'great books', geography, free-enterprise economics, and the 'three Rs'. These elitists believe that teachers must be depoliticized, that politics is to be excluded from educational policy making, that professional education courses are a waste of time for people trained in a subject matter area, and that schools should be run like corporations, factories, or other assembly-line or bureaucratic private operations. The end result of this process is incompetent democratic citizenship. This failed civic curriculum produces political ignorance, lack of interest, and avoidance of participation. It results in incoherent ideologies, intolerance, anomie, alienation, overzealous nationalism and patriotism, and approval of the growth of state fascism and authoritarianism. It does not teach conflict resolution, decision making, problem solving, or critical thinking skills. Other products are middle-of-the-road politics, anti-legitimacy sentiments, cynicism, apathy, and nonvoting. Political media are avoided and the public wrongly believe they are informed based on viewing short, sound-bite news programs. No group work, solidarity, or internationalism is promoted and citizens become xenophobic, militarist, and embrace enemy images, alienation, ennui, racism, anti-multicultural and anti-affirmative action beliefs. Huge defense budgets are not critiqued, but the poor, weak, and 'others' are harangued for their lack of success or prosperity.

By contrast, the participatory democratic view of civic education holds that citizens can learn from experts and nontraditional media all they need to know to share in public policy making. Schooling must help citizens to develop partisanship, make choices, be empowered, engage in social reconstruction, and destroy the insidious hidden, elitist, reproductionist curriculum.

Other purposes of participatory civics are to heighten political interest and involvement, improve citizen knowledge and skills, create democratic schools and school systems free of corporate dominance, and increase citizens' proficiency in decision and policy making, problem solving, and critical thinking. Active citizen roles as leaders and followers, as group members, and in other venues must be learned. The skills of bargaining, persuasion, conflict resolution, and citizen mobilization can be learned in civic education for the masses. The types of courses to be studied are practical politics, international affairs, political problems, civics, political behavior, public opinion analysis, comparative government, and recent history.

For participatory democrats, the hidden curriculum is rejected; teachers are trained in politics and educational studies; state exams, tests, and graduation requirements include political topics. Democracy in the school, family, peer group, work setting, and society is promoted. Considered partisanship becomes an acceptable alternative and a matter of choice. Critical attitudes become part of increasing expertise in decision making and problem solving, both based on adequate political knowledge. Citizen's opinions become fully developed, grounded, and well-reasoned about subjects such as freedom, equality, social welfare, tolerance, racism, multiculturalism, fascism, authoritarianism, democracy, and other key themes and topics. Political behaviors learned illustrate competence in acquiring information, talking about politics, interrogating leaders, defending one's partisanship, establishing congruence between one's personal and policy preferences, and enjoying interest or pressure group and party activity, including practical politics, fund-raising, and campaign management. The competent democrat stands for party, group, association, or political offices. He/she uses conflict resolution skills effectively, consumes quality media, and develops an international and comparative perspective. Through mediation and the peaceful resolution of inevitable disputes, the democrat in the 21st century will use diplomacy, negotiation, and compromise to help others find grass-roots solutions that do not come from the manipulative and powerful elite. (These topics are more fully discussed in Farnen, 1996, pp. 60-4 and Dekker, 1996.)

7 Political Attitudes Across World Regions, Gender, and the Media

INTRODUCTION

This chapter charts variations in authoritarian, democratic, and multicultural attitudes over world regions, by gender, and across the range of media users. We investigate whether attitudes are equally distributed over world regions or if they vary. The first option holds that if the differences between regions are not substantial, attitudes are much the same for the various regions. We call this the 'equality hypothesis'. The opposite or 'diversity hypothesis' assumes differences between key attitudes across regions. A different rate of historical development, contrasting religious and cultural traditions, or different rates of economic development may account for such differences. (See Chapter 2 for attitude scales.)

POLITICAL ATTITUDES ACROSS WORLD REGIONS

Since it would be impossible to present results of 44 countries separately, we reduced the number and pooled related countries into eight world regions. This categorization is to some extent artificial, as any such reduction probably would be (Huntington, 1996). In addition to these eight world regions, we analyzed the respective political attitudes for variation in the economic development of the countries surveyed (developed first world, former communist second world, and developing third world). Both our eight world regions and three developmental worlds are not meant to be exclusive, but rather serve as a comprehensive way to analyze some regional differences in terms of several common features of geography, economics, history, or politics.

Democratic Systemic Worth

The issue of popular support for a democratic system is not well sampled in our survey. Our questions dealt mainly with general political attitudes (see Chapter 2 for the scales and the Appendix for survey questions). But one item stated: 'Democracy is by far the best form of government for our country and people'. This item was also part of a separate main attitudinal factor. It clearly considers the worth of a democratic system.

Differences among the regions are clearly significant, as are differences among the three worlds (both p<.0001; see Table 7.1). The strongest support for formal democracy appears in West European samples, followed by Africans and North Americans. The least support for democracy comes from CIS-Russia and East Europe; Oceania (Australia/New Zealand), Asia, and Latin America have relatively lower levels. Although even the lowest means (scale mean is 4.00) indicate support for democracy, these are surprising results for some samples. For instance, although there is no strong African tradition of democracy, our African samples show even more support for democracy than those in North America or other developed regions. At the other extreme, the former communist samples appear least enthusiastic about democracy. Despite the fact that their systems changed from totalitarianism to democracy in the 1990s, one may not count completely on its inner stability and strength.

Table 7.1. 'Democracy best' and eight world regions/three worlds

	Regions	Means	Number of Respondents	Significance p =
Eight World	North America	5.94	1372	
Regions	Latin America	5.75	908	
	West Europe	6.18	2042	
	East Europe	5.50	1602	
	CIS-Russia	4.74	1393	
	Africa	6.12	395	
	Asia	5.86	1313	
	Oceania	5.70	122	
Total	*Eight World Regions*	5.71	9147	<.0001
Three Worlds	Developed First World	6.01	3952	
	(ex)Communist Second World	5.15	3012	
	Developing Third World	5.92	2183	
Total	*Three Worlds*	5.71	9147	<.0001

Notes: variables DEMO1 x GEO8 and WORLD3; range = 1.00 to 7.00; high mean = prodemocratic; CIS = Commonwealth of Independent States; ANOVA F-between -groups

The three worlds' perspective also supports this interpretation. Not so much the third world, but the second (former communist) is far less positive about the virtues of a democratic system. Whereas other democratic countries previously suffering from dictatorship (Latin America, Asia) changed for the better, East Europeans seem to be unenthusiastic about democracy.

Democratic Attitudes

The democratic attitude factor behaved somewhat differently from support of formal democracy. This may be due to the difference in meaning between formal concepts of democracy and democratic attitudes. The content of the democratic attitude item mainly expresses in various ways decentralization of political power. This is often considered a core issue of democracy.

Table 7.2. Democratic attitudes and eight world regions/three worlds

	Regions	Means	Number of Respondents	Significance p =
Eight World	North America	5.11	1334	
Regions	Latin America	5.52	881	
	West Europe	5.22	2378	
	East Europe	4.94	1581	
	CIS-Russia	4.67	1291	
	Africa	5.76	377	
	Asia	5.34	1252	
	Oceania	5.24	119	
Total	*Eight World Regions*	5.14	9213	<.0001
Three Worlds	Developed First World	5.19	4238	
	(ex)Communist Second World	4.82	2889	
	Developing Third World	5.50	2086	
Total	*Three Worlds*	5.14	9213	<.0001

Notes: variables DEMOAT5 x GEO8 and WORLD3; range = 1.00 to 7.00; high mean = pro-democratic; CIS = Commonwealth of Independent States; p = significance of ANOVA F-between- groups

The differences among the eight regions and three worlds are clearly significant (see Table 7.2). The rank order is less clear, except that CIS-Russian and East European samples again exhibit less democratic attitudinal support. Democratic decentralization may not be very attractive in a large and unstable country like Russia, but why this is also a problem in many smaller East European countries remains puzzling. The African samples express their strong democratic views. Surprisingly, some of our third world samples in general show strong democratic attitudes, at least in terms of decentralizing political power. Developed Western samples are somewhat less supportive.

Psychological Authoritarianism

Psychological authoritarianism includes favoring strong-man politics and harsh punishment and disrespecting deviants and the underprivileged. It consisted of Adorno et al. (1950) F-scale items associated with psychological tendencies, including cultural and political factors (Meloen, 1983, 1993, 1996). To prevent response set, these items were 'hidden' in the survey.

Differences among the eight regions and three worlds are quite significant (see Table 7.3). Much has been published (Meloen, 1991a) about psychological authoritarianism recently, but little time was devoted to making sense of empirically derived authoritarianism levels. In a preliminary analysis of results from 24 countries, a pattern clearly emerged (Meloen, 1983).

Table 7.3. Psychological authoritarianism and eight world regions/three worlds

Regions		Means	Number of Respondents	Significance p =
Eight World	North America	4.23	1320	
Regions	Latin America	4.70	864	
	West Europe	3.52	1869	
	East Europe	4.44	1572	
	CIS-Russia	4.72	1360	
	Africa	5.27	369	
	Asia	4.62	1240	
	Oceania	3.77	116	
Total	*Eight World Regions*	4.34	8710	<.0001
Three Worlds	Developed First World	3.90	3712	
	(ex)Communist Second World	4.57	2949	
	Developing Third World	4.80	2049	
Total	*Three Worlds*	4.34	8710	<.0001

Notes: variables AUT8 x GEO8 and WORLD3; range = 1.00 to 7.00; high mean = pro-authoritarian; CIS = Commonwealth of Independent States; ANOVA F-between-groups

Less developed, often non-Western countries, tended to show higher authoritarianism levels. Our results are similar. West Europe and Oceania show the lowest levels, North America is next, while the third world samples produce the highest levels, somewhat higher than the former communist world. Asian, Latin American, and CIS-Russian samples show high levels of authoritarianism, with the Africans being most authoritarian. By contrast, East European groups show relatively low authoritarianism levels.

Political Repression

Although its content is somewhat related to psychological authoritarianism, this item estimated a willingness to use tough political measures against political opponents and minorities. Therefore, this attitude more explicitly expresses political repression than does the former.

The differences among the eight regions and three worlds are again significant (see Table 7.4). Among the lowest means (suggesting strong rejection of repression) are the Oceanian and North American samples, followed by the Western Europeans and Latin Americans. Political repression measures are not often popular, so all the means are below the scale mean of 4.00. There is one remarkable exception: CIS-Russian samples. Their means are much higher than those from other regions. The core of the former Soviet Union regions still shows most support for tough measures against political and other opponents. In general, this seems to be the case as well for the former communist second world, compared with the first and third worlds.

Table 7.4. Political repression and eight world regions/three worlds

	Regions	Means	Number of Respondents	Significance p =
Eight World	North America	2.93	1311	
Regions	Latin America	3.22	858	
	West Europe	3.04	1880	
	East Europe	3.85	1565	
	CIS-Russia	4.37	1354	
	Africa	3.99	361	
	Asia	3.53	1234	
	Oceania	2.77	120	
Total	*Eight World Regions*	3.50	8683	<.0001
Three Worlds	Developed First World	3.05	3713	
	(ex)Communist Second World	4.09	2936	
	Developing Third World	3.47	2034	
Total	*Three Worlds*	3.50	8683	<.0001

Notes: variables REPRES7 x GEO8 and WORLD3; range = 1.00 to 7.00; high mean = pro-repression; CIS = Commonwealth of Independent States; ANOVA F-between-groups

Militarism

Militarism covaries closely with both political repression and psychological authoritarianism. Militarism has a long history. It is not necessarily at odds with democracy. That is, democracy sometimes needs to be protected via military means. The type of militarism assessed here is related to an attitude of preserving military strength, law and order, and high military spending.

The world regions show significant differences with respect to militarism (see Table 7.5). It is not really surprising that this attitude prevails mainly in the regions of the superpowers in North America and the former Soviet Union (CIS-Russia), opposing sides in the cold war. Apparently, this is one of the remaining cold war attitudes that is not yet completely abandoned. This antagonism may also explain the current high level of prevailing militarist attitudes in Asia, where the Asiatic cold war (with respect to China, Korea, Vietnam) is not yet over. On the low or rejecting side of this value, the West European samples seem the most pacifist, followed by the Oceanian and Latin American ones. However, the second world (former communist countries) shows the most support for militarism, followed by the third world. The developed first world seems the least militaristic, despite high US scores.

Table 7.5. Militarism and eight world regions/three worlds

	Regions	Means	Number of Respondents	Significance p =
Eight World	North America	3.85	1358	
Regions	Latin America	3.12	902	
	West Europe	3.03	2012	
	East Europe	3.50	1588	
	CIS-Russia	3.89	1382	
	Africa	3.29	393	
	Asia	3.88	1285	
	Oceania	3.23	121	
Total	*Eight World Regions*	3.51	9041	<.0001
Three Worlds	Developed First World	3.36	3900	
	(ex)Communist Second World	3.69	2987	
	Developing Third World	3.55	2154	
Total	*Three Worlds*	3.51	9041	<.0001

Notes: variables MIL3 x GEO8 and WORLD3; range = 1.00 to 7.00; high mean = pro-militarism; CIS = Commonwealth of Independent States; ANOVA F-between-groups

Table 7.6. General authoritarianism and eight world regions/three worlds

	Regions	Means	Number of Respondents	Significance p =
Eight World	North America	3.84	1239	
Regions	Latin America	3.96	804	
	West Europe	3.41	1777	
	East Europe	4.21	1529	
	CIS-Russia	4.56	1313	
	Africa	4.61	326	
	Asia	4.26	1130	
	Oceania	3.43	111	
Total	*Eight World Regions*	4.02	8229	<.0001
Three Worlds	Developed First World	3.64	3512	
	(ex)Communist Second World	4.37	2859	
	Developing Third World	4.21	1858	
Total	*Three Worlds*	4.02	8229	<.0001

Notes: variables AUT20 x GEO8 and WORLD3; range = 1.00 to 7.00; high mean = pro-militarism; CIS = Commonwealth of Independent States; ANOVA F-between -groups

General Authoritarianism

The general authoritarianism factor included psychological authoritarianism, political repression, and militarism. They work together to create a tendency toward general authoritarianism. Not surprisingly, regional differences are also strongly significant (see Table 7.6). The lowest general authoritarianism levels were found in West European and Oceanian samples, followed by North and Latin American ones. North America, a bastion of anti-authoritarianism in the 1970s, seems to have been bypassed since West Europe and Oceania score lower. Altemeyer's (1988, 1996) research results indicated rising levels for North America in the 1980s. Lower levels for Western Europe (Lederer, 1982; Lederer and Schmidt, 1995; and Meloen and Middendorp, 1991) support this view.

Clearly, authoritarianism levels are not entirely stable. At the highest levels, CIS-Russia and Africa stand out as most authoritarian. In the Asian and East European samples, there seems to be less support for general authoritarianism, although these levels are below those in CIS-Russia and Africa. The former communist world samples again show the highest levels, followed by the third and first world with lower levels.

Multiculturalism

This concept refers to equal treatment and equal rights for various ethnic, religious and national groups. It is the opposite of racism or ethnocentrism (considering ones own group different and superior, with total disregard for the welfare of others). Multiculturalism emerged in our analysis as a separate major factor. Regional differences were clearly significant (see Table 7.7), but with a different pattern. West European samples show the most respect for multiculturalism, followed by African, Asian, and Latin American ones. By contrast, the CIS-Russian and North American groups show the least multiculturalism, followed by the East European and Oceanian samples. For both the North American and Oceanian samples, such relatively low levels are somewhat surprising. In sum, samples from the former communist world seem least inclined toward multiculturalism, the third world the most.

General Multiculturalism

This is the second main factor in our analysis of political attitudes; it includes multiculturalism and democratic attitudes. The pattern of this factor resembles the former one on specific multicultural attitudes (see Table 7.8). Strong support for general multiculturalism is found among samples from Africa, Latin America, West Europe, and Asia; North America and Oceania are in the middle; CIS-Russia and East Europe are the least enchanted with this factor.

All groups agree to some extent (means above scale means); they only differ in the extent to which they support general multiculturalism. Differences among the three worlds support the view that the former communist world shows the greatest distance toward central ideas of democracy and multiculturalism. Comparatively, the CIS-Russian groups in particular are the most consistent in their anti-democratic scepticism: lowest on democracy, lowest on multiculturalism. East European groups are in second place.

Table 7.7. Multiculturalism and eight world regions/three worlds

	Regions	Means	Number of Respondents	Significance p =
Eight World	North America	5.45	1292	
Regions	Latin America	5.73	859	
	West Europe	5.85	1960	
	East Europe	5.50	1563	
	CIS-Russia	5.41	1362	
	Africa	5.81	341	
	Asia	5.76	1237	
	Oceania	5.62	118	
Total	*Eight World Regions*	5.63	8732	<.0001
Three Worlds	Developed First World	5.69	3772	
	(ex)Communist Second World	5.46	2942	
	Developing Third World	5.78	2018	
Total	*Three Worlds*	5.63	8732	<.0001

Notes: variables MCULT3 x GEO8 and WORLD3; range = 1.00 to 7.00; high mean = pro-democratic; CIS = Commonwealth of Independent States; ANOVA F-between-groups

Table 7.8. General multiculturalism and eight world regions/three worlds

	Regions	Means	Number of Respondents	Significance p =
Eight World	North America	5.32	1273	
Regions	Latin America	5.65	840	
	West Europe	5.61	1917	
	East Europe	5.29	1546	
	CIS-Russia	5.12	1270	
	Africa	5.78	331	
	Asia	5.61	1194	
	Oceania	5.48	116	
Total	*Eight World Regions*	5.44	8487	<.0001
Three Worlds	Developed First World	5.50	3701	
	(ex)Communist Second World	5.22	2833	
	Developing Third World	5.68	1953	
Total	*Three Worlds*	5.44	8487	<.0001

Notes: variables MCDEMO13 x GEO8 and WORLD3; range = 1.00 to 7.00; high mean = pro-democratic; CIS = Commonwealth of Independent States; ANOVA F-between-groups

Political Leaders

Respondents rated political leaders they admired (9.00) or disliked (1.00) on a 9-point scale (with a scale mean of 5.00). Both mean and median scores are shown (see Table 7.9). Not surprisingly, the respondents disliked dictators (Hitler, Hussein, Mao, Stalin) and admired leaders who nonviolently resisted the injustices of colonialism, apartheid, or racial discrimination (Gandhi, Mandela, King) or tried to reform a totalitarian system (Gorbachev). Remarkably, while socialist dictators (Stalin, Mao) are viewed very negatively, our respondents (including leftists) rated Marx more positively, even higher than Reagan. But Marx was more a social philosopher than a political leader. Therefore, he is not seen as responsible for the horrendous political crimes of the 20th century committed while taking his name and philosophy in vain. Napoleon is less negatively rated than might be expected, judging his poor historical reputation. This cannot be due to the wars he started or to his claim that he completed a social transformation (the 'French Revolution').

In a few countries where our survey was conducted, some national political leaders were added to our basic list. In Italy, Benito Mussolini (see Table 7.10) was added. He was rated very negatively, but less so than his WWII ally, Adolph Hitler. Mussolini's 1990s heir, Gianfranco Fini, turned the neo-fascist post-war MSI Party (Movimento Sociale Italiano) into the Aleanza Nationale. Fini's rating is neither positive nor negative, probably due to his rather 'democratic' image since he foreswore fascist traditions. More positively rated is Antonio Gramsci, an Italian socialist who resisted Mussolini's fascism and wrote Marxist political philosophy while he was in jail.

Table 7.9. Ratings of political leaders

Political Leader	Country	Mean Rating	Median	Number of Respondents
Mohandas 'Mahatma' Gandhi	India	7.26	8	8723
Martin Luther King	USA	7.11	8	8681
Nelson Mandela	South Africa	6.72	7	8696
John F. Kennedy	USA	6.65	7	8572
Franklin D. Roosevelt	USA	6.14	6	8535
Mikhail Gorbachev	USSR	6.04	6	8717
Dwight D. Eisenhower	USA	5.48	5	8444
Karl Marx	Germany	5.41	5	8699
Napoleon Bonaparte	France	5.40	5	8684
Ronald Reagan	USA	5.28	5	8625
Mao Tse Tung	PR China	4.11	5	8678
Joseph Stalin	USSR	3.03	2	8676
Saddam Hussein	Iraq	2.43	1	8709
Adolph Hitler	Germany	2.05	1	8736

Notes: range 1.00 to 9.00; high mean = admires leader

Not surprising is the popularity of Pope John Paul II in Poland since he was born there. Remarkably, Solidarity union leader Lech Walesa (who unseated the communists) is not rated very positively. Since he was president during this survey, it may have affected his low rating. Josef Pilzudski, the authoritarian ruler of Poland before WWII, still is admired. This may be due to Poland's position between Germany and Russia. Strong men who helped create an independent Poland (such as Napoleon) have become popular there; but Stalin, who suppressed the Poles, was fully despised.

In Turkey, Kemal Ataturk (the modern country's founder) received a very positive rating. By contrast, many survey answers from Russia, Ukraine, and Belorussia indicated cynicism toward politicians and rated them all negatively. Even the heros of most of the world (Gandhi, King, Mandela) received low or less positive ratings. In Russia, only anti-communist writer Alexander Solzhenitsyn was rated slightly positively. Reformers like Yeltsin (Russia's first democratic president), Gorbachev, and Shevardnadze (former Soviet foreign affairs minister) were only viewed slightly less negatively than Rutskoi (a *coup d'etat* general), Zhirinovsky (extreme right), and Stalin. The alienation toward politicians in Russia goes far beyond the generally cynical attitude toward politicians found in many democracies.

Table 7.10. Leaders in specific countries.

Political Leader	Country	Mean Rating	Median	Number of Respondents
Benito Mussolini	Italy only	3.12	1	122
Gianfranco Fini	Italy only	5.16	5	121
Antonio Gramsci	Italy only	5.97	5	122
Lech Walesa	Poland only	4.55	4	299
Josef Pilzudski	Poland only	6.68	7	299
Pope John Paul II	Poland only	7.09	8	299
Napoleon Bonaparte	Poland only	6.56	7	299
Joseph Stalin	Poland only	1.86	1	299
Kemal Ataturk	Turkey only	7.78	9	401
Boris Yeltsin	Russia only	3.93	4	450
Edward Shevardnadze	Russia only	4.10	3	249
Alexander Rutskoi	Russia only	3.47	3	370
Vladimir Zhirinovsky	Russia only	2.43	2	370
Alexander Solzhenitsyn	Russia only	5.55	6	370
Mikhail Gorbachev	Russia only	4.72	5	448
Joseph Stalin	Russia only	2.65	2	451

Notes: range 1.00 to 9.00; high mean = in favor of leader

Dictators and Reformers

The first factor includes support for four dictators: Hitler, Stalin, Hussein, and Mao. Since most of them were strongly rejected (low rating), one might also consider this factor as rejecting dictatorship. Variations over the world regions are once again significant (see Table 7.11).

A somewhat different distribution than previous ones emerges here. East European groups very strongly reject these dictators. Since these countries suffered most under communism, this result is understandable. Next are the West European samples, followed by North American and Oceanian. The least rejection is found in our African groups that tend to be more neutral.

In Latin America and Asia, some rejection is prevalent. The CIS-Russian groups tend to be average in this respect. In general, third world groups seem less convinced of the evil of dictators, compared with groups from the West and former communist states. Of course, only one (Hussein) can be considered to represent the third world type of dictator.

Table 7.11. Dictators and eight world regions/three worlds

	Regions	Means	Number of Respondents	Significance p =
Eight World	North America	2.71	1247	
Regions	Latin America	3.68	884	
	West Europe	2.52	1971	
	East Europe	2.31	1373	
	CIS-Russia	2.92	1356	
	Africa	4.13	342	
	Asia	3.44	1219	
	Oceania	2.76	114	
Total	*Eight World Regions*	2.90	8506	<.0001
Three Worlds	Developed First World	2.68	3723	
	(ex)Communist Second World	2.61	2746	
	Developing Third World	3.68	2037	
Total	*Three Worlds*	2.90	8507	<.0001

Notes: variables DICTATOR x GEO8 and WORLD3; range = 1.00 to 9.00; high mean = pro dictator; CIS = Commonwealth of Independent States; ANOVA F-between-groups.

The reformer factor has in common the concept of nonviolent attempts to change the sociopolitical situation in the countries of the included leaders: King, Mandela, Gandhi, and Gorbachev. Despite their differences, they represent policies to increase freedom and democracy for their people.

The regional differences in the ratings of these reformers are significant (see Table 7.12). They are most admired in Western Europe, even though none of these leaders were of Western European origin. African and Latin American groups followed and, at some distance, the Asian ones. The lowest

Democracy, Authoritarianism, and Education

admiration was found among CIS-Russian samples; East Europeans were next lowest. North American and Oceanian groups tended to be slightly above average. The first and third world groups did not differ much, but the former second world samples were clearly less supportive of democratic reformers.

Table 7.12. Political reformers and eight world regions/three worlds

	Regions	Means	Number of Respondents	Significance p =
Eight World	North America	6.93	1257	
Regions	Latin America	7.38	883	
	West Europe	7.47	1988	
	East Europe	6.25	1369	
	CIS-Russia	5.37	1344	
	Africa	7.42	348	
	Asia	7.03	1209	
	Oceania	6.92	113	
Total	*Eight World Regions*	6.78	8511	<.0001
Three Worlds	Developed First World	7.23	3755	
	(ex)Communist Second World	5.81	2730	
	Developing Third World	7.26	2026	
Total	*Three Worlds*	6.78	8511	<.0001

Notes: variables REFORMER x GEO8 and WORLD3; range = 1.00 to 9.00; high mean = pro-democratic; CIS = Commonwealth of Independent States; ANOVA F-between-groups

Rating US Presidents

Supporting four US presidents (Franklin D. Roosevelt, Eisenhower, Kennedy, Reagan) emerged as one factor in our analysis. It may suggest pro- and anti-American sentiments. Regional differences are significant here as well (see Table 7.13). It is not entirely surprising that these presidents are most admired in North America or that African, East European, and CIS Russian samples closely mirror this feeling. Less supportive are those from West Europe, Oceania, Asia, and Latin America.

Over all, those from the former communist regions seem much more enthusiastic about these four men than are those from the third or the rest of the first (except for North America) worlds. All ratings of American presidents were positive cross-nationally, indicating no clear anti-Americanism in any regional samples.

Table 7.13. US presidents and eight world regions/three worlds

	Regions	Mean	Number of Respondents	Significance p =
Eight World	North America	6.62	1246	
Regions	Latin America	5.64	881	
	West Europe	5.37	1821	
	East Europe	6.01	1344	
	CIS-Russia	6.07	1358	
	Africa	6.47	333	
	Asia	5.62	1212	
	Oceania	5.46	112	
Total	*Eight World Regions*	5.88	8307	<.0001
Three Worlds	Developed First World	5.86	3578	
	(ex)Communist Second World	6.03	2719	
	Developing Third World	5.72	2010	
Total	*Three Worlds*	5.88	8307	<.0001

Notes: variables USPRES x GEO8 and WORLD3; range = 1.00 to 9.00; high mean = pro-presidents; CIS = Commonwealth of Independent States; ANOVA F-between-groups

Self-Rating as Right-Wing or Multicultural

Considering oneself conservative, right-wing, militarist, authoritarian, and elitist showed a clear pattern of covariance. The differences between regions for these self-ratings are all statistically significant (see Table 7.14). Our West European samples show the fewest right-wing tendencies, followed by the Oceanian and Latin American samples. By contrast, CIS-Russian, African, and East European groups show more right-wing tendencies, while the North American and Asian ones tend to be 'middle of the road'. Those from former left-wing dictatorships (East Europe, Russia) seemed to move right; those with experience of right-wing dictators show more left-wing inclinations. The first world samples are the least right-wing, those from the former communist regions the most, while the third world are rather neutral bystanders.

The second self-rating factor included considering oneself multicultural, internationalist, and cosmopolitan. This view reflects broad- and world-mindedness as opposed to provincialism and narrow-mindedness. The difference among world regions is significant (see Table 7.15).

Although all groups tended to support a self-image of multiculturalism, it was most obvious in West Europe and Oceania. The least multicultural self-image was found among African groups. This sharply contrasted with their attitudes toward multiculturalism, where the African groups were among its strongest supporters. Asian groups showed little self-reported multiculturalism. CIS-Russian and East European groups came next. North American and Latin American samples were average. In the developed world, respondents thought themselves most multicultural, somewhat less so in the second world, and least so in the third world.

Table 7.14. Self-rating as right-wing and eight world regions/three worlds

	Regions	Means	Number of Respondents	Significance p =
Eight World	North America	4.11	1227	
Regions	Latin America	3.90	884	
	West Europe	3.63	2279	
	East Europe	4.28	1590	
	CIS-Russia	4.39	1369	
	Africa	4.38	330	
	Asia	3.98	1212	
	Oceania	3.77	113	
Total	*Eight World Regions*	4.03	9004	<.0001
Three Worlds	Developed First World	3.82	4027	
	(ex)Communist Second World	4.33	2976	
	Developing Third World	4.01	2001	
Total	*Three Worlds*	4.03	9004	<.0001

Notes: variables SRIGHT5 x GEO8 and WORLD3; range = 1.00 to 7.00; high mean = pro-right-wing; CIS = Commonwealth of Independent States; ANOVA F-between-groups

Table 7.15. Self-rating as multicultural and eight world regions/three worlds

	Regions	Means	Number of Respondents	Significance p =
Eight World	North America	4.73	1255	
Regions	Latin America	4.85	891	
	West Europe	5.54	2002	
	East Europe	4.57	1594	
	CIS-Russia	4.54	1375	
	Africa	3.92	339	
	Asia	4.19	1242	
	Oceania	5.39	114	
Total	*Eight World Regions*	4.77	8812	<.0001
Three Worlds	Developed First World	5.15	3784	
	(ex)Communist Second World	4.56	2986	
	Developing Third World	4.37	2042	
Total	*Three Worlds*	4.77	8812	<.0001

Notes: variables SMCULT3 x GEO8 and WORLD3; range = 1.00 to 7.00; high mean = pro-multicultural; CIS = Commonwealth of Independent States; ANOVA F-between-groups.

POLITICAL ATTITUDES AND BACKGROUND VARIATION

Gender

Political attitudes of men and women are often not the same. Evidence that authoritarian attitudes of women and men differ has often been reported (Meloen and Middendorp, 1991). However, we were not prepared for the very significant worldwide differences we found between men and women (see Table 7.16).

Table 7.16. Political attitudes of men and women (total sample)

Variable	Code	Means		Significance
		Women	Men	P =
Democratic System	DEMO1	5.73	5.67	.03*
Democratic Attitudes	DEMOAT5	5.20	5.08	.0001***
Psychological Authoritarianism	AUT8	4.27	4.41	.0001***
Political Repression	REPRES7	3.40	3.61	.0001***
Militarism	MIL3	3.37	3.66	.0001***
General Authoritarianism	AUT20	3.93	4.12	.0001***
Multiculturalism	MCULT8	5.69	5.57	.0001***
Pro-dictator	DICTATOR	2.80	3.00	.0001***
Pro-reformer	REFORMER	6.85	6.71	.0001***
Pro-US Presidents	USPRES	5.89	5.88	.85ns
Self-right-wing	SRIGHT5	3.05	3.33	.0001***
Self-multicultural	SMCULT3	4.96	4.75	.0001***

Notes: number of women = 4362-4761; number of men = 3892-4318; p = ANOVA F-between-groups; ns = not significant; * p<.05; *** p<.001

Women more strongly support the democratic system and attitudes, are less psychologically authoritarian, give less support to political repression and militarism, are less generally authoritarian, have stronger multiculturalist attitudes, give less support to dictators and more to reformers, and consider themselves less right-wing and more multicultural. Only in attitudes toward American presidents do men and women show similar attitudes. The differences in these attitudes are not related to the main background variables in our survey since our results indicate there is no difference between men and women regarding social class (p = .19 ns) or father's education (p = .86 ns). Thus, these attitudinal differences are not a result of sampling error.

The Media

Mass media influence is important for the health of democratic politics. We asked respondents which type of media they used to obtain political information: TV, radio, newspapers, word of mouth, or magazines. Most of the media information sources were unrelated to the key political attitudes of our survey (a correlation below .10); therefore, we present results from only two of them (TV and newspapers) in Table 7.17. We find that TV use is associated with stronger democratic attitudes, less support for dictators, but also more psychological authoritarianism, more militarism, and, in a different context, more support for US presidents. From this, one may conclude that there is no consistent international TV effect.

Newspaper readers tend to be more pro-democracy (as a system), less psychologically authoritarian, less pro-repression, less militarist, less supportive of general authoritarianism, more multiculturalist, less pro-dictator, and more pro-reformer. They are also less right-wing and consider themselves more multicultural. This seems to be both more consistent and moving in a pro-democratic direction. TV and newspaper effects may vary in relation to the specific political attitudes we assessed.

Table 7.17. Political attitudes and the mass media (total sample)

Variable	Code	Television		Newspaper	
		Signif.	*watchers are:*	*Signif.*	*readers are:*
Democratic system	DEMO1	.56ns	-	.001**	>pro-democracy
Democratic attitudes	DEMOAT5	.03*	>democratic	.13ns	-
Psy. Authoritarianism	AUT8	.0001***	>authoritarian	.0001***	<authoritarian
Political repression	REPRES7	.06ns	-	.0001***	<pro-repression
Militarism	MIL3	.0001***	>militarist	.0001***	<militarist
Gen. authoritarianism	AUT20	.0001***	>authoritarian	.0001***	<authoritarian
Multiculturalism	MCULT8	.11ns	-	.0001***	>multiculturalist
Pro-dictator	DICTATOR	.0001***	<pro-dictator	.009**	<pro-dictator
Pro-reformer	REFORMER	.62ns	-	.0001***	>pro-reformer
Pro-US presidents	USPRES	.001**	>pro-US pres.	.002**	< pro-US pres.
Self-right-wing	SRIGHT5	.78ns	-	.0001***	<right-wing
Self-multicultural	SMCULT3	.93ns	-	.0001***	>multicultural

p = ANOVA F-between-groups; ns = not significant; > = more; < = less; viewers/readers compared with nonviewers/nonreaders; * p<.05; ** p<.01; *** p<.001

Political Party Choice

One's political party choice was not part of our standard questionnaire; it was added in only a few countries. Relationships between authoritarian attitudes and party choice have often been investigated (Meloen, 1983, 1993, 1994a, b; Meloen, van der Linden, de Witte, 1996). Party choice is of interest when a relation can be shown between anti-democratic or racist parties and political attitudes. In Italy and Belgium, fascist parties were active during our survey.

In Belgium, the Vlaams Blok belongs to the extreme right. This party has been successful since the early 1990s in Flanders, mainly advocating anti-immigrant issues (particularly anti-Islam, -Turks, or -Moroccans). It drew 10 per cent of the votes in local and national elections. A few of its supporters were included in our survey of about 200 Belgians (see Table 7.18).

Our left-wing respondents showed stronger democratic attitudes, less general authoritarianism, more multiculturalism (along with more left-wing self-ratings), while rejecting strongly right-wing extremist ideology. The right seems more skeptical about these issues. The few right-wing extremists stand out as more authoritarian, less multicultural (a key issue in their ideology), and self-described as more right-wing. These results support earlier and similar investigations in Belgium (Meloen, van der Linden, and de Witte, 1996).

Table 7.18. Political attitudes and political party choice (Belgium)

Party choice	Democratic attitudes DEMOAT5	General auth- oritarianism AUT20	Multi- culturalism MCULT8	Self- right-wing SRIGHT5	Right-wing extremist REX6
Left Wing	5.14	3.02	5.83	2.18	1.79
Undecided	4.68	3.39	5.57	2.89	2.00
Right-Wing	4.61	3.66	5.41	3.23	2.25
Extreme Right	4.87	3.98	5.26	3.47	2.19
Total	*4.80*	*3.38*	*5.60*	*2.77*	*2.01*
Significance p =	*.01**	*.0001****	*.019**	*.0001****	*.0001****

Notes: p = ANOVA F-between-groups; Left Wing = SP, AGALEV, PVDA; Right-Wing = CVP, VLD, VU; Extreme Right = Vlaams Blok; N total around 200; Vlaams Blok only 6 respondents; for explanation of scales, see Chapter 2; REX6 = Hans de Witte's right-wing extremism scale; * p<.05; *** p<.001

Table 7.19. Political attitudes and political party choice (Italy)

Party choice	Democratic attitudes DEMOAT5	General auth- oritarianism AUT20	Multi- culturalism MCULT8	Self- right-wing SRIGHT5	Rating Fini extreme right FINI
Left-Wing	5.41	3.84	6.21	1.91	3.50
Undecided	5.32	4.02	6.20	2.03	4.47
Right-Wing	5.18	4.40	5.93	3.08	5.63
Extreme Right	4.93	4.64	5.94	3.43	8.10
Total	*5.23*	*4.15*	*6.09*	*2.50*	*5.15*
Significance p =	*.22ns*	*.0013***	*.17**	*.0001****	*.0001****

Notes: p = ANOVA F-between-groups; Left-Wing = PDS, Communists, Socialists; Right-Wing = Forza Italia; Extreme Right = Aleanza Nationale; N total around 110; range 1.00-7.00, except Fini rating 1.00-9.00; for explanation of scales, see Chapter 2; ns = not significant; * p<.05; ** p<.01; *** p<.001

In Italy, the post-war neo-fascist MSI was replaced by the Aleanza Na-tionale. This party claimed not to be fascist any more, although the same leaders (such as Gianfranco Fini) remained in power and endorsed much of its old program. Our survey included 110 respondents from southern Italy (see Table 7.19), where the Aleanza Nationale was quite popular with voters in this region and among our student respondents (about 30 per cent; support was higher than national levels). The extreme right has the lowest level of democratic attitudes, the highest authoritarianism, and strongest self-rating as right-wing. Not surprisingly, this group shows the most admiration for its leader, Fini. The left tends to show stronger democratic attitudes, less general authoritarianism, high (but not the highest) multiculturalism, and most left-wing self-ratings with the highest rejection rates for the neo-fascist Fini.

CONCLUSIONS

Our results indicate that pro-democratic attitudes are not as common in every world region as one might expect. They do not seem to be evenly distributed over the globe. Our results strongly supported the 'diversity hypothesis' and strongly rejected the 'equality hypothesis'. In some regions or countries, consistent major political attitudes about democracy, authoritarianism, or multiculturalism are more prevalent than in others.

The CIS-Russia region presents the worst case scenario in our survey. It has the least support for democracy and multiculturalism and has high levels of authoritarianism, militarism, and repression of political attitudes. If CIS-Russians tended to say 'yes' to the questions in general (response set), they certainly did not do so for questions on democratic issues and political reformers. Their overriding attitude toward politics is negative. Perhaps this indicates they may soon support extremist leaders, strong-man politics, and future *coups d'etat*.

We see an unstable picture in third world regions such as Africa. In the 1990s, a tendency toward democratization appeared there, but the attitudes we found do not coincide with this tendency. Authoritarian attitudes are still virulent there; simultaneously, democratic ideas and multiculturalism are also supported. Our educated African respondents are aware of authoritarian strong-man traditions and past political suppression of other cultures. The strongest supporters of democracy now come from West Europe and Oceania, both surpassing North America, which once was called the 'arsenal of democracy' (the US still has the most complete Western arsenal, if not the world's model democracy). We also found consistently that women showed stronger democratic attitudes worldwide. This surprising and remarkable result needs to be given more attention in the professional literature.

8 Democracy, Authoritarianism, and Educational Levels

INTRODUCTION

Here, we examine the relationship between authoritarianism and level of education with a secondary analysis of several relevant international surveys.

AN INVERSE RELATIONSHIP

The relationship between level of education and authoritarianism has often been studied (Lederer, 1982, 1983; Albinski, 1959; Hesselbart and Shuman, 1976; McFarland and Sparks, 1985; Photiadis, 1962; Shaver, Hofmann, and Richards, 1971; Wrightsman 1977; Stone, Lederer, and Christie, 1993; Raaijmakers, Meeus, and Vollebergh, 1986). Soon after *The Authoritarian Personality* (Adorno et al., 1950) appeared, this relationship was found in some large-scale surveys. It appeared to be a consistent empirical finding since then. This relationship suggested that support for authoritarianism as an anti-democratic force is associated with lower levels of general education. However, a satisfactory explanation was elusive. Moreover, most studies used college or university students, while (relatively rare) random surveys often used short (sometimes very unreliable) scales (Meloen, 1983 1993). Even less discussion involved categories representing consecutive educational levels. Finally, most studies originated in free Western countries, hardly any from non-Western ones. But how universal is this relationship? How international is it? Are there any exceptions to the reported inverse relationship? To explore this, we re-analyzed some national random sample surveys.

European Anti-Semitism Survey

The first survey (Tumin, 1961) investigated racism, anti-Semitism, and authoritarianism in post-WWII (West) Germany compared with Britain and France. The adult population was randomly sampled while anti-Semitism was a sensitive issue in Germany. We do not know how accurate the sampling was since little is known about the survey; it was not reported or published. The survey's author was never identified; only the data file and questionnaire are available at Amsterdam's Steinmetz Archives (as 'T. Melvin', Princeton University). Melvin Tumin (1961) wrote an inventory of anti-Semitism.

A short (four-item) authoritarianism scale included 'spare the rod and spoil the child' and 'what this country needs is a strong leader who won't put up with any nonsense', both variants of standard authoritarianism items. Only composite scale results were available and no reliability could be computed. The scales used for measuring racist thinking, anti-Semitism, and authoritarianism all intercorrelated positively and significantly, but the correlations were rather low (+.16 to +.22; all p<.001). In Germany and France, these relationships were stronger (+.22 to +.36; all p<.001), especially between authoritarianism and racism. We also recomputed the relationship between this authoritarianism scale and respondents' educational levels (see Table 8.1). There were so few highly educated respondents in this study that 'upper secondary' and 'university education' had to be pooled into 'higher education'. The correlation was indeed negative, significant, but surprisingly low, lower than in many other studies (here: between -.11 and -.21).

Table 8.1. Authoritarianism by school level in three countries (1961)

School Level	Total		West Germany		Britain		France	
	mean	*N*	*mean*	*N*	*mean*	*N*	*mean*	*N*
Primary	3.79	1148	3.45	406	3.75	394	4.23	348
Intermediary	3.42	218	3.04	70	3.34	83	3.92	65
Higher	3.33	101	2.39	18	3.53	43	3.53	40
Correlation	*-.14*	*1467*	*-.20*	*494*	*-.11*	*520*	*-.21*	*453*
Significance	***		***		**		***	

Notes: 4-item composite authoritarianism scale; range: 1-5 (low-high authoritarian); random national samples West Germany, France, and Britain **p<.005; ***p<.001; source: Melvin, 1961; Steinmetz Archives, Amsterdam, the Netherlands

This result confirms that level of education is inversely related to authoritarianism. It applies to all three countries, being strongest in Germany and France, but less so in Britain (except there, the highest educated are not the least authoritarian). However, the least educated groups in each country tend to have the highest levels of authoritarianism. This suggests that one possible effect of higher education may be nonauthoritarian or tolerant attitudes. People exposed longer to education may more uniformly acquire such attitudes. Over time, this explanation became quite popular (Meloen, 1983).

The Civic Education Survey

A major attempt to assess the relationship between education and authoritarian and intolerant attitudes was the classic civic education study (Torney, Oppenheim, and Farnen, 1975) conducted by IEA in the early 1970s in ten countries (US, FRG, Finland, Sweden, the Netherlands, Italy, Ireland, Israel, and New Zealand; incomplete data from Iran were not included). One of its goals was to investigate the effect of civic education on political attitudes. Surveyed were 30 006 middle and secondary school students as well as their teachers. Neither schools nor students were randomly selected, but this was offset because other characteristics improved representativeness such as selection criteria, the large numbers of respondents, the specific respondent group of elementary and high school students, and its international character. A ten-item anti-authoritarianism attitude scale was included (see Table 8.2), but not all its results were reported. We reanalyzed this scale (which was worded mainly in the authoritarian direction) and its empirical relationships using archived IEA data files.

Table 8.2. IEA anti-authoritarianism attitudes scale (1970-72)

1. Hotels are right in refusing to admit people of certain races or nationalities.
2. Regular elections in our country are unnecessary.
3. People of certain races or religions should be kept out of important positions in our nation.
4. War is sometimes the only way in which a nation can save its self respect.
5. The people in power know best.
6. So many people vote in a general election that when I grow up, it will not matter much whether I vote or not.
7. It is wrong to criticize our government.
8. I don't really care what happens to others so long as I am alright.
9. People should not criticize the government, it only interrupts the government's work.
10. Talking things over with another nation is better than fighting (reverse scoring).

Source: IEA civics data, Torney et al., 1975; 10 items; N = 27,685 respondents; alpha = .75, mean inter-item correlation = .23; alpha-30 = .90, or a strong scale

This scale was reliable (Cronbach alpha .75) and qualified as strong. The relation between the scores on this anti-authoritarianism scale and students' educational level was substantial (+.48; see Table 8.3), with anti-authoritarianism levels rising considerably from the lowest to the highest grade. This was also true in each country separately, with correlations between +.11 (US) and +.64 (West Germany). Especially in West Germany, extra effort was taken to stimulate democratic attitudes among students. This may have resulted in the strong relationship there. At the time, both in the UK and the FRG, only a bright minority finished secondary education, contrasted with the US comprehensive system which then had practically universal attendance.

Strong relationships existed with tolerance and favoring women's rights, as well as with general tolerance (a combination of anti-authoritarianism, tolerance, women's rights), including support for civil liberties, freedom of the press, tolerance of different races and religions, and freedom to criticize the government. Educational levels also appeared to be strongly related to tolerance, but less so with favoring women's rights. Not surprisingly, anti-authoritarianism, tolerance, and women rights attitudes intercorrellated substantially (+.43 to +.56; all p<.0001). These results suggest that elementary and high school students, as they receive more general education, do become less authoritarian and more democratic-minded. This is not an isolated phenomenon, but rather a consistently observed international one.

Table 8.3. Anti-authoritarianism by school level: nine countries (1970-72)

Educational Level	Anti-auth-oritarianism	Tolerance	Women's rights	General tolerance	Number of respondents
	Mean	*Mean*	*Mean*	*Mean*	
1st-4th Grade	33.9	35.9	36.2	34.7	1047 - 1072
5th-6th Grade	35.0	36.5	37.1	35.5	4396 - 4452
7th-8th Grade	39.8	40.2	40.6	39.8	2785 - 2816
9th Grade	40.0	39.7	38.3	39.6	6087 - 6176
10th-11th Grade	41.5	41.3	41.6	41.2	3557 - 3574
12th Grade	42.8	42.5	42.5	42.4	6244 - 6270
13th-14th Grade	43.5	43.2	42.6	43.1	3624 - 3635
Correlation	*.48****	*.41****	*.24****	*.51****	27741-27995

Notes: high mean = anti-authoritarianism, tolerance, pro-women rights, and general tolerance; sample = secondary schools in US, FRG, the Netherlands, Italy, Finland, Sweden, Ireland, Israel, New Zealand; source: IEA Civics data, Torney et al. (1975); *** p<.0001

The level of education here is the grade the student was in, which is closely related to the student's age. We reanalyzed the relationship between age and anti-authoritarianism and found it to be linear, highly significant, and substantial (+.49; see Table 8.4).

Table 8.4. Anti-authoritarianism and age groups

Age Groups (years)	Anti-authoritarianism	
	Mean	*Number of respondents*
9-11	34.8	5347
12-14	40.0	3753
15-16	40.3	7196
17-18	42.6	6871
19-23	44.0	3836
Correlation	*.49****	*27003*

Notes: high mean = anti-authoritarianism; sample = schools in the US, West Germany, the Netherlands, Italy, Finland, Sweden, Ireland, Israel, New Zealand; source: IEA Civics data, Torney et al. (1975); *** p<.001

Age and school level are hard to disentangle; as long as students are in school, both variables are almost identical in practice. Only when some students leave school will the exposure to education be different for those who stay and those who go. These survey results show a relatively strong relationship between supportive attitudes about anti-authoritarianism and democratic tolerance on the one hand and increased level of education on the other.

The Belgian Election Study

A 1991 Belgian study provides additional evidence about voters (voting is obligatory by law in Belgium). The authors used a seven-item authoritarianism scale. All the items were taken from Adorno et al. (1950) and the scale showed adequate reliability (Cronbach alpha .77). The sample was randomly drawn from the electorate, the adult population of Belgium. We computed the relationship for the two main Belgian language groups (Dutch in Flanders, French in Walonia) separately, as well as for the population as a whole.

Table 8.5. Authoritarianism by school level: Belgium (1991)

Educational Level	Belgium Total		Dutch Speaking		French Speaking	
	Mean	*N*	*Mean*	*N*	*Mean*	*N*
Primary	5.54	760	5.42	532	5.80	223
Lower Secondary	5.12	1000	5.00	662	5.35	333
Higher Secondary	4.69	1239	4.57	787	4.89	450
College	4.27	765	4.14	448	4.45	316
University	3.97	311	3.89	165	4.05	146
Correlation	-.45***		-.47***		-.46***	

Notes: N = number of respondents; mean = mean on 7-item Adorno type F-scale; recomputed range: 1-7 (low-high authoritarian); national random sample, in Belgium, 18+ years population; source: Belgian Election Study, Steinmetz Archives, Amsterdam, the Netherlands; *** p<.001

Authoritarianism was negatively related to educational levels for Dutch (-.47) and French speakers (-.45) in Belgium (see Table 8.5). The strength of the relationship is much higher than in the studies we analyzed previously. Correlations are equally high in French- and Dutch-speaking areas, indicating that linguistic and cultural differences seem not to play any part in the inverse relationship between educational level and authoritarianism. Results confirm that on a national scale, this inverse relationship exists, even in recent years.

Hungarian Anti-Semitism Study

Relevant random sample studies are lacking in former communist countries, with the exception of two (both unavailable for reanalysis; an early 1980s Polish study, Koralewicz, 1992; and an early 1990s Russian study, Popov, 1995). Hungarian investigators (Erös, Fabian, Enyedi, and Fleck, 1996; Enyedi, Erös, and Fabian, 1997) surveyed anti-Semitism, ethnocentrism and anti-'gypsy' (Roma) attitudes in Hungary in 1994. They used a national random sample and included authoritarianism concepts from Adorno et al. and Altemeyer (seven F-scale and 12 RWA-scale items). The F-scale was unidirectional, while the RWA-scale was balanced. (A balanced scale has both positive and negative statements which measure the same attitude.) Both scales showed adequate reliabilities (Cronbach alpha of .76 and .77, respectively; see Table 8.6). The relationships between authoritarianism, anti-Semitism, and ethnocentrism also were significant.

Table 8.6. Authoritarianism by school level: Hungary (1994)

Educational Level	F Scale (Adorno et al.)		RWA Scale (Altemeyer)	
Completed	*Mean*	*N*	*Mean*	*N*
Less than 8th class	3.53	70	2.99	66
8th class or equivalent	3.31	199	2.77	193
Vocational training	3.14	193	2.51	173
Technical school	2.79	129	2.37	119
Secondary school	2.70	87	2.35	74
College	2.50	69	2.26	70
University	2.15	45	2.16	45
Correlation	*-.54****		*-.48****	

Notes: N = number of respondents; mean = mean of 7-item Adorno type F-scale; range 1.00 -4.00 (low-high authoritarian); 12-item Altemeyer RWA-scale, range 1.00-4.00 (low-high authoritarian); national random sample in Hungary, 1994; source: Erös CEU-files; *** p<.001

Both concepts of authoritarianism reveal the same inverse relationship with the respondents' educational level (-.54 and -.48, respectively). This result indicates that the inverse relationship between educational level and authoritarianism is not limited to Western countries, but also to a post-communist country like Hungary. Also, using balanced or unidirectional scales makes no difference here. This inverse relationship cannot be an artifactual (yes-saying) result of using the F-scale.

The Middendorp Surveys

The series of Middendorp studies are unique since he repeated his surveys four times (1970, 1975, 1980, 1985, and 1992; Middendorp, 1978, and 1991; Meloen, and Middendorp, 1991). Each survey included national random samples of some 2000 Dutch respondents. Among the variables included was an authoritarianism scale consisting of seven Adorno et al. items. Although this scale was short, its reliability was substantial (Cronbach alphas were between .66 and .72) and the scale proved to be factor-analytically one-dimensional.

The relationship between educational level and authoritarianism existed in every Middendorp survey. No clear trend in time toward a stronger or weaker relationship was found. The stability of the relationship is quite remarkable (-.37 to -.44; see Table 8.7). Father's educational level was asked in four surveys. It appeared that the respondents' authoritarianism scores also were related to his/her father's educational level (see Table 8.8).

Table 8.7. Authoritarianism by school level: the Netherlands (1970-92)

School	1970		1975		1980		1985		1992	
Level	*Mean*	*N*	*Mean*	*N*	*Mean*	*N*	*Mean*	*N*	*Mean*	*N*
Primary	4.91	881	4.67	939	4.49	851	4.49	718	4.55	606
Secondary	4.37	547	4.23	480	4.00	540	3.96	559	3.77	546
Grammar	3.79	326	3.70	286	3.58	348	3.47	379	3.20	393
University	3.46	114	3.30	91	3.22	114	3.11	128	2.98	187
Correlation	-.41		-.38		-.37		-.39		-.44	
Significance ***			***		***		***		***	

Notes: N = number of respondents; mean = mean of 7-item Adorno/Middendorp F-scale (see Chapter 2); recomputed range: 1.00-7.00 (low-high authoritarian); repeated random national samples in the Netherlands, with identical items and questions; sources: Middendorp files, Steinmetz Archives, Amsterdam, the Netherlands; also see Middendorp, 1978, 1991; Meloen and Middendorp, 1991; *** p<.001

Table 8.8. Educational level and authoritarianism: the Netherlands (1970-85)

Correlated Variables	1970	1975	1980	1985
Authoritarianism x education father	-.28	-.29	-.29	-.32
Education respondent x education father	+.55	+.55	+.54	+.62

Notes: source: Meloen and Middendorp, 1991; four national random samples in the Netherlands; N=1791-1905 respondents in each survey; education of father with education of respondent over four surveys (1970-1985) correlates +.57; n = 4613 respondents; all correlations were highly significant

These correlations were only slightly lower (-.28 to -.32) than those between one's own authoritarianism and educational level. Also, they were just as stable over time. This may not be very surprising since the educational levels of both respondent and father were also substantially related (+.54 to +.62) in Middendorp's surveys. This indicates that the parents' educational level is substantially related to the respondents' level of authoritarianism. The parents' educational level is related to the respondents' educational level as well. Additionally, these results suggest that the relationship between educational level and authoritarianism does not change very much, even over decades. It also expresses the importance of one's educational level. So far, one's educational level has been shown to be the most important of all the social, background, demographic, or dependent variables related to authoritarianism.

CONCLUSIONS

The inverse relationship between level of education and authoritarian attitudes was reviewed and reassessed using cross-national data sets of very large or random samples from North America and Western Europe taken from the 1960s to the 1990s. An inverse relationship appears to exist almost universally since it was shown to be present in each sampled country from the 1960s to the 1990s. It also is a very stable phenomenon and changes very little over decades.

ACKNOWLEDGMENTS

We express our gratitude for the use of data for a secondary analysis to the International Association for the Evaluation of Educational Achievement (IEA); to Professor Ferenc Erös and his colleagues Zsolt Enyedi, Zoltan Fabian, and Zoltan Fleck of the Hungarian Academy of Sciences and the Central European University in Budapest; to Professors Jacques Billiet and Swyngedouw of the Belgian General Election study groups (ISPO and PIOP) at the University of Leuven; to the late Cees Middendorp; and to the Steinmetz Archives in Amsterdam for providing access to the Middendorp and 'T. Melvin' data.

9 Testing Simpson's Thesis: Authoritarianism and Education

INTRODUCTION

We said in Chapter 8 that authoritarianism is almost universally related to lower levels of education. In this chapter, we explore and test a notable exception to this rule, one which Simpson (1972) advanced.

SIMPSON'S HYPOTHESIS

Simpson (1972) investigated the effect of education on authoritarianism in an international context. Although this effect was considered to be well established, Simpson suggested that in non-Western societies, it might not be self-evidently true. He analyzed four large national random sample surveys of over 3600 adult respondents in the US, Finland, Mexico, and Costa Rica. A four-item authoritarianism scale was included. Simpson's main thesis was that different types of education will have different effects. He showed that in the US and Finland, an increase in the number of years one is educated was associated with a decrease in authoritarianism. But for Costa Rica, the effect was much less clear; for Mexico, the decrease was almost nonexistent. He argued that Mexican education, with its emphasis on rote learning, would not stimulate children enough to become less authoritarian, more independent, and more critical. Since democratic education was more effective in the US and Finland in this respect, authoritarianism levels for adults were also lower than in Mexico. A high societal level of authoritarianism there seems to be one effect of its educational system. Democratic attitudes may not easily develop there. For many decades, Mexico was virtually a one-party (the PRI) state with little political opposition. Simpson concluded that more years of education will not necessarily reduce authoritarianism in certain circumstances. He emphasized that the quality of the educational system in a country is also very important, as is the type of education available.

Simpson's hypothesis can be rephrased as: the effect of education will be different and presumably greater in countries with a stronger democratic tradition. The rate of decline in authoritarianism will serve as a measure for this. The educational system will be effective in teaching democratic attitudes if there is a substantial decline in authoritarianism. The main idea is that democratic ideas and actions have to be learned and practiced. Consequently, democratic attitudes can reduce existing and parallel authoritarian traditions.

133

METHODS OF ANALYSIS

Validating Simpson's thesis is no simple task. It requires cross-national surveys with random samples and measures for both the level of education and authoritarianism. Western and non-Western countries should be included since Simpson's thesis especially notes differences in developed and underdeveloped nations. The nature of their democratic systems should also vary. We did not have the means to do this in our own survey. However, one survey available for secondary analysis meets most of our criteria: Inglehart et al.'s world values survey conducted in over 40 countries (see Table 9.1) in 1981 and 1990-92 (Inglehart, 1997). It includes an indicator for the level of one's education. An authoritarianism scale was not included, but one may be constructed from items used. We reanalyzed this survey to test Simpson's thesis.

Table 9.1. World regions in the world values survey

World Region	Number of Countries	Number of Respondents		
		Total Ns	*Survey 1 (1981)*	*Survey 2 (1990-92)*
North America	2	7148	3579	3569
Latin America	4	8657	2842	5815
West Europe	16	41 110	16 594	24 516
East Europe	10	12 216	1464	10 752
CIS-Russia	2	5250	1262	3988
Africa	2	5333	1596	3737
Asia	5	8966	2174	6792
Oceania	1	1228	1228	-
Total World	*42*	*89 908*	*30 739*	*59 169*

Notes: source: World Values Study, 1981, 1990-92; Steinmetz Archives, Amsterdam, the Netherlands

The survey includes two waves of data-collection: in 1981 (with data mainly from Western countries) and in 1990-92 (adding non-Western, former communist, and third world countries). Most of the important countries in the major world regions were included (such as the US, Brazil, Argentina, Germany, the UK, France, Italy, Poland, Russia, Turkey, South Africa, Nigeria, India, China, and Japan). In every country, a random sample was taken of the population with 1000 to 2000 respondents. There were 24 countries that were surveyed twice (in 1981 and from 1990-92).

Respect for Authority Scale

No authoritarianism scale was included in this survey. However, several items were closely related to what is generally understood as authoritarianism in both an empirical and theoretical sense. Theoretically, the most important aspects according to Adorno et al. (1950) and Altemeyer (1988) are authoritarian conventionalism or moralism; authoritarian submission to authorities; and authoritarian aggression toward inferiors, the opposition, minorities, and outgroups. Relevant items were selected and statistically analyzed.

Authoritarian conventionalism was interpreted as conservative moralism that includes a number of 'conventional' moral issues (divorce, homosexuality, and prostitution) easily understood in every culture. In the survey, these issues were rated in a bipolar way, expressing tolerance for or rejection of these behaviors. Authoritarian submission was operationalized with items indicating trust or distrust of various authorities. Authorities that seemed most relevant for authoritarianism were the armed forces, the church, and the bureaucracy. Trusting such authorities generally means submission to their will and actions. For authoritarian aggression, no items were available; however, we included some items that seemed to indicate the opposite of authoritarian aggression (anti-authoritarian assertions). These items related to participating in overt actions such as demonstrations and boycotts. They can be considered to challenge established authorities. Meloen (1991b) demonstrated that this behavior was indeed negatively related to authoritarianism.

The authoritarianism-related items showed reliabilities far beyond the level of a constructed artifact. The reliability of a ten-item scale was substantial (Cronbach alpha .74) and comparable to other short authoritarianism scales. A 15-item version showed a very respectable reliability (Cronbach alpha .80). Since both versions included the question on valuing a 'greater respect for authority', this was called the 'respect for authority' (RFA) scale.

The three theoretical factors of authoritarian conventionalism, submission, and aggression are equally represented (each with one-third of the items). The scale is balanced against response set since some items are worded in a conservative (submission), some in a liberal (aggression), and the rest in a bipolar format (conventionalism). It is also important that this scale includes values, attitudes, and behaviors. This makes it a more complete measure. Most authoritarianism scales so far consisted of attitudes (Altemeyer, 1988, 1996; Lederer and Schmidt, 1995; exceptions are: Rigby, 1984, 1987; see also Meloen, van der Linden, and de Witte, 1996). We mainly used the ten-item version (RFA10) with over 62 000 respondents.

The face validity seemed quite adequate. Concurrent validity was supported as well. The RFA scale showed positive and significant correlations with issues such as 'not willing to have as neighbor' (people such as homosexuals, criminals, the unstable, AIDS patients, and Jews). Also, political self-ratings of left- or right-wing identity showed that the high RFA scorers tend to position themselves mainly at the far right, with only a small group at the far left (a J-curve). As can be expected, high RFAs tend also to be materialistic and lows, postmaterialistic. Most background variables tend to be comparable to those found using other authoritarianism scales. The geographical variation over eight world regions was similar to the one found with our general and psychological authoritarianism scales (see Table 9.2).

Table 9.2. World regions and respect for authority scale (RFA)

World Regions	Total	Survey 1 (1981)	Survey 2 (1990-92)
North America	4.71	4.89	4.53
Latin America	5.00	5.11	4.96
West Europe	4.45	4.58	4.37
East Europe	4.66	4.95	4.61
CIS-Russia	4.82	-	4.82
Africa	5.33	5.32	5.33
Asia	4.95	4.63	5.03
Oceania	4.59	4.59	-
Total World	*4.67*	*4.73*	*4.65*
Number of Respondents	*69 406*	*22 475*	*46 931*

Notes: source: World Values Study, Steinmetz Archives, Amsterdam, the Netherlands

Respect for authority (and lower authoritarianism) was lowest in West Europe and Oceania; highest in CIS-Russia and Africa. The means are slightly lower in the last survey. Respect for authority barely changes at all while differences between regions are quite stable. The RFA scale meets our criteria in measuring authoritarianism as a concept; it also has empirical results very similar to those which more conventional authoritarianism scales produce.

Educational Levels and School Leaving Age

The second variable needed for our analysis is a measure of the respondent's level of education; however, this depends very much on a country's educational system. Comparing educational systems of several countries seems to be an almost impossible task. In cross-national research, it is necessary to use precisely the same indicators and measurements. Fortunately, one such question was available: the age the respondent left school. Although it can be argued that this is not precisely the same as one's educational level, it is very closely related. The longer one stays in school, the more effective education can be in the end. The question asked was also very simple and easy to understand. With no adequate alternative available in this survey, we used the best available proxy for a respondent's level of education.

RESULTS

First, we analyzed the relation between RFA-authóritarianism and educational level and computed the mean authoritarianism scores for each educational level or respective school leaving age (see Table 9.3). The results for eight world regions as well as for the total scores are presented. The levels of education and the authoritarianism mean scores show the expected inverse relationship, highly significant in all cases. This is also true for each country in this survey. The rates of authoritarianism were highest for those who left school the earliest and lowest for those who left the latest.

Although this relationship was both predicted and expected, its universality is nothing less then overwhelming. In almost all included countries and across all world regions, there is a general decline in authoritarianism as people receive more education and stay in school for a longer time.

Table 9.3. RFA and level of education in eight world regions: mean scores (1981; 1990-92)

School Leaving Age (years)	North America	Latin America	World Region Western Europe	Eastern Europe	CIS-Russia	Africa	Asia	Oceania
up to 12	5.59	5.20	5.07	5.76	5.69	6.00	5.46	5.13
13-15	5.32	5.19	4.85	5.03	5.38	5.39	5.27	4.93
16-18	4.87	5.01	4.50	4.51	4.85	5.38	4.83	4.58
19-20	4.63	4.91	4.12	4.57	4.81	5.23	4.97	4.23
21+	4.28	4.79	3.85	4.30	4.66	5.19	4.81	3.98
Total	*4.70*	*5.04*	*4.45*	*4.61*	*4.80*	*5.32*	*4.97*	*4.60*

Notes: source: World Values Study, Steinmetz Archives, Amsterdam, the Netherlands; means of RFA10 by level of education; scale range is 1.00 low to 7.00 high authoritarianism

In most countries, the correlations are not even close to zero. They vary from -.12 to -.52, with an overall mean of -.27. All the correlations are again highly significant (see Table 9.4). In general, the relation is most strongly negative in Western countries (around -.35), while in several less-developed as well as former communist countries, these same correlations are lower. In Russia, Belarus, India, and China, the correlations are much lower. East Europe seems less affected overall and approaches the average levels of Western countries. East Asian countries (Japan and South Korea) show correlations comparable to those found in Western countries.

The 24 countries were surveyed twice. The results indicate considerable stability in this educational level-authoritarianism correlation over time (over ten years). It is both substantial and remarkable (in 1981, -.33, p<.001; in 1990-92, -.31, p<.001).

Table 9.4. RFA and level of education in eight world regions (1981; 1990-92)

	Total World			World Region					
		North America	*Latin America*	*West Europe*	*East Europe*	*CIS-Russia*	*Africa*	*Asia*	*Oceania*
N	62 525	5897	6240	29 385	8057	2920	3769	5167	1090
Corr	-.27*	-.34*	-.17*	-.35*	-.28*	-.22*	-.12*	-.17*	-.35*

Notes: source: World Values Study, Steinmetz Archives, Amsterdam, the Netherlands; correlation of RFA10 by level of education; * p<.001; N = number of respondents; Corr = correlation between RFA10 and level of education

Interpreting the strength of the inverse relationship between authoritarianism and educational level is not easy since some prosperous non-Western countries (Japan, Korea) show a 'Western pattern'. Obviously, this relationship is not entirely a 'Western' phenomenon.

TESTING SIMPSON'S THESIS

We are now ready to test Simpson's thesis. Essentially, he suggested that the inverse relationship between authoritarianism and level of education may not be entirely universal and varies between countries. In less-developed countries, education may be less successful in countering authoritarian tendencies and in promoting democratic ones. He concluded this when he found different effects of education in developed (US and Finland) and underdeveloped (Mexico and Costa Rica) countries. Differences between countries can be interpreted as differences in economic development, but also as differences in the degree of democracy. Therefore, we will test Simpson's thesis in several ways, distinguishing between levels of economic development and democracy. A higher correlation indicates a stronger relationship and, thus, a stronger educational effect.

Our expectation is that the observed decline of authoritarianism will be greatest in nontotalitarian countries, those with the lowest state authoritarianism and highest levels of freedom. This decline will also be strongest in the developed world, as compared with the developing world, and will show the least decline in underdeveloped regions.

Economic Development

The first difference is the level of socioeconomic development in the world. The countries included in the survey were pooled (with respect to their development) into three groups: the developed or first world countries, developing or second world countries, and underdeveloped or third world countries. The first world includes Western countries (North America, West Europe, Oceania) and East Asia (Japan, Korea), the second world, mainly the (ex) communist countries (East Europe, CIS-Russia, China), and the third world (Latin America, Africa, Middle East, South Asia).

Table 9.5. Testing Simpson's thesis: three developing worlds (1981; 1990-92)

Age Leaving School	Developed 1st World		Developing 2nd World		Underdeveloped 3rd World	
	RFA Mean	N	RFA Mean	N	RFA Mean	N
up to 12	5.10	3024	5.27	2372	5.75	204
13-15	4.87	9008	5.10	2970	5.53	1176
16-18	4.58	12 350	4.70	5436	5.38	2186
19-20	4.23	4340	4.70	2134	5.32	775
21+	3.95	9339	4.54	5064	5.19	2139
Total	4.50	38 061	4.79	17 984	5.34	6480
Correlation	-.33***		-.25***		-.15***	

Notes: source: World Values Study, Steinmetz Archives, Amsterdam; means of RFA10 by level of education; scale range 1.00 low to 7.00 high authoritarianism; N = number of respondents; RFA = Respect for Authority scale; correlations are between RFA10 and educational levels; *** $p < .001$

In each of the three worlds, education has an effect on authoritarian attitudinal levels. However, results depict stronger correlations in the first world (-.33) than in the second (-.25) or third (-.15; see Table 9.5). The effect in the first world is twice as strong as in the third. The second world is clearly in the middle. Simpson's thesis is supported strongly. Education in developed countries is much more effective in lowering authoritarianism.

Level of Democracy

We also pooled countries according to their past (or present) experience with totalitarianism, state authoritarianism, and freedom.

First, we divided the countries into democratic and nondemocratic, which included those with a totalitarian or militarist regime, one-party state, or dictatorship either now (China) or in the recent past (CIS-Russia, East Europe, and Africa; see Table 9.6). In nontotalitarian countries, we find a stronger relationship (-.30) than in totalitarian states (-.22). The authoritarianism lowering effect of education is stronger in nontotalitarian countries than in totalitarian ones. However, this effect is not entirely absent in totalitarian countries.

Table 9.6. Testing Simpson's thesis: totalitarianism (1981; 1990-92)

Age Leaving School	Nontotalitarian RFA Mean	N	(Ex)totalitarian RFA Mean	N
up to 12	5.12	3147	5.29	2453
13-15	4.89	9183	5.21	3979
16-18	4.61	12 729	4.86	7243
19-20	4.32	4681	4.79	2568
21+	4.07	10 272	4.65	6270
Total	*4.54*	*40 012*	*4.90*	*22 513*
Correlation	*-.30****		*-.22****	

Notes: source: World Values Study, Steinmetz Archives, Amsterdam; means of RFA10 by level of education; scale range 1.00 low to 7.00 high authoritarian; N = number of respondents; RFA = Respect for Authority scale; correlations are between RFA10 and educational levels; *** p<.001

The second indicator is state authoritarianism. The countries were divided into high, medium, and low state authoritarian levels, according to respective scores on this scale (Meloen, 1996; see Table 9.7). These three levels of state authoritarianism also make a difference. The results are very similar. Once more, the correlation is much stronger in low state authoritarian countries (-.33) than in those with high state authoritarianism (-.17). In the former case, it is almost twice as strong.

Table 9.7. Testing Simpson's thesis: state authoritarianism levels (1981; 1990-92)

Age Leaving School	Low State Authoritarianism RFA Mean	N	Medium State Authoritarianism RFA Mean	N	High State Authoritarianism RFA Mean	N
up to 12	5.24	982	5.11	2453	5.28	1559
13-15	4.83	5497	5.00	4940	5.38	2014
16-18	4.51	9864	4.72	5169	5.15	4158
19-20	4.20	3850	4.56	1471	5.04	1689
21+	3.92	7781	4.25	3285	4.90	4527
Total	*4.39*	*27 974*	*4.75*	*17 318*	*5.34*	*13 947*
Correlations	*-.33****		*-.26****		*-.17****	

Notes: source: World Values Study, Steinmetz Archives, Amsterdam; means of RFA10 by level of education; scale range 1.00 low to 7.00 high authoritarianism; N = number of respondents; RFA = Respect for Authority scale; correlations are between RFA10 and educational levels; *** p<.001

The third indicator was the Freedom House rating (1993). The countries were subdivided into those with little (low), some (medium), and complete (high) freedom according to the Freedom House categories (see Table 9.8).

Table 9.8. Testing Simpson's thesis: freedom levels (1981; 1990-92)

Age Leaving School	High Freedom RFA Mean	N	Medium Freedom RFA Mean	N	Low Freedom RFA Mean	N
up to 12	5.09	2952	5.25	1648	5.37	886
13-15	4.87	8870	5.13	1899	5.42	1880
16-18	4.57	12 235	4.73	2810	5.11	4147
19-20	4.22	4247	4.69	1096	4.99	1736
21+	3.94	9218	4.46	1751	4.85	5124
Total	*4.49*	*37 522*	*4.85*	*9204*	*5.34*	*13 773*
Correlations	*-.33****		*-.27****		*-.21****	

Notes: source: World Values Study, Steinmetz Archives, Amsterdam; means of RFA10 by level of education; scale range 1.00 low to 7.00 high authoritarianism; N = number of respondents; RFA = Respect for Authority scale; correlations are between RFA10 and educational levels; *** $p<.001$

Results for the three levels of freedom closely resemble those for totalitarianism and state authoritarianism. This is not too surprising because these indicators include closely related concepts.

CONCLUSIONS

We tested the quality and strength of the relationship between authoritarianism and level of education using Simpson's (1972) thesis. The results of our analyses support Simpson's thesis concerning the strength of the relationship between authoritarianism and level of education. In less-developed and less-democratic countries, this relationship is much weaker (down to half its strength elsewhere). This indicates a much weaker effect of education in combating authoritarianism and strengthening democratic attitudes in such countries.

We may conclude that this analysis generally supports the thesis that education in more democratic countries is quite effective in countering authoritarianism and supporting democratic attitudes, more so than is the case in less-democratic countries. Less-developed and some (ex)communist countries not only suffer from relatively high levels of authoritarianism, but often also from less educational effectiveness in terms of students'/citizens' acquisition of democratic attitudes. Education apparently has a different effect in underdeveloped countries, but this is also the case in countries that previously suffered from an authoritarian political regime or dictatorship.

10 Authoritarianism, Democracy, and Educational Orientations

INTRODUCTION

In this chapter, we return to our own survey and examine attitudes toward education among our survey respondents with respect to teaching styles, content, and educational policy choices. We will report on the associations between one's political views and certain education-related attitudes.

VIEWS ON EDUCATION

We present answers for the total sample regarding nine statements on education and teaching. Some reflect content of teaching, others style of teaching, teaching methods, and educational goals. Five were worded in a liberal, progressive direction (+), four in a conservative, nationalist one (-). We also examine students' answers and their consistency in the various world regions.

Teach Individual Freedom (+): *Our schools ought to teach us more about promoting individual freedom, popular participation, keeping the peace, and achieving economic equality and justice for all (item 22).* This liberal statement is supported by an overwhelming proportion (88 per cent) of the total sample of students (see Table 10.1).

Table 10.1. Teach individual freedom by world region

	Regions	% agree	% neutral	% disagree	Number of respondents
Eight	North America	85	9	6	1367
World	Latin America	92	4	4	906
Regions	West Europe	91	4	5	2032
	East Europe	85	7	9	1604
	CIS-Russia	81	11	7	1392
	Africa	94	2	4	394
	Asia	92	4	5	1299
	Oceania	87	8	5	122
Three	Developed First World	89	6	5	3936
Worlds	(Ex)Communist World	83	9	8	3013
	Developing Third World	93	3	4	2167
Total	World	88	6	6	9116

Notes: GEO8 and WORLD3 by IT22; Chi-square eight regions and three worlds, p<.0001; horizontal %

Only 6 per cent rejected it and 6 per cent remained neutral. The support for this item varies from 81 to 94 per cent over the eight world regions. Most of the support comes from Latin American, African, Asian, and West European samples (91-94 per cent). Least support is found in East European, CIS-Russian, North American, and Oceanian/Australian groups (81-87 per cent). The strongest dissent comes from East Europe and Russia (7-9 per cent). Those from the developing countries support teaching of freedom the most (93 per cent); those from the former communist states the least. Third world countries strongly favor such education even though they may have experienced less freedom in the past. The former Communist world is less enthusiastic, probably because of continuing deep-rooted ideological or cognitive schema or the effects of political socialization under communism that led respondents to view individual freedom very skeptically.

Schools Teach Too Much About Other Peoples (-): *Our schools already teach us too much about other lands, peoples, cultures, and races (item 23).* This conservative, nationalist statement includes an exaggerated interest in one's own group and a disregard for other groups (ethnocentrism or xenophobia). This strikes a positive chord among 24 per cent of the students who agree with this view (see Table 10.2).

Table 10.2. Schools teach too much about other peoples by world region

	Regions	% disagree	% neutral	% agree	Number of respondents
Eight	North America	77	10	13	1372
World	Latin America	44	16	41	907
Regions	West Europe	82	7	12	2039
	East Europe	78	7	15	1606
	CIS-Russia	60	9	31	1392
	Africa	38	5	57	392
	Asia	54	7	39	1308
	Oceania	86	7	7	121
Three	Developed First World	78	8	14	3947
Worlds	(Ex)Communist World	70	8	23	3015
	Developing Third World	46	10	45	2175
Total	*World*	*68*	*8*	*24*	*9137*

Notes: GEO8 and WORLD3 by IT23; Chi-square eight regions and three worlds, p<.0001; horizontal %

Nevertheless, most students (68 per cent) do not agree, while 8 per cent were undecided. The regional pattern is different here because Oceanian, North American, and European groups (West and East) strongly reject this statement (77-86 per cent). But the CIS-Russian, and Asian groups (60 and 54 per cent), and especially Latin American and African samples (44 and 38 per cent) registered very little opposition. In fact, in the African group, a majority of 57 per cent agreed with this statement, whereas all other groups disagreed. The African and Latin American samples exhibit the strongest ethnocentrism levels. This ethnocentrism appears to be widely embraced among third world groups, with protagonists (46 per cent) and antagonists (45 per cent) almost equal. By contrast, levels of rejection in the first and second world are much stronger (78 and 70 per cent) than agreement levels (14 and 23 per cent).

Teach Peace (+): *Our schools ought to teach us more about the United Nations, comparative government, and keeping the peace through international organizations and peacekeeping alliances (item 24).* Knowledge of international political bodies seems necessary to understand our complex world. This is also the view most students hold (76 per cent; see Table 10.3). Only a minority (13 per cent) rejects it, while 10 per cent has no opinion. Teaching peace gets most support from the Asian, West European, and Latin American samples (81-83 per cent), somewhat less from North American and Oceanian groups (77-79 per cent), followed by African and CIS-Russian groups (73-74 per cent). Absolutely the least support comes from our East European samples (62 per cent); they also show the strongest rejection levels (25 per cent), much higher than in any other group. This bellicosity may help us understand why peacekeeping has not been fully successful in some parts of East Europe (former Yugoslavia, former Soviet-Russian republics). The second world in general shows little support for teaching peace, much less so than the first and the third worlds.

Table 10.3. Schools should teach peace by world region

	Regions	% agree	% neutral	% disagree	Number of respondents
Eight	North America	79	14	8	1372
World	Latin America	81	9	10	907
Regions	West Europe	83	9	9	2040
	East Europe	62	13	25	1607
	CIS-Russia	73	12	15	1388
	Africa	74	8	18	394
	Asia	83	7	11	1300
	Oceania	77	9	14	121
Three	Developed First World	81	11	8	3948
Worlds	(Ex)Communist World	67	13	21	3012
	Developing Third World	81	7	12	2169
Total	*World*	*76*	*10*	*13*	*9129*

Notes: GEO8 and WORLD3 by IT24; Chi-square eight regions and three worlds, p<.0001; horizontal %

Schools Should Prohibit Minority Languages (-): *With respect to minority languages and cultures, our schools ought to prohibit such languages for individual learning, classroom instruction, and separate school subjects (item 25).* This is an important nationalist issue in multicultural societies where linguistic, ethnic, and cultural minorities exist. Most students do not think one should prohibit minority languages and cultures from playing a part in schools (74 per cent; see Table 10.4). However, a sizable minority (16 per cent) supports such exclusionary measures, while 10 per cent had no opinion. This statement is rejected by large majorities of students in all world regions, but less so in Africa and Asia (60 and 62 per cent), where agreement is also strongest, as it generally is in the third world. Rejection is much stronger in West and East Europe (82 and 81 per cent) and strongest in Latin America (86 per cent). Most of our respondents seem tolerant about this aspect of ethnic and linguistic diversity.

Table 10.4. Schools should prohibit languages by world region

	Regions	% disagree	% neutral	% agree	Number of respondents
Eight	North America	69	15	16	1365
World	Latin America	86	5	9	904
Regions	West Europe	82	9	10	2014
	East Europe	81	7	12	1606
	CIS-Russia	68	14	19	1389
	Africa	60	13	28	390
	Asia	62	10	26	1300
	Oceania	77	16	7	121
Three	Developed First World	76	12	12	3936
Worlds	(Ex)Communist World	75	10	15	3013
	Developing Third World	69	8	24	2167
Total	*World*	*74*	*10*	*16*	*9089*

Notes: GEO8 and WORLD3 by IT25; Chi-square eight regions and three worlds, p<.0001; horizontal %

Minority Parents as School Partners (+): *With respect to members of minority groups, parents of minority children should become partners with the schools by helping to determine the school curricula and policies and by becoming more directly involved in the schools (for example, by teaching a course; item 26).* An endorsement of cooperation with ethnic and cultural minorities is expressed here. There are fewer supporters (60 per cent) than in the previous question and more undecided respondents (22 per cent; see Table 10.5), whereas rejections are at the same level as before (18 per cent). The regional pattern is more stable since in most regions, except for CIS-Russia (49 per cent), a slim majority agrees with this stand (53-66 per cent). Africans have high levels of rejection (33 per cent), but the least support overall (55 per cent) comes from the second world samples.

Table 10.5. Favor minority parents as school partners by world region

	Regions	% agree	% neutral	% disagree	Number of respondents
Eight	North America	56	25	19	1367
World	Latin America	70	15	15	903
Regions	West Europe	62	24	14	2016
	East Europe	61	21	19	1603
	CIS-Russia	49	31	20	1391
	Africa	53	14	33	394
	Asia	66	17	18	1299
	Oceania	56	29	16	122
Three	Developed First World	61	24	15	3918
Worlds	(Ex)Communist World	55	25	19	3011
	Developing Third World	64	15	21	2158
Total	*World*	*60*	*22*	*18*	*9087*

Notes: GEO8 and WORLD3 by IT26; Chi-square eight regions and three worlds, p<.0001; horizontal %

Back to Basics (-): *Concerning teaching and testing methods in the schools, students should be grouped by ability, should learn basic facts, and should take competitive subject examinations so everybody knows where they stand in a course and teachers can be held accountable (item 27).* This statement expresses a preference for basic, factual, objective, and clear-cut education rather than open-ended or subjective educational procedures.

Table 10.6. Approve back to basics by world region

	Regions	% disagree	% neutral	% agree	Number of respondents
Eight	North America	34	17	49	1365
World	Latin America	29	11	59	906
Regions	West Europe	48	15	36	2025
	East Europe	32	9	59	1604
	CIS-Russia	23	13	64	1388
	Africa	28	11	61	390
	Asia	23	10	68	1296
	Oceania	44	19	37	122
Three	Developed First World	42	16	42	3925
Worlds	(Ex)Communist World	28	11	61	3009
	Developing Third World	23	9	67	2162
Total	*World*	*33*	*13*	*54*	*9096*

Notes: GEO8 and WORLD3 by IT27; Chi-square eight regions and three worlds, p<.0001; horizontal %

Surprisingly, most students (54 per cent) support this view, but there is a sizable (33 per cent) opposition, while 13 per cent have no opinion (see Table 10.6). In Canada and the US, this conventional idealized view of the teaching-learning process is part of the conservative 'back to basics' movement which expresses a form of educational authoritarianism, endorsing conventional practices, student submission to teacher authority, and aggressive reactionary reforms. This statement is supported by a slim majority in some world regions, but not in our West European and Oceanian groups (36 and 37 per cent in favor); while rejection is strongest here (48 and 44 per cent). In North American groups, support does not reach an absolute majority (49 per cent). The third and second world groups tend to support learning basic facts as priorities, but this is much less the case in the first world (a 42/42 per cent split). Perhaps there is less emphasis on learning basic facts in the postindustrial regions than in the developing world. The item summarizes an essential feature of the North American culture wars over current educational practices.

Table 10.7. Schools should encourage critical learners by world region

	Regions	% agree	% neutral	% disagree	Number of respondents
Eight	North America	59	21	20	1361
World	Latin America	57	18	26	905
Regions	West Europe	70	14	17	2022
	East Europe	57	15	28	1605
	CIS-Russia	78	13	9	1389
	Africa	76	12	12	387
	Asia	82	8	11	1294
	Oceania	64	17	19	122
Three	Developed First World	66	16	18	3918
Worlds	(Ex)Communist World	67	14	19	3011
	Developing Third World	72	12	17	2156
Total	*World*	*68*	*14*	*18*	*9085*

Notes: GEO8 and WORLD3 by IT28; Chi-square eight regions and three worlds, p<.0001; horizontal %

Schools Should Encourage Critical Learners (+): *Concerning teaching and testing methods in the schools, process is more important than content so that students are active, involved, and critical learners and so that assessment of results is based on less formal means, including student self-assessment (item 28).* The opposite of 'back to basics', this item emphasizes progressive teaching goals and procedures. Most students (68 per cent) do not see a contradiction with the former statement and answered in favor (see Table 10.7). A minority did not agree (18 per cent), with 14 per cent undecided. Interestingly, many students do not yet differentiate between factual, rote, passive, or criticism, process, and active learning styles; but a majority worldwide support both factual and critical learning, wanting the best of both worlds. All regions strongly support this conclusion. West Europeans and Oceanians (70 and 64 per cent) do so; much stronger support is found among CIS-Russians (78 per cent), Africans (76 per cent), and Asians (82 per cent). The least support comes from East European, Latin, and North American students (57, 57, and 59 per cent). The third world groups endorse more critical learning, more so than do both the first and second world samples, but they are probably least exposed to this pragmatic teaching style (despite the African adage 'it takes a village to raise a child') in formal schooling.

Teaching Patriotism (-): *Concerning history, social studies, and civic education, teaching about other countries' history, government, cultures, and peoples is far less important than teaching about patriotism, our nation's glorious history, and our outstanding military achievements (item 29).* The nationalistic content here is much more than benign patriotism; it includes glorifying nation and supporting militarism. Most students (69 per cent) reject such nationalism (see Table 10.8). Still, 23 per cent support nationalist education with 8 per cent undecided. This stance is broadly rejected since in all world regions, majorities disagree. Latin American, Asian, African, and CIS-Russian groups are most in favor of teaching patriotism (25-35 per cent), rejecting it least (57-63 per cent). West European, Oceanian, and North American samples most strongly reject teaching patriotism (72-82 per cent). There seems to be a relation here with economic development levels. The first world has least support for patriotism in education, the third world the strongest, with the second world in between. This may help to explain why some wars break out where they do, while other world regions are more peaceful.

Eliminate Curricular Nationalism (+): *Concerning history, social studies, and civic education, we should eliminate isolationist, provincial, and nationalistic themes from the curriculum so that students can learn more about international topics (such as the UN, EEC, PLO, OAU, CSCE, GCC, and OPEC; item 30).* This progressive liberal view is supported by 45 per cent, while 39 per cent rejected it, with 15 per cent undecided (see Table 10.9). It indicates clear divisions within the total group of students. Only theCIS-Russia, West European, and Asian groups show a bare majority of anti-nationalistic supporters (50, 51, and 53 per cent), while the Latin American sample shows a slim majority in the pro-nationalist direction (53 per cent). Most support for the anti-nationalist position comes from the second world. Apparently, this is a controversial issue. Many students do not think nationalism should be eliminated. Extreme nationalism has been an important issue in South America (Argentina, Chile), but not in North America. Perhaps the political residue of super-nationalistic Reagan-Bush years reveals its effects here. The often highly nationalistic content of contemporary US education, media, and politics may also play a part in these results (Pat Buchanan's 'America first' campaign in 1996).

Table 10.8. Favor teaching patriotism by world region

	Regions	% disagree	% neutral	% agree	Number of respondents
Eight	North America	72	11	17	1367
World	Latin America	57	10	33	906
Regions	West Europe	81	6	13	2039
	East Europe	69	6	25	1605
	CIS-Russia	63	12	25	1390
	Africa	61	10	30	394
	Asia	59	6	35	1299
	Oceania	82	10	8	122
Three	Developed First World	76	8	16	3943
Worlds	(Ex)Communist World	66	9	25	3012
	Developing Third World	59	8	34	2160
Total	*World*	*69*	*8*	*23*	*9115*

Notes: GEO8 and WORLD3 by IT29; Chi-square eight regions and three worlds, p<.0001; horizontal %

Table 10.9. Eliminate educational nationalism by world region

	Regions	% agree	% neutral	% disagree	Number of respondents
Eight	North America	32	28	41	1357
World	Latin America	32	15	53	903
Regions	West Europe	51	13	36	2025
	East Europe	49	10	41	1605
	CIS-Russia	50	19	31	1390
	Africa	44	12	45	389
	Asia	53	11	37	1291
	Oceania	34	26	41	121
Three	Developed First World	42	19	40	3917
Worlds	(Ex)Communist World	50	14	37	3012
	Developing Third World	47	11	42	2152
Total	*World*	*45*	*15*	*39*	*9081*

Notes: GEO8 and WORLD3 by IT30; Chi-square eight regions and three worlds, p<.0001; horizontal %

EDUCATIONAL ORIENTATIONS

Of the nine educational statements, most students selected progressive, pragmatic, liberal answers and rejected the more conservative ones. This pattern seems fairly stable over all regions, with some exceptions. Apparently, these postmodern and new age students are much more alike than one might expect. Some variations within these patterns may be a result of particular local circumstances, such as the extent to which patriotic fervor is a societal custom in the political culture, schools, or society as a whole.

The stability of these results may also indicate a pattern (or common denominator) of teaching attitudes that runs through these issues. These core 'attitudes' lie under any surface 'opinions' about education and society.

Two Types of Educational Attitudes

To find the common factors in the answers to attitudes about teaching styles, a factor-analysis was conducted (see Chapter 2). Two factors were found, a progressive/liberal and a conservative/nationalist one. All items worded in a nationalist direction loaded on one factor; all liberal worded items on the other. We concluded there were two scales: one conservative or nationalist and one liberal or progressive. At least two teaching style orientations or cognitive schemata seem to be present when we use our empirical data to verify their existence. The two scales, conservative/nationalist education (EDNAT4) and liberal/progressive education (EDLIB5), correlated negatively and significantly, but at a rather low level: -.08 (p<.001; N = 8844). Both theoretical concepts (liberal and nationalist education attitudes) may be less one another's opposites than appears to be the case at first sight (for example, students favoring both factual and critical learning styles). Our data analysis supports the existence of these two different educational orientations.

Liberal and Nationalist Educational Attitudes

Respondents' answers indicated that 74 per cent supported the goals of liberal/progressive education (see Table 10.10). Simultaneously, they rejected less strongly (58 per cent) those at the other end of the spectrum comprising nationalist education (see Table 10.11). In general, there is more agreement on liberal education issues than on nationalist ones (which elicit more controversy among respondents). We also examined variation over the included world regions. The strongest support for liberal education attitudes comes from Asian and West European groups (83 and 81 per cent). The least support (but still substantial) comes from East Europe, Oceania, and North America (65-69 per cent). Latin American, CIS-Russian, and African groups show average support. The third world samples show the most enthusiasm, those from the second world the least, but recorded differences are relatively minor.

If we contrast these results with the answers about nationalist educational attitudes, it becomes clear why liberal education is not exactly the opposite of nationalist education. Again, West Europeans (78 per cent) and Oceanians (76 per cent) are most rejecting of nationalist education. Africans and Asians (34-38 per cent) reject it the least and show the strongest support for nationalist education (21-26 per cent). Apparently, Asian groups support both liberal and nationalist educational goals to a larger extent than elsewhere. These respondents may not see any incompatibility or cognitive dissonance between teaching peace and freedom or glorification of the nation and the military.

Table 10.10. Support for liberal education by world region

	Regions	% disagree	% neutral	% agree	Number of respondents
Eight	North America	4	27	69	1335
World	Latin America	3	25	71	890
Regions	West Europe	2	17	81	1980
	East Europe	6	29	65	1599
	CIS-Russia	4	20	77	1383
	Africa	4	24	73	378
	Asia	2	15	83	1260
	Oceania	4	30	66	120
Three	Developed First World	3	22	76	3845
Worlds	(Ex)Communist World	5	25	70	2999
	Developing Third World	3	20	78	2101
Total	*World*	*3*	*22*	*74*	*8945*

Notes: GEO8 and WORLD3 by EDLIB5; Chi-square eight regions and three worlds, p<.0001; horizontal %

Table 10.11. Support for nationalist education by world region

	Regions	% disagree	% neutral	% agree	Number of respondents
Eight	North America	63	28	9	1350
World	Latin America	47	40	13	896
Regions	West Europe	78	17	5	1989
	East Europe	64	28	8	1601
	CIS-Russia	46	39	15	1383
	Africa	34	45	21	378
	Asia	38	36	26	1281
	Oceania	76	23	1	120
Three	Developed First World	70	23	7	3936
Worlds	(Ex)Communist World	55	33	11	3013
	Developing Third World	38	39	23	2167
Total	*World*	*58*	*30*	*12*	*8998*

Notes: GEO8 and WORLD3 by EDNAT4; Chi-square eight regions and three worlds, p<.0001; horizontal %

With respect to the three developing worlds, it is interesting that national-ist education attitudes tend to be most strongly rejected in the first world, least in the third, with the second in between. It seems that level of development may be more closely associated with less nationalist educational goals, not with more liberal ones. Our overall results on liberal and nationalist education attitudes indicate some regional variations in support for nationalistic educa-tion. By contrast, there is rather uniform support among all students surveyed for liberal education.

GENERAL BACKGROUND

The background for both education attitudes was explored using correlational analysis. For both attitudes, we computed Pearson correlations with relevant variables that were included in our survey for this reason (see Table 10.12).

The nationalist education attitude was relatively strongly related to gen-eral authoritarianism (+.54), to psychological and Adorno-type authoritarian-ism (both +.50), and somewhat less so to political repression (+.44) and militarism (+.33). General authoritarianism appeared to be the best predictor for this nationalist education attitude. The relation of nationalist education to multiculturalism was much weaker, both for democratic multiculturalism (-.20) and multiculturalism (-.27). No relation (despite its significance) was shown with democratic attitudes (-.03) and only a weak one with a pro-demo-cratic system attitude (-.12). A positive relation with the dictators' rating (+.23) and a negative one with the reformers' rating (-.22) were not very strong, but were in the expected direction. Neither interest in politics nor con-sidering oneself religious was substantially related. Composite ratings of self-right-wing (+.30) and self-multicultural (-.28) were not very strong, but were also in the expected direction. Social background variables (age, social class, father's education, and town size in youth) were unrelated. Only a weak cor-relation with being male or female indicated that a relationship may exist.

The liberal education attitude appears not to be exactly the opposite of the nationalist one here as well. This factor is mainly correlated with demo-cratic multiculturalism (+.44), multiculturalism (+.43), democratic attitudes (+.28), attitudes toward democratic reformers (+.24), support for the demo-cratic system (+.18), and self-ratings of being right-wing (-.28) and multicul-tural (+.26). All other background variables tend to have only very weak associations with liberal education attitudes, while social background vari-ables are virtually unrelated.

These results show quite clearly that both teaching style preferences have a somewhat different pattern of correlates, each emphasizing a number of different issues. The nationalist style is related to authoritarian, repressive, militarist, and dictatorial tendencies, while the liberal/progressive one is much more strongly related to multiculturalism and democratic attitudes and preferences for a democratic political system and democratic reformers. Both these clusters of correlates support the face and concurrent validity of these two separate education attitudes.

Table 10.12. Correlations of liberal and nationalist education

Variable	Code	Liberal Education	Nationalist Education
General Authoritarianism	AUTH20	-.06***	.54***
Psychological Authoritarianism	AUT8	-.03*	.50***
Adorno Authoritarianism	F10	-.03**	.50***
Political Repression	REPRES7	-.10***	.44***
Militarism	MIL3	-.13***	.33***
Democratic Multiculturalism	MCDEMO13	.44***	-.20***
Multiculturalism	MCULT8	.43***	-.27***
Democratic Attitudes	DEMOAT5	.28***	-.03**
Democratic System	DEMO1	.18***	-.12***
Dictator	DICTATOR	-.05***	.23***
Reformer	REFORMER	.24***	-.22***
Self-Political	SPPOLIT	-.06***	.01ns
Self-Religious	SRELIG	-.07***	.11***
Self-Right-Wing	SRIGHT5	-.28***	.30***
Self-Multicultural	SMCULT5	.26***	-.28***
Education Father	EDUCFA	-.05***	.04**
Age	AGE	.05***	-.04***
Male/Female	SEX	-.03**	.13***
Social Class Parents	SOCCL	-.01ns	.06***
Town Size Youth	TOWNYTH	.02ns	.08***

Notes: Correlations EDLIB5 and EDNAT4 with Variables; * p<.05, ** p<.01, *** p<.001, ns = not significant

Social Background

Our social background variables do not seem to be related, whereas they have been found to be so in many other random sample studies. However, a direct relation of outcomes with level of education is not likely in this survey because of the sample's educational homogeneity. There is little variation among university students in achieved levels of education. Most respondents come from the (sub)urban, (upper) middle class and have college-educated parents. Therefore, none (or little) variance exists for education in our survey. Because of this lack in social background variation, the relation with parental variables may also be too weak to produce sizable correlations.

Political Environment

National political circumstances may influence our attitudes. Therefore, we included indicators of the social and political environment behind or undergirding educational attitudes. To test this assumption, we used political indicators (ratings of country performance). The means for each country on both liberal and conservative-nationalist education attitudes were correlated with the 1992 and 1995 freedom ratings (Freedom House, 1993, 1995), 1991 state authoritarianism (Meloen, 1996, 1999), 1991 gross human rights violations (Gupta et al., 1993) and the 1985 human freedom index (UNDP, 1991).

The results we found are nothing short of remarkable (see Table 10.13). The nationalist education attitude correlated significantly with all the country performance ratings. This indicated more support for nationalist education in countries with less freedom, stronger state authoritarianism, and more human rights violations. The correlations were high and significant (.50 to .75). This makes sense since the political context in each country contributes to the predominance of related education attitudes there. For example, the higher the levels of state authoritarianism and the less freedom, the stronger the attitudes in favor of nationalist-conservative educational policies.

Table 10.13. National levels with liberal or nationalist education: intercorrelations

Variable	Code	Liberal		Nationalist	
		Corr.	Countries	Corr.	Countries
Freedom Index 1992	FREE92	-.04ns	44	.57***	44
Freedom Index 1995	FREE95	.02ns	44	.50**	44
State Authoritarianism 1991	STAUT91	.28ns	32	.73***	32
State Authoritarianism 1991+	STAUT91+	.01ns	43	.52***	43
Gross Human Rights Violations 1991	GHRV91	.25ns	35	.75***	35
Human Freedom Index 1985	HFI85	.27ns	33	.59***	33

Notes: correlations EDLIB5 and EDNAT4 with variables; Corr. = correlation; ** p<.01, *** p<.001; ns = not significant

However, no statistical relationship between the liberal education attitude and these external variables appeared. None of the correlations with liberal education reached acceptable levels of statistical significance. Apparently, if the political environment influences such attitudes, it seems more likely to occur for nationalist education attitudes than for liberal ones.

STABILITY OF RELATIONS

Relations between background variables and educational attitudes may only exist at the aggregate ('world') level in this survey, not for the separate world regions where our samples originated. Are these (cor)relations stable and do they exist in every world region of this survey? We tested this stability by computing correlations separately for each world region. Our samples from Africa and Oceania have relatively few respondents, so results from these regions show less stability. For the liberal education attitude (see Table 10.14), we found that a significant relation with democratic multiculturalism shows the most stability over the eight world regions (around .40 and significant in every region).

Table 10.14. Liberal education intercorrelations by world region

Regions		General authorit- arianism	Democratic multicul- turalism	Democratic system	Self right- wing	Self multi- cultural
Eight	North America	-.08**	.48***	.06*	-.31***	.25***
World	Latin America	.05ns	.40***	.10**	-.21***	.15***
Regions	West Europe	-.10***	.43***	.11***	-.25***	.31***
	East Europe	-.12***	.46***	.21***	-.29***	.27***
	CIS-Russia	-.11***	.45***	.29***	-.23***	.25***
	Africa	.16**	.25***	.18**	-.07ns	.15**
	Asia	-.01ns	.40***	.23***	-.26***	.24***
	Oceania	-.25**	.65***	-.08ns	-.41***	.47***
Three	Developed First World	-.12***	.46***	.10***	-.31***	.31***
Worlds	(Ex)Communist World	.01ns	.43***	.21***	-.23***	.22***
	Developing Third World	.02ns	.36***	.18***	-.21***	.22***
Total	*World*	*-.06***	*.44***	*.18***	*-.28***	*.26***

Notes: correlations EDLIB5 with variables listed above; * p<.05, ** p<.01, ***p<.001

Somewhat less stable is the relation with the composite self-rating on multiculturalism (a lower correlation, but significant in every region), while the relation with the composite self-rating as right-wing seems more variable (in its negative strength and in seven out of eight regions). The relation with the pro-democratic system rating is quite variable (ranging from .06 to .29, yet significant in nearly every region). The relation with general authoritarianism is rather weak and unstable (.16 to -.25) and is hard to generalize about. Thus, the relation of liberal education attitudes was stable and sizable over the eight world regions for democratic multiculturalism and considering oneself multicultural. This pattern also exists for the three developing worlds, although these relationships tend to be slightly weaker in the third world.

The nationalist education attitude shows stable relationships in all the world regions with general authoritarianism (around .50, significant in every region; see Table 10.15). The relationships with self-ratings as right-wing or multicultural are slightly more variable (but also significant in every region).

Democratic multiculturalism shows some variability in its relationship to nationalist education (.08 to -.43), although a weak relationship was observed in most regions.The relation with the pro-democratic system item is rather unstable (weak to nonexistent). Therefore, the nationalist education attitude is related to authoritarianism and self-ratings as right-wing and as (not being) multicultural. This pattern is also found in the first, second, and third worlds.

Table 10.15. Nationalist education intercorrelations by world region

	Regions	General authorit- arianism	Democratic multi- culturalism	Democratic system	Self right- wing	Self multi- cultural
Eight	North America	.49***	-.29***	-.04ns	.30***	-.31***
World	Latin America	.48***	-.13***	.06ns	.21***	-.31***
Regions	West Europe	.55***	-.37***	-.08***	.35***	-.32***
	East Europe	.49***	-.22***	-.16***	.27***	-.13***
	CIS-Russia	.32***	-.25***	-.14***	.22***	-.27***
	Africa	.43***	.08ns	-.02ns	.23***	-.13*
	Asia	.59***	-.002ns	-.03ns	.28***	-.20***
	Oceania	.61***	-.43***	.11ns	.49***	-.49***
Three	Developed First World	.56***	-.31***	-.09***	.38***	-.35***
Worlds	(Ex)Communist World	.44***	-.24***	-.19***	.27***	-.22***
	Developing Third World	.55***	-.08***	-.01ns	.28***	-.21***
Total	*World*	*.54***	-.20***	-.03**	.30***	-.28***

Notes: correlations EDNAT4 with variables; * p<.05, ** p<.01, *** p<.001

CONCLUSIONS

From our analysis, we may conclude that relatively stable relationships over the world regions exist for liberal education attitudes/policy choices as related to multiculturalism and for considering oneself as multicultural or left-wing. Nationalist education attitudes/policy choices are more closely related to authoritarianism and considering oneself as right-wing, and as (not being) multicultural.

11 Content of Education: Testing the Farnen/Meloen Thesis

INTRODUCTION

This chapter describes the results of an empirical test of the Farnen/Meloen thesis on student preferences about the content and style of education and their relationships to relevant political attitudes. Our main research problem is that education has clear political effects because some students stay in the school system longer than others and, therefore, the population varies in average levels of education and in the distribution and consumption of educational resources. Our thesis in this study has been that not only does achieved educational level have effects, but it also matters what is being taught, the content of teaching, and the process of education in general.

We analyzed this process for political socialization themes and operationalized the political content of education with questions about teaching explicitly around democratic issues, individual freedom, international peace-keeping bodies, and respect for minorities. We included some issues about teaching style (such as rote learning, testing methods) and teaching goals. We developed two education scales: conservative-nationalism and liberal-progressivism (see Chapters 2 and 10) to study possible effects of teaching goals, styles, and content on democracy, authoritarianism, and multiculturalism.

We reported that there was an inverse relationship between increased levels of education and reduced authoritarianism (see Chapters 8 and 9), thus suggesting that more education leads to stronger democratic attitudes. However, Simpson's thesis also maintained that education in some countries was more effective than in others in stimulating democratic and nonauthoritarian attitudes. We found some support for his thesis in a reanalysis of one worldwide survey. Simpson believed this difference in effectiveness was due to the way the school system was organized and the content of what was taught. Passive or rote learning, instead of teaching students to be active and critical, does not stimulate their growth as democratic citizens, he argued.

This issue is the focus of our analysis here. We propose the following guiding research questions (the Farnen/Meloen thesis): Does statistical analysis show a relation between one's teaching style and attitudinal preferences (liberal-progressive or conservative-nationalist), with multicultural democratic attitudes, with evaluations of dictators and democratic reformers, and with one's support for democracy? Are any other factors involved that influence or mediate this process, such as background variables (gender, parental environment), media use (TV and newspapers), and political self-ratings?

TESTING THE FARNEN/MELOEN THESIS

We will test our main thesis in a series of statistical analyses, using the LIS-REL ML-method, with liberal-progressive education (EDLIB5) and conservative-nationalist education (EDNAT4) as our basic indicators for one's teaching style and content preferences (see Chapters 2 and 10). We will show some results in diagrams, depicting only significant relationships (arrows) as well as their statistical model coefficients. We must caution that these LISREL analyses cannot prove theoretical relationships. Its use can only answer the question whether the statistics allow us to consider the worth, rationality, or reasonableness of certain proposed solutions or interrelationships.

Authoritarianism and Multiculturalism

First, we tested the basic relationship between liberal-progressive or conservative-nationalist educational attitudes and both authoritarianism (AUTH20) or multicultural democratic attitudes (MCDEMO13), the main survey factors (see Figure 11.1; see also Chapter 2). It appears that conservative-nationalistic attitudes about education are substantially related to general authoritarianism (.54), but not with multicultural democratic attitudes (-.09). It does not strongly undermine democratic attitudes directly, but it does indirectly, by strengthening authoritarian attitudes; in turn, these decrease the power of democratic attitudes (-.14). Liberal-progressive education preference is related only to multicultural democratic attitudes (.43) and seems to have no direct or indirect relationships to authoritarianism. This result supports our thesis and indicates that conservative-nationalistic teachings are more successful in strengthening authoritarian attitudes and weakening democratic multicultural ones than is the case for liberal-progressive education in increasing democratic attitudes. Liberal-progressive education also barely weakens authoritarian attitudes. Apparently, the legitimation of conservative-nationalistic education has much more powerful effects on students.

Educational Level of the Father

In our second analysis, we added as a separate influence the educational level of the respondent's father (see Figure 11.2). This was the only indicator of the educational level showing any statistical variation. Obviously, the students themselves did not show much variation in level of education since most of them were still in school. Their 'levels' may be considered relatively homogeneous as compared to the rest of the population that has not enjoyed college, tertiary, or university education.

Figure 11.1. Authoritarianism and education attitudes in all world regions
Notes: Chi-2 = 1.41; df = 1; p = 0.24; AGFI = 1.0; N = 7535

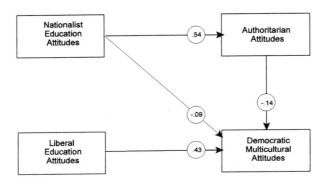

Figure 11.2. Authoritarianism and education attitudes in all world regions

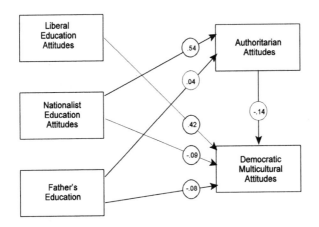

Notes: Chi-2 = 1.06; df = 1; p - 0.30; AGFI = 1.0; N = 7807

We assumed the level of parental (here, the father's) education would vary from primary and secondary schools up to college or university levels. This was the case, but there was a societally disproportionate number of students with parents who had received higher education (see Chapter 2). This is no surprise, but it severely limits variation in our indicator for level of education. Nevertheless, we wanted to find out whether this limited factor still showed some competing influence with respect to the other political attitudes used in our model. Therefore, we added this factor to our model (see Figure 11.2), but found no substantial changes. The relationships with father's education showed little effect. Level of education was not related to authoritarian attitudes or democratic multicultural ones. The main relationships between one's preference for liberal-progressive or conservative-nationalistic educational choices and authoritarian or democratic attitudes were unaltered.

This test of the level of education was the best possible from among the available indicators in our survey. For a true test of the two competing factors (level versus content of education), a random sample of various national populations would be needed. Since the recent random sample surveys that we analyzed (see Chapter 9) had no indicators for liberal or conservative types of educational preferences, using them here for this test was not possible.

Three Worlds of Development

There may be differences in results for more- and less-developed countries, but also for democratic and (former) communist ones. To test this, we reconfigured our model using data from the developed first world only (mainly the West, Japan, and Australia) in a first world model. We did the same for the second world and the remaining countries of the third world.

The first world model shows satisfactory and significant statistics (Chi-2 = 2.29; df = 1; p = 0.13; AGFI = 1.0; N = 3364). We find very few changes in the relationships depicted in our model. This model differs little from the basic one (including data from all the world regions). The second world model also shows significant relations as expected (Chi-2 = 0.50; df = 1; p = .048; AGFI = 1.0; N = 2719) as does the third world model (Chi-2 = 1.3; df = 1; p = 0.19; AGFI = 0.99; N = 1724). Again, both models are very similar to the total and first world ones. All causal relations are significant. The strongest is between liberal-progressive education and democratic multicultural attitudes on one hand and between nationalist education and authoritarian attitudes on the other. The main relationships are confirmed between support for liberal-progressive education and democratic multicultural attitudes (.38 to .42) and between conservative-nationalist education and authoritarian attitudes (.44 to .56).

The results indicate that our basic model is relevant for each of the three worlds of development. This also supports our general 'assumption' that relationships between our factors would be more or less the same in the main world regions and would not be too specific for only one region (the West).

Gender and Parental Environment

In the next analysis, gender and social background were added to examine competitive effects on authoritarian and democratic attitudes. Gender differences might explain some of the variation in effects on political attitudes. Among our respondents, the groups of male and female students were about equal in number. Therefore, this variable is adequately represented in our survey. An index of parental environment was constructed from the students' ratings of their father's education, parental social class, and size of the town in which they grew up. Unfortunately, the index showed hardly any relationship with democratic or authoritarian attitudes. Probably this index was too homogeneous since the students disproportionally came from the upper middle class, with college/university-educated fathers, and from (sub)urban areas. Once more, random national samples are needed to test these effects more definitely among the adult population. The test indicates that this model is supported (Chi-2 = 1.26; df = 1; p = 0.26; AGFI = 1.0; N = 7535), but that neither gender nor parental environment show any effect (-.04 and -.07). As a consequence, the main relationships seen in the basic model are unchanged.

The Media

In this analysis, more powerful (in theory, at least) variables were added. The media may exert quite an effect on attitudes and could change the relationships in our model. We included the questions on TV and newspapers as sources of political information. But including both variables did not change the model (Chi-2 = 1.08; df = 1; p = 0.30; AGFI = 1.0; N = 7535). TV appears to be positively related to both authoritarianism (.04) and democratic (.05) attitudes; newspapers are positively related to democratic attitudes (.03) and negatively to authoritarian ones (-.06). These relationships are significant, but too weak to be relevant. Therefore, we are unable to find a substantial or even a weak effect of the media on democratic and authoritarian attitudes. Our basic model hardly changed after we added these two factors.

Self-Ratings as Apolitical and Religious

Rating oneself as political or apolitical and as religious or not were also used to test our model. The self-rating as religious was included to indicate the strength of religious beliefs. Asking for religious denominations in an international survey may lead to a very long list of religions. Also, it is doubtful if one can compare religions very well between countries. Our indicator seemed to be quite adequate, with most respondents indicating 'religious' (49 per cent) and a minority 'not religious' (36 per cent; 15 per cent no opinion).

For the second self-rating, students were asked whether they viewed themselves as political or not political. Contrary to popular beliefs about the interests of students, 50 per cent viewed themselves as political, while 33 per cent rated themselves as 'not political' (17 per cent had no opinion).

We added both variables to our basic model and again found little change (Chi-2 = 0.36; df = 2; p = .84; AGFI = 1.0; N = 7535). Being political or not does not influence these two political attitudes. The religious self-rating shows a very weak relation with authoritarian attitudes (.13). Therefore, religion may exert a slight productive influence on authoritarianism.

Figure 11.3. Education attitudes and political leaders in all world regions

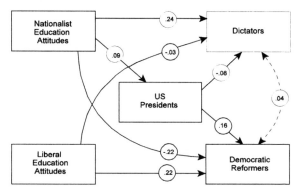

Notes: Chi-2 = 2.32; df = 1; p = 0.13; AGFI = 1.0; N = 7535

Dictators, Reformers, and US Presidents

Our analysis (see Chapter 2) included three types of leaders: dictators (Hitler, Stalin, Mao, Saddam Hussein), democratic reformers (King, Gandhi, Mandela, Gorbachev), and US presidents (Eisenhower, Kennedy, F. D. Roosevelt, Reagan). We tested the effects of education on the evaluation of these leaders (see Figure 11.3). We expected that conservative-nationalist education would lead to a more positive (or better stated, less negative) evaluation of dictators. This proposition was supported, but not very strongly (.24). Liberal-progressive education showed a positive effect on rating democratic reformers more positively (.22). However, nationalist education counterbalanced this effect by negatively influencing these reformer ratings to about the same extent (-.22); liberal-progressive education did not have a substantial effect on the ratings of dictators (-.03). Again, we find that effects of conservative-nationalist education tend to be stronger than those of liberal-progressive education.

This analysis of political leaders shows that different types of education have predictable effects on evaluations of democratic and dictatorial leaders. All our respondents were included and the results are not limited to views within US society or the West as a separate group. Apparently, similar views on some topics are shared among many young people across the globe.

Figure 11.4. Democratic system and education attitudes in all world regions

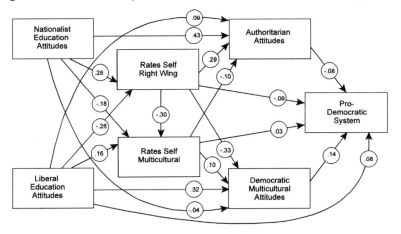

Notes: Chi-2 = 1.58; df = 2; p = 0.45; AGFI = 1.0; N = 7353

Political Self-Ratings and Pro-Democratic System Attitudes

Our final test is the most complex (see Figure 11.4). It includes the basic model with some extensions. The first assumption added is that self-definitions will mediate between the education received and attitudinal outcomes. Educational information is individually processed. The self-ratings represent self-definitions and are a psychologically active part of the individual, who otherwise would be a passive recipient of education. Conservatives and liberals will not passively accept everything taught, but will process this according to their political self-definitions as conservative or liberal. This assumes a stimulus (education) to spur individual processes (self-definition) to produce reactions (attitudes) and types of reasoning. Thus, coherent political attitudes are assumed to be the outcome of this process. We used the self-rating scales for viewing oneself as right-wing (SRIGHT5 as conservative, right-wing, authoritarian, militarist, and elitist), or multicultural (SMCULT3 as internationalist, cosmopolitan, and multicultural) (also see Chapter 2).

The second assumption is that one's evaluation of democracy as a political system can be externally influenced. These attitudes, the type of education preferred, and self-definitions play this role. The item 'considering the democratic system as the best for our country and people' was used as the final 'dependent variable' in this analysis. This was the only item in our survey about democracy as a political system. However, predicting the role single items will play is more difficult than with using attitudinal clusters or scale results.

We tested these assumptions in a rather complex model (see Figure 11.4). It appeared that self-definitions provided an additional path from education types to attitudes. Self-definitions can be considered as an intermediary. Nationalist education showed a significant path to the self-rating as right-wing (.28), followed by another significant path to authoritarian attitudes (.29). However, the direct influence of nationalist education on authoritarian attitudes remains substantial (.43). The same appeared to be true for liberal education, where the self-definition of multiculturalist adds to the explanation of democratic multicultural attitudes, with somewhat lower coefficients. The relationship between liberal education and multicultural democratic attitudes is still substantial (.32), but that between liberal education and self-rating as multicultural is much weaker (.16). This is also the case for the relationship between the self-rating as multicultural and democratic attitudes (.10).

The lesser influence of liberal education is partly explained by the overriding crossover influence of nationalist education and self-rating as right-wing. This self-definition shows considerable negative influence on the self-definition as multicultural (-.30), but also on democratic multicultural attitudes (-.33). Liberal education does have some crossover influence on self-ratings as right-wing (-.26) but, in general, liberal effects tend to be weaker. They lead to a positive influence on authoritarian attitudes (.09, very weak, but significant), the only anomaly in this model, and a result still hard to adequately explain. In all other instances, the relationships are in the predicted directions.

The attitude toward the democratic system variable can be predicted positively by democratic multicultural attitudes, the self-definition as multicultural, and the liberal education attitude. Negative influences are authoritarian attitudes and self-rating as right-wing. But all the influences appear to be very weak (-.09 to +.14), the democratic multicultural attitudes being the strongest force here. Our measures to assess support for the democratic system were somewhat limited in explanatory power (as mentioned in Chapter 2).

CONCLUSIONS

In this international survey, we investigated the relation between education and authoritarian or democratic attitudes. Previous research often showed a relation between one's higher level of general education and lower authoritarianism in the range of .30 to .40. An adequate explanation is still lacking, but several were suggested. One alternative explanation is that there is a substantial effect of preferences for certain educational content reflecting authoritarian or democratic attitudes, apart from the general effects of level of education achieved. This proposition was stated as the Farnen/Meloen thesis.

The results of our statistical analyses tend to support our thesis. Liberal and conservative-nationalist education can have effects on authoritarian and democratic multicultural attitudes. In general, one's content and style of educational choices are related to political relevant attitudes. The basic model (see Figure 11.1) remains valid, even though a series of competing explanations were presented in our analysis. This model applies not only to the West, but also to the former communist second world, and to the third world. Students also prefer democratic reformers or dictatorial leaders to the extent to which they accept or reject liberal-progressive or conservative-nationalist teaching tendencies. Political self-definitions mediated between education orientation types and political attitudes. Therefore, students are not passive recipients of education, but use personal self-definitions that, together with the effects of education, lead to the development or reinforcement of democratic or authoritarian attitudes.

12 Suggestions for Political Socialization Research and Political Education Reforms

INTRODUCTION

In this chapter, we discuss the consequences for political socialization research and educational reform of our findings about authority, international democratic and multiculturalist attitudes, regional results, and teaching-learning styles. We examine current educational trends and curriculum reform projects regarding the need to teach about democracy, authoritarianism, militarism, fascism, racism, tolerance, nationalism, and participatory politics.

OVERVIEW OF IMPORTANT FINDINGS

We found that democratic or authoritarian attitudes are diversely, not equally, distributed over different world regions. Therefore, areas of the world wanting to increase their democratic and decrease their authoritarian quotients can learn from others. Eastern Europe and CIS-Russia can learn something from developed first world countries, such as Western Europe, about building democratic attitudes and support for democracy through educational reforms. North Americans and others could learn something about reducing both types of authoritarianism from Western European and Australian educational practices. Australia, North America, and Western Europe could teach us how to reduce acceptance of political repression, reduce militarism, and increase tolerance and multiculturalism. CIS-Russia could learn about increasing multiculturalism from almost any other country or regional group. General and democratic multiculturalism models can be found in Western Europe, Africa, Asia, and Latin America so that North Americans and others could take a page from their political textbooks. Taken as a whole, the results show that Western Europe and Australia are the new repositories of considered anti-authoritarianism and strong democratic values and attitudes.

Also important are our findings about gender and media. Women around the world are less authoritarian and more democratic, lending credence to the long-term trend connecting increases in women's rights and gender equality as a critical supporting feature in increased democratization both in and out of school. The influence of using print as contrasted with electronic (TV) media is also significant for promoting democratic political education across the world regions. Increased newspaper use is a feature of democratic political education deserving more cross-national attention.

Our results also support the general proposition that increased educational achievement in itself is another way for reform-minded regions to increase the societal level of democratization and anti-authoritarianism. Mere educational reform (apart from offsetting effects of recent levels of authoritarianism and improving socioeconomic development) is not likely to affect such changes by itself. Yet, we maintain that students can unlearn or be re-socialized away from authoritarianism and encouraged to develop along democratic and participatory political modes of thinking, learning, and behaving.

Encouraging liberal educational attitudes through political education clearly helps promote multiculturalism among students across the world, both in terms of the subject as an attitudinal cluster and as a basis of one's self-identity. Political education also needs to counter nationalism and preference for nationalistic educational policy options to increase multicultural orientations to counter dangerous right-wing tendencies and authoritarianism. Since pro-democratic values are currently so strong worldwide, this aspect of the ideal political curriculum can easily be reinforced, but it still needs reform in the directions indicated earlier (toward strong, active, and participatory democracy).

Our other relevant findings (regarding the Farnen/Meloen thesis about educational policy preferences and authoritarianism/democracy) indicate a clear course for civic education and democratic development. Liberal-progressive and conservative/nationalistic teaching/learning/content preferences and styles are not polar opposites; so, it is not enough to just teach a pro-democracy curriculum. Instead, we must use critical educational methods to directly refute fascism and authoritarianism. Teachers, parents, peers, print media, religion, and other socialization agents can help youth build their self-image as democrats, internationalists, multiculturalists, progressive liberals, active participants, and anti-dictatorial, not excessively religious persons and pro-reformers.

SUGGESTIONS FOR CURRICULUM REFORM

Cross-national research on political socialization and education (mainly in the US and Europe) can be used to construct generalizations about youths' developmental patterns as well as important influences on the growth of their political knowledge, attitudes, and behaviors (Farnen, 1996, pp. 94-8).

Some political loyalties (patriotism, ethnicity, racism, religiosity, and trust) are formed in the primary school years. They may be modified, but many last a lifetime. By the upper elementary or middle school years, one's attitudes and knowledge become more differentiated, flexible, and factual, but not sophisticated. Thereafter, students adopt sociopolitical ideas, solidify their attitudes, are conceptually more consistent, and can differentiate between the real and ideal worlds. By the end of secondary school and the start of university, they accumulate political knowledge, recognize contradictions, develop political efficacy, or allow cynicism or alienation to interfere with developing a positive view of their governments. By early adulthood, political involvement or distancing can take hold and reasoned political attachments are formed. Thereafter, they move on to early middle age detachment, then more active involvement, followed by relative stability in politics and views. During the middle school years (ages 12-14), students are open to critical self-examination of their commitments to democracy, free speech, or authority (Jenness, 1990, pp. 192-5).

Politics Courses

Teachers can help students increase their democratic attitudes. In classroom and school discussions, they may explore decision making and problem solving experiences, group activities, and the whys and wherefors of political participation along with the role of the hidden curriculum. This is an alternative to rote, read and recite, and disciplinary restrictions.

Politics courses (especially current events' discussions) may result in more positive evaluations of one's government. Subjects must be current, varied, and reinforced. Experimental curricula can include concepts such as democracy versus authoritarianism, critical inquiry, conflict resolution, decision making, problem solving, and public policy analysis. Some student groups (vocational, college-bound, minority, coeducational) score better on parts of exams not solely because of their gender, race, or ethnicity, but based on their personal interests and experiences in and out of school. They can study civil rights and liberties as current events to encourage educational prowess. Proficiency in the language of instruction and belonging to an education-oriented family can be important for public policy formulation and skills. Minority youth can be encouraged to read more (especially current events), take more civics courses, view less violent/entertainment TV, and participate in school governance.

Such revised civics curricula must address basic political questions such as: How do we develop and improve our political cognitions and solve political problems? How is public policy made in authoritarian and democratic political systems? If authoritarianism is a root cause of undemocratic personalities and behaviors, how can it be offset? How do people effectively participate in democratic group settings to resolve inevitable public and private conflicts?

Improving Democracies

Barber (1995, pp. 411-8) discusses how to create and improve democracies. His suggestions list basic concepts for civic educational reform and a core curriculum in democratic education. Students need to learn fundamental policy alternatives which can make democracy happen worldwide:

- Agree on essentials: control violence, promote liberty and equality, respect the rule of law and the rule of reason, and practice free elections.
- Establish national and international assemblies to strategize and organize for the advance of democracy, focus on common essential issues, and develop newfound strength in such associations.
- Curtail national/international trade with nondemocracies (Russia and PRC) until they reform and can receive aid from and join the free trade (WTO) democratic partnership.
- Wage war rarely and only based on elected representatives' decisions. Nondemocracies should not engage in arms trade with democracies. The democracies should have a united front if one is attacked. If war breaks out in a nondemocracy, democracies should unite to end or contain it (Bosnia and Kosovo).
- Disallow immigration from nondemocracies (except for short-term political asylum) until their leaders or people convert to democratic government.
- Communicate truthfully and interactively among democracies themselves and with the people of nondemocracies. Include good news and bad so that the advantages of a democratic government become clear.

Federal democracy should be tried as an alternative to bring together parts of a nation (such as the Russian federation) or to join with different nations (such as the CIS) to produce a federal democratic system which can control interethnic violence. There are also four 'speculative' ideas about improving democracy which need to be tested, including:

- Rule by open voting and elections; reasonable political information, communication, and journalism; and free public education to produce a democratic citizenry.
- Rule of constitutional law, equality before the law, and clearly written and publicized laws.
- Limit government to promote liberty, equality, and a competitive capitalist economy, with the government as a referee to ensure fair play.
- Control violence, deromanticize war and crime, and found an international military union of democracies to spread and protect democracy worldwide. These controversial propositions need to be 'researched, assessed, and debated' in civics classrooms throughout the world, according to Barber.

Reforming Civic Education

Barber maintains (Monroe et al., 1990, pp. 34, 37-40) that 'scientism is dead in social science'. The new concern of political science, its basic unifying idea, is 'politics', itself. This new political science focuses on 'inequalities and disparities'; questions of race, gender, and class; and the politics of everyday life in 'a liberating conversation of everyone in society about the nature of that society'. Farnen (1990, pp. 287-93) offered a policy process, systems analysis, and problem-solving model to reconstruct civic education. It incorporates teaching and learning (texts, teachers, school organizations), individual orientations (values, skills, knowledge) across different levels of analysis (from group to global) with respect to different political environments, systems, and problems (public policy, decision making). It includes discussions at the university or highest secondary school level about underlying conflicts and tensions between individual conscience, higher-law principles, civil disobedience, passive resistance, minority rights, concurrent majorities, veto groups and consociationalism, and the social compact, itself.

If applied to the question of national identity/minorities, using this model would raise many basic questions. These would relate to nationalism, racism, human rights, majority rule, pluralism, immigration, and 'problem' areas across the standard school curricula in any country. They are essential parts of the political culture/environment, decision-making process, and policy analysis which is the heart of the participatory democratic system.

Another basic question is: What has the student been taught or know about national identity and its influence on one's positive self-image (concept of self and one's citizenship) at the individual or everyday level? This opens the door to multiple levels of analysis across age groups and types of students in different classroom settings. Students and teachers can learn about sources of knowledge (flags, songs, symbols); the extent to which they share these myths; the obvious differences and similarities that occur across societies (ceremonies, holidays, movements, heroes, traitors); and the close connections between one's self-ascriptions ('who am I'?) and societal definitions of ideal citizens, patriots, minorities, majorities, races, national 'enemies', and 'others'. Such a procedure would replace the stock answers and conventional wisdom which the teacher and commercial texts are expected to supply while fulfilling their major role of system preservation and legitimization. However, if answers to fundamental questions are handled in an orderly and increasingly sophisticated (cognitively complex and abstract reasoning) manner across age groups or ability levels, the result might begin with self-doubt and criticism and would surely end with strengthened personal patriotism, loyalty, and a sense of security.

This approach focuses on underlying principles. For example, civil disobedience is often seen as a 'problem' area, 'failure', or source of democratic 'weakness'. However, a more detailed consideration will reveal that such actions are legitimate parts of the democratic policymaking process in a pluralistic democratic society. The goals of tolerance, compromise, respect, appreciation, empathy, enlightenment, and liberation are often forgotten when civic disobedience and demonstrations occur. These are sources of strength in a democratic polity and civil society. They provide realistic examples of citizen involvement, participation, petition, assembly, freedom, and rights. It is the job of the police not to stop the demonstrators, but rather to protect them from those who would restrict their free exercise of these basic rights. The law and order seen as so typical of many authoritarian Asian societies with their so-called 'guided democracies' is not the model democrats seek to emulate. Instead, conflict is normal and its resolution temporary; discussion reveals means for its amelioration, not its extinction (Farnen, 1996, pp. 98-100).

A more basic question for examining the civic domain is: What is the nature and purpose of humans, societies, states, politics, and governments? This is often raised in critical theory literature, but is seldom asked in schools. How does civil authority relate to questions of power, legitimacy, justice, freedom, and equity? This question guides civic education reform along a new (but actually, very ancient) course. Students may see some correspondence between the form of government, the state, and the economy (market capitalism and democracy). Often not asked is: Why would not a prominent instrument of the state (like the military, the church, or the schools) reflect this same nexus? None of the undergirding institutions (state, economy, schools) is politically neutral. Thus, schools are contested grounds, just as are the state, family, mass media, churches, and society itself. Now that communism is deeply buried, it is safe for us to put politics back into education. Poor working conditions make poor citizens and even poorer democrats when hegemonic co-optation occurs in the workplace (Peterson, 1990, pp. 44-8).

Both politics and education and the politics of education are legitimate areas for reform. The politically liberating, emancipatory, and transformational role of schooling is the way in which democracy is linked to education. Politics *and* education is external to the schools and deals with state financing, standards, testing, referenda, planning, certification, research and development grants, and financial aid. It is a big business in most countries. Politics *of* education is internal to the schools and deals with the hidden curriculum, civic education, political socialization, organizational hierarchies and power relationships, teachers' unions, textbook selection (state and local), parent/teacher organizations, and similar topics. When schools fail to teach democracy, this is an educational and political failure and a challenge to democratic political theory (Merelman, 1980, pp. 319-20).

Class, gender, and minority status in schools and society is another theme for an educational reform agenda to address male/female political differences and similarities, whether class has political implications, and how minority status impacts on citizens' views of multiculturalism, militarism, or nationalism. The critique of patriarchy, racial and ethnic discrimination, and aggressive behavior toward the powerless are valid parts of a curriculum reform which would enlighten the classroom and allow all students to participate equally.

Schooling's social dimension (group, team, and cooperative work) has already been mastered in some third world countries, but is still seriously neglected in first world schooling with its individualized approaches. Teaching, cooperation, teamwork, and group creativity are important features of this aspect of democratic education. 'Team' control of the work plan, standards, problem solving, decision making, self-evaluation, and other tasks is important for both postindustrial and developing countries. As first world economies move from the Ford/Taylor models of efficiency to new ones of productivity (such as quality circles), school graduates lacking experience in group activities will be disadvantaged.

Ethnographic studies provide descriptive analyses of lived lives in school cultures. The school can be a political laboratory to study the hierarchy, cultural dominance, and class hegemony operating in schools nationally and worldwide. Parallel to these trends are the economic correspondence and reproduction of workers' principles functioning in schools which are partially offset by students' resistance to domination. This demonstrates the transformative possibilities of democratic schooling. If we deal with matters of education and class, race, gender, ethnicity, urbanism, and everyday life, we need researchers, teachers, and students trained in the use of ethnographic methods (videotapes, interviews, observations, survey research, and focus groups).

Needed Research

Anyon (1981) and Willis et al. (1988) conducted national and cross-national political socialization and educational policy research. Anyon studied the curriculum of two working class, one middle class, and two elite schools and found evidence of the hidden curriculum. Worker schools were dull, routine, offered no choices, encouraged student conflict and resistance; middle class schools were more open to choices, bureaucratic, service-oriented; elite schools taught leadership, power, and ownership, imparting 'symbolic capital'. Such schools reproduce social inequality. Not limited to North America or West Europe, this is also characteristic of schooling in Eastern Europe

(Poland, Hungary), Latin America, Africa, and Asia, except for students who study in other nation's elite schools. Willis et al. (1988) studied Wolverhampton's isolated, rootless youth who lack self-identity. Specific policy proposals coming from this project included coordinating local youth policy, combating victimization, structuring unemployment, self-defining problems, empowering students, and risk taking.

Political socialization research also has to become more qualitative and in-depth or we shall miss the nuances and reasons behind responses such as why minority students score lower in the US on national assessment tests. We should not just test them, consign them to the bottom of the pile, and start preparing the next test. Videotaping classroom instruction with a professional panel observing and interpreting the results (as is frequently done in the FRG) would also be a good place to start this new analytical procedure.

It may be time to revive the 1980s debates which explored the 'hidden', 'dual', and explicit curricula in schooling in the US political science literature without the benefit of a genuine radical critique or participation of critical theorists in this debate. There is still an information gap between research on nationalism, national identity, national minorities, and ethnic and racial groups on the one hand and the appropriate civic, tolerance, multicultural, or interracial education needed to fulfill the democratic goals of equality, justice, equity, and human rights on the other. Farnen (1994a, pp. 63-86 and 443-62) concluded:

- The nature of the minority, nationality, ethnic group, and multicultural public policy question varies so much from country to country that there are no universals in policy applications or models of civics or political education which will work across all borders.
- New components of civic education should include foundation topics such as race, color, caste, religion, nationality, citizenship, language, visa status, national ideology, and political culture.
- Published research (such as cultural/media or linguistic/discourse studies) for understanding anti-racist models which work cross-nationally is limited and lacks a common or consistent philosophical or theoretical approach.
- We lack sufficient international information on multicultural, bicultural, or tricultural (multiple), ethnocentered, and bilingual education and cultural incorporation to develop knowledge of internationalism, nationalism, appropriate teaching styles, and minority incorporation.
- The political socialization literature published to date is of limited utility because less research on topics such as patriotic symbols is needed and more on how hegemony, rules, power, color, race, gender, diversity, and language relate to one another in different political systems/cultures.
- While there are some useful models for bilingual and multicultural education in English, Dutch, Swedish, and OECD literature, their successful

application in other settings and countries remains in doubt because of key differences in political culture which require international working groups to resolve.

- Guidelines are lacking for teaching 'reasoned patriotism' and civil courage rather than 'pseudo-patriotism'. Such teaching should be balanced, rational, transformative, enlightened, critical, and democratic. Yet, we still lack the proper goals, processes, objectives, and materials which focus on democracy, multiculturalism, internationalism, and anti-authoritarianism.

The Multiculturalism Debate

A 1994 Roper national poll of adults found that teaching multiculturalism in US schools was 'acceptable for anyone' (77.5 per cent), indicating a near universal approval of the topic with a clear mandate for educators to focus on unity and diversity. The National Council for the Social Studies (NCSS, 1992) produced curriculum guidelines for multicultural education in the US (including topics such as diversity, positive cultural interactions and understandings, social conflict resolution, pluralism, decision making, participation, and political efficacy, and appropriate assessment procedures). Reactions to these standards engendered political criticism with charges of cultural relativism and an 'anti-Western' bias, while disputing the value of diversity (Fauts, 1993). One critic claimed the guidelines were too nationalistic and contributed to confusion between multicultural and international education. Goals were also seen as not intellectual enough (Rényi and Lubeck, 1994). Radical left Afrocentrists claimed these guidelines did not go far enough to attack white racism, power inequality, and abject poverty among US minorities; conservative forces rejected them as challenging US unity (Kaltsounis, 1997).

In our view, these NCSS multicultural guidelines provide a useful direction for civics curriculum reform. But we find problematic the idea that there exists a special ethnic thinking or common learning style (which has not been proven to exist, apart from those identified in the famous Meyer-Briggs inventory) and the fact that the US curriculum has already been revised to focus on history and geography, not on political education or critical thinking. To us, these guidelines should adopt the information processing and problem solving/decision making styles of learning for all students which Voss et al. (1991), Corretero and Voss (1994), and Farnen (1994d) described for history, geography, the social sciences, and political education, including group activities and processes. Although critical educators such as Giroux (1993) were charged with having their own agenda in the multicultural debate along with a rabid passion for Afrocentrism, we found little evidence for this false allegation.

International Differences

International comparisons among educational systems (Alexander, 1992) show how different countries' particular cultural imperatives affect their human rights education programs (Ray et al., 1994). School systems are decentralized (US, Canada, Australia, FRG) or centralized (Japan, the Netherlands, Sweden, France) in terms of their governance. In centralized systems, it is much easier to control curriculum standards, teacher qualifications, examinations requirements, textbooks used, inspectorates, and funding for public and private schools. Most developed countries have no more than 10 per cent of students in private schools. In some (the Netherlands, 67 per cent; Belgium, 56 per cent), the proportion of state-funded religious schools is higher. Some school systems in developed countries serve a single ethnic and linguistic group (over 90 per cent in France, Hungary, and Japan), whereas others are much more diverse (in the US, Canada, Australia, and Spain).

While the US does not split secondary schooling into strict academic (university) and vocational/technical (terminal) programs, many others (Austria, Germany, Japan) do. Days spent in school vary from the fewest (Ireland, US) to the most (Taiwan, Japan), ranging from 173 to 222 days. Homework varies from the lowest (US) to the most (France, Italy, Spain, Russia) as does educational expenditures from the highest (US, Switzerland) to the lowest (New Zealand, Ireland) or a per pupil variance from \$4315 to \$1365 (1987-88). Most countries have national or state examinations (for entrance or graduation), requiring mastery of subject matter; the US has only minimum competency tests in some states and a state-level national assessment program. Most countries have essay, oral, or practical exams; the US has standardized, commercially produced tests. Employment is closely related to education in some countries (Japan, FRG). Such differences in school systems also lead to different outcomes. Secondary school completion rates are highest in Ireland, FRG, and Denmark; once the highest, the US has dropped to the mean (74 per cent). Post-secondary education enrollment is highest in the US, with most countries at half the US rate.

School Reform and Minorities

Some countries have school systems which are caught up in long-term civil strife (in Columbia, rural areas even obtain school funds from the drug trade). In CIS-Russia, schools promoted minority toleration to prevent hostilities and violence. Russia is involved not only in increased democratization, but also with efforts to protect resident minorities. Democratic civic education reforms , replaced Marxism/Leninism in secondary schools. Germany must constructively deal with large minority populations (Sinti-Roma, guest workers and their families, asylum seekers, an immigrants from other EU and eastern countries, folk German returnees, and eastern Germany) who seek jobs and demand public services such as education. German civic education teaches responsibilities to others as well as human rights. In China, there is a movement toward a new rights and obligations curriculum and pedagogy as part of the modernization process.   ·

India suffers most from sexism, the caste system, militarism, ethnic clashes, and rural/urban disparities. Education addressed these problems through school financial aid, an equality curriculum, and teacher training and examination reforms. Indian equality goals are for access, treatment, and results by reducing discrimination. Canada institutionalized its legal protections for minority rights in 1971 and 1982. Then, multiculturalism became state policy and the Charter of Rights and Freedom prohibited discrimination and protected cultural rights. Schools there guard against racism and intolerance in textbooks, pay attention to human rights in teacher and in-service education, and revised or modified educational objectives (such as a new school prayer convention).

With UNESCO help, Colombia consistently addressed its problems with discrimination. Chief among the agencies providing for job opportunities through improved education are the schools, rural and urban alike. Cultural differences are recognized and fully accepted in Colombia as is also the case in China, India, Russia, Germany, Norway, and Canada, where disunity in the society is severe enough to require mediation of such differences.

The Czech Republic engaged in a new educational reform which allows choices for students, teachers, and society to use creativity to realize one's full human potential. Russia is involved in some of these same reforms to free the 'human imagination and spirit' using multidisciplinary formats. Germany and Canada are perhaps the best models for what can be achieved when equal opportunity and education are combined to release one's human potential. Education is abundant, poverty is offset by social security, learning is unconstrained, and personal fulfillment is possible.

In sum, some educational systems represent civilizations which emerged recently (China, Czech Republic) or some time ago (Columbia, Canada, India) from colonialism, had recent wars (Russia, Serbia, Argentina), are very poor (Kenya) or very rich (US, FRG), or have distinct cultural divisions (Russia, FRG, Canada, and India). Others value aboriginal status (Columbia, Russia, Canada, Australia, New Zealand), have significant rural/urban divisions (Columbia, India, China, Russia), or place severe ideological constraints on educational options (China, Slovak Republic, Russia, Serbia, Cuba) (Ray et al., 1994, pp. 1-15). These demographic, political, cultural, or background variables significantly affect the extent, quality, or reform potential for civic educational change.

Directions for Civic Education

Among the world's constitutional democracies, several trends are influencing the direction of civic education. According to Patrick (1997), these include:

- Conceptualizing civic education in terms of knowledge of democracy in a comparative perspective, cognitive learning and participation skills, and character traits regarding respect for others, civility, honesty, self-control, tolerance, empathy, and reasoned patriotism.
- Focusing on core concepts such as the rule of law, participatory democracy, and civil rights and liberties.
- Studying cases of political behavior and legal disputes.
- Developing problem solving, information processing, and decision making skills.
- Using comparative and international perspectives on government and citizenship to reduce ethnocentrism.
- Developing participatory skill through cooperative learning in groups to enhance civic 'virtue' and citizen competencies such as leadership, resolution of conflict, compromise, negotiation, and informed criticism.
- Using literature to illustrate democratic personality and character traits such as social justice, reasoned patriotism, and problem solving skills.
- Connecting processes of cognitive learning to a body of civic knowledge levels linking content to process in a dynamic way.

McGinn (1996) said the US recently spent more on improving voter education in South Africa than increasing voter knowledge and participation at home. The US is adept at exporting civic education, with democracy and capitalism as its two principal components. However, this product is increasingly being met with suspicion and mistrust. Not only is it too perfectly prepackaged, but the US is one of the poorest examples of democracy in action since so many of its people hate their governments and their elected representatives and do not even vote. It is hard for fledgling democracies to learn from a poor role model that democracy is a political process requiring active participation (as individuals and in groups), political equality, tolerance, and civic engagement to resolve public issues.

Regardless of its causes, there is less public participation in all democracies (not just in the US) and education has not prevented it. With educational emphasis shifting from students 'doing' democracy to learning about it to pass exams, they are not learning how to challenge authority claims, assumptions, and practices. Since other institutions (such as federal and state legislatures) now preach an anti-democratic message along with the national corporations, TV, and the multinationals, schools may not be solely at fault. Apologists advocating 'let's develop economic and social security, then we will try out democracy' base their contentions on erroneous information; the only likely result of this policy is postponing democracy without any guarantee of continuing economic security. Furthermore, using the national unit of analysis in comparative education promotes competition and ill will while hindering other worthwhile causes such as worldwide democratization. (Essential similarities in international educational content and temporal allocations may actually be greater than cross-national dissimilarities.) This effort also promotes more diversity and integration as well as increasing politicization of citizens in real political activity which is 'the best school for democracy'.

In Latvia, there are serious ethnic, educational, and citizenship conflicts between the Latvian majority and Russian minority. Current problems merely continue the administrative/teacher authority and student passivity common in the USSR days. Old civics textbooks were revised simply by replacing the old constitution, symbols, and laws with new ones. Other aspects of the school system are being democratized: more teachers and students now share in decision making, student participation is encouraged, teachers are trained to interact with students, and the educational process has opened up.

The former communist GDR now comprises five new *Bundesländer* in the FRG. Since reunification, Sander (1994) examined political education curriculum trends implemented in eastern Germany using Western models. Since the former civic education teachers are considered 'ideologically handicapped', new ones had to be trained by western German experts. Results were disappointing. For example, in the entire FRG, civics courses are only taken seriously in Hessen, North-Rhine Westphalia, and Brandenburg (perhaps because of its proximity to Berlin). In the new *Länder*, civics courses focus mainly on institutions, civil rights, and duties; they neglect the GDR past, social conflict, critical analysis, political problem solving, and distinguishing theory from practice. The result is an 'unpolitical' political education. Only Brandenburg emphasizes developing political awareness, self-determination, political cooperation, and problem solving. 'Political education can and should construct democracy', but none of the new state guidelines provide for this. Civic education is undertaught, subject matter specialists are not hired, and it is of 'peripheral importance' in all parts of the country.

Current Models

Several current models, definitions of, and perspectives on civic education stem from US, Western, and Eastern European conferences and documents.

Merelman (1996) identifies four models of civics in political education: hegemonic (keeps political power where it is), critical (exerts public control over the powerful), transformative (blends the first two), and symbolic (reassures powerful people that all is right with the youth). New US civics standards stress shared values, not participation; oversimplify how American political values are interrelated; want shared values to reduce diversity and increase social unity/cohesion; and use elites to express these values. Criticism or participation are not encouraged, so wealthy power holders benefit most. Even these values are idealized, exclusive, authoritative, and inconsistent in fact, if not in theory. These standards offer no place for strikes and protests, just for civic, labor, religious, and other 'legitimate' groups. While political conflict is the rule in real-life politics, it is not so in these standards. Perhaps it was the culture wars on race and recent diversity claims which produced such hegemonic standards. In sum, new US national standards represent shared values (unity), merit, constraint, expertise versus diversity, equality, freedom, and democracy, respectively.

Four US political science professors have examined the voluntary *National Standards for Civics and Government* (1994). The first faulted the standards for scholarly sloppiness and errors; Merelman (1996, p. 56) called it 'a symbolic ritual masked as an educational policy for reinforcing cultural hegemony'; and the last pair found that increased educational attainment levels resulted in more political knowledge, interest and involvement in politics, and support for constitutional law, but not for the worth of political debate or compromise (which US civics texts do not teach). The latter group also wanted US secondary school government courses (now taught only in 21 states) to include information on divided public opinions which produce policy conflicts and interest group representations. Other recommended topics are debate and compromise, the lengthy public decision-making process, and that 'conflict will always be a part of democratic reality' (Hibbing and Theiss-Morse, 1996).

The Civitas Project (*National Standards for Civics and Government*, 1994) suggests that US secondary schools teach about government and its tasks, the political system and its foundation, democracy and the Constitution, US politics and world affairs, and citizen roles. It stresses the rule of law, limited government, constitutions, comparative political systems, political culture, democratic values, individualism, humanism, and participation.

The 1992 and 1994 Council of Europe reports (Farnen, 1996, pp. 66-9) mention our major themes of democracy, authoritarianism, and multiculturalism (1992) and civic education topics (1994) such as concern for identity, linguistic power, minority education, loyalty, racism, ethnic groups, nondiscrimination, prejudice, bilingualism, Sinti/Roma youth, civic education as a forum for discussions, and the democratic teacher's role. A UNESCO (1995) report emphasized the importance of civic education in Central and Eastern Europe as a 'key to the democratization process in general, and to education reform in particular'. Schools should teach and practice democracy in the classroom. The region has no common definition of civic education, but has a 'minimum political consensus' on concepts to be included such as 'human rights, liberty, tolerance, democracy, participation, decision making, the rule or law, media education, international interdependence, and global responsibility'.

This UNESCO (1995) report stressed some dangers confronting civic education such as historical chauvinism and indoctrination. There should be a special subject and trained teachers for civics. Building respect for minority rights and transforming authoritarian schools into democratic institutions are two other goals for civic education in the area. Support for teachers, texts, resources, and an 'open' teaching style were necessary to ensure success. National governments should encourage growth of national associations, legally establish civics in the curriculum, set up examinations systems, encourage curriculum development in a democratic fashion, provide supplementary teaching material (not just textbooks), establish university chairs, initiate incentives for good teaching, and involve media experts and other subject areas in the field. A plan for UNESCO involvement was proposed.

A final consideration of the implications of our study for political education and socialization research returns us to Altemeyer's (1996) RWA work. He experimented with high-RWA University of Manitoba students to try to reduce their level of prejudice. He used Rokeach's value confrontation procedure (based on providing feedback to students about their own and group mean scores and the selfishness demonstrated in their choices) which resulted in long-lasting attitudinal changes. Altemeyer used these same freedom and equality rankings regarding aboriginal/natives in Manitoba. Apparently, it is possible to effect value change since Altemeyer's most recent follow-up study showed RWA support for an aboriginal scholarship and higher than expected support for aboriginal demands. In another such experiment, nonpersonal value confrontation methodology did not accomplish these same purposes/results.

CONCLUSIONS

Among the principal matches and comparisons between our research and recent political socialization/education findings are the following:
1. We advocated studying politics, society, and educational policy or the politics of/and education to show that schools should not be depoliticized with respect to democracy and multiculturalism. This is especially true since the cold war's end. Politics is essential in a democracy and permeates

every part of our social fiber. There is a worldwide pattern of expanding democratization, democratic education, its content, theoretical structures, emphases, and impacts. However, if everyone is becoming a democrat in theory (if not in practice), then many people are capable of being authoritarians in practice (if not in theory). We found evidence that authoritarianism can be unlearned or modified. This includes direct confrontation with RWAs, their values, and perhaps their religious fundamentalism. Therefore, teachers must combine forces to teach the advantages of democracy and multiculturalism, together with the disadvantages of fascism/authoritarianism, militarism, nationalism, and dogmatism. Most important is to do this using a democratic/progressive teaching/learning style.

2. An international conference should be called to critique important findings, coordinate research and publications, and establish a common agenda. Conference reports and publications show that many organizations working abroad make an impact on educational challenges and problems. Regularly, new information becomes available from UNESCO, the Center for Civic Education, and the National Issues Forum at the Kettering Foundation. Groups such as the Research Committee on Political Socialization and Education (RC21) of the International Political Science Association should cooperate with national groups such as APSA and NCSS to encourage national and international networking in these areas of common significance to political scientists and civic educators.

3. More national and international research should be conducted on important questions: What political views may be modified in school? When are they most malleable? Are the middle school years critical? How can students be helped to accept democracy and anti-authoritarianism for themselves rather than through indoctrination? How can we encourage ethnic and racial minorities to improve their political education and participant orientations through schooling? What about Barber's (1995) and McGinn's (1996) suggesting that democracy and comparative education are worthy of critical study and implementation globally? Which local, cultural, and national factors (such as finances, patriarchy, religion, gender, race, ethnicity, teacher training, textbooks, resources, or infrastructure) are crucial to an educational reform agenda? Without such an analysis, any educational reform efforts will likely fail. Some school systems face survival issues (Serbia, Kosovo, Bosnia, Uganda, Rwanda, Ethiopia, Columbia, Burma), others discrimination, and still others matters of conscience as their biggest problems. Now, the fundamentalists, state-guided 'democrats', authoritarians, and right-wing conservatives are much better organized than the advocates of progressive democratic liberalism. This situation sorely needs correction.

4. Useful models of analysis (Farnen, 1990) can inform us of systematic components to examine in such reform efforts. For example, there are US, Swedish, Dutch, German, and other civic education models which provide a basis for further reconceptualizing political education and politics. Model building would allow us to critique so-called guided democracies in Asia, Latin America, and Africa systematically, thereby exposing their deficiencies, inadequacies, and dangers. Countries such as India may be on the course to democracy, yet hardly deserve to brandish this label.

5. We also suggested expanding group work, using ethnographic studies, changing the political socialization research agenda, reconsidering critical studies and reconceptualizing critiques of the schools, and developing new civics materials on militarism, nationalism, internationalism, authority, and democracy to enhance civic participation, strong democracy, and civic competence. The hidden class-based curriculum still exists and needs to be exposed for what it is. Suggestions for particular content elements for political education have also been made regarding patriotism and pseudo-patriotism as topics for study along with diversity/multiculturalism/hegemony/symbolism (as Merelman, 1996, amply demonstrates).

13 Conclusions: Democracy, Authoritarianism, and Education Worldwide

INTRODUCTION

This chapter summarizes major findings from our research efforts. We restate our conclusions and suggest some ideas for future research.

RESEARCH QUESTIONS AND BASIC CONCEPTS

The Main Issues

Our primary aim was to investigate the relation between educational processes and acquiring certain political attitudes. We related authority/democracy/multiculturalism issues to political concepts such as militarism, nationalism, liberalism, and conservatism. Besides the concept of political culture, we discussed the role of political socialization and democratic civic education in this process. We maintained that a democratic political culture gone bad produces a rightist ideology (psychological and political authoritarianism). A cognitive map we presented showed the interrelationships among key concepts such as socialization agents, social context, cognitive learning processes, authoritarianism, political cultures, and research approaches. This conceptualization guided our overall research effort.

International Survey

To answer our research questions, we collected (between 1991 and 1997) data from 44 countries (nearly 10 000 student respondents) about democratic attitudes, authoritarianism, multiculturalism, liberal and nationalist tendencies in education, support ratings for well-known dictators and reformers, political self-ratings, and social background questions (see Appendix for survey). The aim of this extensive pilot study was to evaluate student attitudes in light of a widespread impetus toward international democratization during the 1990s. Statistical analysis supported the worldwide existence of the main concepts and attitudes toward democracy, authoritarianism, and multiculturalism. General and psychological authoritarianism, dictator and reformer ratings, and both multicultural attitudes and the composite self-rating of multiculturalism appeared as strong variables. Moderately performing were the concepts of democratic attitudes, general multiculturalism, and political repression. Attitudes about the democratic system, militarism, the composite self-rating as right-wing, and questions on liberal and nationalist education could be improved in a more definitive project testing these concepts internationally in future on random national samples of the adult population. But such an enterprise would require major financial support. A test showed that the translations were well understood. Our survey instrument proved adequate and performed well for our purposes.

NEW RESEARCH AND ANALYSES

Political Systems Worldwide

Comparing the political and educational systems of the 44 countries in our survey, we saw that those countries (especially in Africa) beset by economic underdevelopment and poverty (lacking a democratic political culture, tradition, educational system, or socialization process) had (and will likely continue to have) a strong tendency toward personal and systemic authoritarianism. The same is true of Eastern European countries (especially CIS-Russia) where prospects for authoritarian rule far outweigh any chances for democracy, freedom, educational and economic reforms, and growth of a democratic civil society and political culture. Two prime examples of this democracy deficit are Serbia and Croatia, with all the authoritarian hallmarks including contempt for liberal democracy. One characteristic of undemocratic and authoritarian countries is the high level of violence, conflict, and bellicosity associated with their civilian- and military-linked regimes. These states fight with neighbors over borders or ethnic nationality issues and must repeatedly quell riots and rebellions at home (China, India, Serbia, Croatia, Kenya, Uganda, Nigeria). The political systems of these states produce authoritarian-type educational systems maintaining ideological conventionalism, submission to the state, and appropriate state-sanctioned aggression when the regime in power gives the order.

Our comparisons of government, education, and defense expenditures reveal that countries which spend much on defense (Kenya, Uganda, Taiwan, India, Nigeria, Serbia) are not democratized and usually spend relatively little on education (partly because their economies cannot support both guns and butter). Countries with high per capita expenditures on education are usually democracies (Sweden, the Netherlands, Canada, the US, Germany, Belgium) and usually have a strong system of democratic civic education (particularly true in Sweden, the Netherlands, and Germany).

Many examples of transitional democracies and full-fledged authoritarian regimes can be found in Africa, Asia, and Latin America; however, most of the nearly 190 political systems in the world remain mixtures of both democratic and authoritarian elements. They move toward one extreme or the other as rulers, elites, the military, the bureaucracy, or other groups alter the political system to suit their interests with or without popular consent.

Types of Democracy

We discussed theories about 'strong' versus 'weak', liberal, social democratic, guided, economic, and consociational forms of democracy. Some of these theories were tried and rejected, others are unlikely to produce democracy, some are impractical, and others are practical strategies to make multiethnic democracies work. We also observed that about half the world's population live in democracies (an encouraging statistic), but this is as much an indication of democracy's frailty and no proof of the inevitable 'end of history'. Indeed, not every person who lives in a democracy is a democrat since sizable parts of the population support authoritarianism in almost every country.

Authoritarianism: Cross-National Perspectives

We reviewed the work of Altemeyer, Lederer, McFarland, and others on authoritarianism in North America, Western and Eastern Europe, and Russia. We looked at longitudinal and cross-generational trends of authoritarianism and found that the US and Canada once had low levels which are now rising, while German and Dutch levels are decreasing. Portents of authoritarianism can be seen in the growth of militaristic fundamentalism and militia groups preaching white supremacy, racism, and anti-Semitism. The mass media provide us with a living textbook to study authoritarianism in all its dimensions.

We examined the political receptivity and perceived economic threat arguments for increased societal authoritarianism and found both applicable to the US and the FRG, respectively; that is, fascism's appeal may have one primary basis in one country and quite another in a separate country. Religion, ethnicity, nationalism, and war are other rationales used to promote an 'authoritarian cycle' of events, reinforce undemocratic social learning trends, or bolster long-term lineage relationships based on authoritarian models.

The changing nature of socialization and resocialization over a lifetime makes it unlikely that individual authoritarianism is entirely permanent, unchanging, or completely parentally determined. Perhaps times favorable to authoritarianism allow its more frequent public expression and appearance. Yet, we need not assume that these attitudinal or psychological structures are immune from learning, change, or modification, just as political cultures and environments are evolving along new-age, global, postindustrial, and post-modern lines. Therefore, as we maintain, education can be an offsetting factor in terms of further exposure to it, a special civic education curriculum, or direct cooperation with authoritarians interested in personal self-reconstruction.

Socialization and Educational Practices

Our summary of socialization practices (mainly in the Western world) indicated that political learning takes place throughout the life cycle, but that the middle school years are key for developing political attitudes toward race, authority, and democracy. Here, civic educational reform should be targeted, combined with renewed cooperative regional research projects assessing the worth of such curriculum reforms and charting the course of political learning/socialization efforts predominant at the moment. What is needed is a combination of democratic educational goals and objectives, collateral socialization research, curriculum reforms, assessments of learning outcomes, and systematic feedback and revision of the process.

Political Attitudes in World Regions

Our results strongly confirmed the 'diversity' rather than 'equality' hypothesis. Democratic attitudes are not uniform in every world region and are not evenly distributed. In some regions or countries, consistent political attitudes on democracy, authoritarianism, and multiculturalism are more prevalent.

We concluded that CIS-Russian states provide the worst-case scenarios and African states very unstable examples of prospects for increased democratization and reduced authoritarianism. The successor ideology to communism is not likely to be democracy, but rather a kind of militaristic-undemocratic-racist-fascistic-authoritarianism. So Zhirinovsky is not as unusual a political figure in Russia as the Western press would have us believe. He is a typical Russian, an anti-democratic 'Uncle Ivan'. Eastern European countries (particularly Belorussia, Slovakia, Russia, Croatia, Serbia) are prime candidates for increasing authoritarian rule and decreasing democratization. They lack a democratic political culture and civic education tradition there. But the growth of nationalism and interethnic rivalries indicates the critical need for political education reform, for a focus on civil rights, liberties, and tolerance toward ethnic minorities and national groups living in those countries.

We found that the US and Canada no longer excel in low levels of authoritarianism; that honor now belongs to Western Europe. Perhaps this result is understandable in the US which took on the burden of Western military leadership, thus promoting its own aggressive militarism. This requires strong nationalistic traditions to ensure continual popular support. No wonder that even if the US pro-democratic propaganda machine still functions well, the storehouse of popular authoritarianism has been overfilled owing to cold war anti-communism, intolerance, superpatriotism, and unremitting militarism.

If the US cannot model itself on Latin America, neither can South Americans reproduce either the US political or educational systems since their political cultural traditions are so different (elitism, Catholicism, strong-man rule). Many of the same traditions are found in the southern part of Western Europe which shares many undemocratic characteristics (excessive religiosity, elitism, military rule) which promote the growth of authoritarianism. Only with respect to northwestern Europe (particularly Germany, the Netherlands, Sweden) do we find active social democracies, low authoritarianism, pro-democracy, low nationalism and militarism scores, fairly high multiculturalism approval, and favorable views of liberal-progressive educational policies. Here, we believe, we can find an appropriate model for North and South America (as well as Africa and Asia) to follow for combating authoritarianism through positive public policies such as civic education reform.

As for the future of democratization and the disappearance of fascist authoritarianism in the rest of the regions we surveyed, the spirit of military dictatorship runs high in Africa and is unlikely to be easily dislodged by either educational or political reform. Such changes are likely to be supported at only the minimal level by improving literacy, holding free and fair elections, or improving the status of women. A similar situation prevails in India, where ethnic divisiveness at home and rivalries with Pakistan and China outweigh all other considerations; achieving real democratization always remains elusive. Turkey has this same intense hatred of Greece plus the domestic revival of religious fundamentalism (an anti-democratic trend). These countries (plus China and the Balkans) are unlikely to be fully democratized any time soon. Their political cultures do not provide socialization experiences or social learning opportunities to combat authoritarianism, improve democratization, increase tolerance, and promote multiculturalism, all necessary components of the participant civic culture with its universal and open educational system.

Educational Level and Authoritarianism

The inverse relationship between level of education and authoritarian attitudes was reanalyzed using cross-national data sets of large or random samples from North America and Western Europe from the 1960s and 1990s. An inverse relationship appears to exist almost universally. It also is a very stable phenomenon, hardly changing over decades. We do not make a causal claim since several explanatory factors which vary from country to country may be responsible. These include variations in content of education, ideology, educational systems, socio-economic forces, and trends in national development. Nevertheless, this reverse relationship appears to be an almost universal phenomenon in all national and cross-national surveys.

Simpson's Thesis Tested

The quality and strength of the relationship between authoritarianism and level of education were tested based on Simpson's (1972) thesis. Our analyses support Simpson's thesis. In less developed and less democratic countries, this relationship is much weaker (down to half its strength elsewhere). This indicates a much weaker effect of education in combating authoritarianism and strengthening democratic attitudes in such countries. We may conclude that this analysis (at least partly) supports the thesis that education in more democratic countries is more effective in countering authoritarianism and supporting democratic attitudes than is the case in less democratic countries. Less developed and some (ex)communist countries not only suffer from relatively high levels of authoritarianism, but often also from less educational effectiveness in the citizens' acquisition of democratic attitudes. Education apparently has a different effect in underdeveloped countries as well as in countries that suffered from lengthy authoritarian or dictatorial rule.

Authoritarian and Democratic Educational Orientations

From our analysis, we may conclude that relatively stable relationships over the world regions exist for the liberal-progressive education attitude as related to multiculturalism and for considering oneself multicultural or left-wing, while the nationalist education attitude is more closely related to authoritarianism and considering oneself right-wing, and as being not multicultural. Liberal-progressive education attitudes display a stable interregional relationship to democratic multiculturalism and self-rating as multicultural. Nationalistic/conservative educational policy preferences are significantly and positively related in all regions with general authoritarianism (positive), self-rating right-wing (positive) and self-rating (negative and more weakly) *vis á vis* democratic multiculturalism and pro-democracy attitudes. One plausible explanation for this latter result is that everyone today is a theoretical democrat (such as our Indian, if not Russian, respondents), but many more are really practicing authoritarians (as is also true in India and Russia). That is, if everyone verbalizes adherence to democratic norms, then there is little variance since this variable is so overpowering and universally positively valued (the so-called 'ceiling-effect' that reduces correlations).

Farnen/Meloen Thesis Tested

In this international survey, we investigated the relationship between education and authoritarian or democratic attitudes. Previous research often showed a relation between one's higher level of general education and lower authoritarianism (in the range of .30-.40). A convincing explanation for this is still lacking. An alternative approach is that there is a substantial effect of preferences for certain educational content reflecting authoritarian and democratic attitudes, apart from the general effects of level of education achieved. This proposition was stated as the Farnen/Meloen thesis. We presented this thesis to the effect that we posit a relationship between one's preferences for policy options/attitudes about liberal-progressive-multicultural-internationalist educational choices and pro-democratic, self-rating as multiculturalist, and multiculturalism, anti-authoritarian, pro-reformer, and anti-dictator on one hand versus conservative-nationalist-monoculturalist-provincial orientations on the other.

The results of our statistical analyses support our thesis. Liberal and conservative-nationalist education can have effects on authoritarian and democratic multicultural attitudes. In general, one's content and style of educational choices are related to politically relevant attitudes. The basic model remained valid, even though a series of competing explanations were included in the analysis. This model exists not only in the West, but also in the (ex)communist second and third worlds. Students prefer democratic reformers or dictatorial leaders, just as they endorse liberal or conservative-nationalist teaching tendencies. Political self-definitions mediated between educational preferences and political attitudes. Students are not passive recipients of education, but use personal self-definitions that (along with the effects of education) lead to expressions of democratic or authoritarian attitudes.

Since the effects of conservative-nationalist styles seem much stronger then teaching democratic multiculturalism, we concluded it is equally necessary to teach pro-democracy and anti-authoritarianism if either course is to have its intended effect. It is also important (as both our findings and Altemeyer's indicated) to try to impact on students' political self-definitions during adolescence when these self-images coalesce and assume greater personal importance.

CONSEQUENCES FOR POLITICAL EDUCATION

Political Education That Makes a Difference

Throughout this book, our fundamental focus has been on two major points: political attitudes (democratic, authoritarian) and educational policy options. How these two political orientations interact nationally, regionally, and cross-nationally has been examined with considerable success. We found the same basic relationship patterns between these two variables. Cross-nationally, we found again the already familiar pattern of (political/psychological) authoritarianism, nationalism, militarism, and anti-multiculturalism. We found that merely increasing the amount of education is not sufficient to overcome (political/psychological) authoritarianism. Instead, we concluded that one's preference for a liberal, democratic, progressive, and multicultural educational policy option or ideology may be a better predictor of lower authoritarianism than are either more education or more of a certain type of social sciences or humanities educational content. Based on our findings, we also concluded that merely teaching pro-democracy is not enough since anti-authoritarianism (political/psychological) must also be taught to strengthen one's democratic ideology as a whole; one without the other will produce less-committed democrats.

Our other conclusions about political education can also be summarized. We concluded that some of our findings help to outline typical cognitive maps about authority, democracy, and ethnicity in given countries and regions of the world. These cognitive schema can be used to plan educational strategies for civic education reform of textbooks, teaching styles, curriculum, and content. Additional socialization research can help detect which societal inputs play a supporting role (newspapers) and which may not (radio, TV).

We also focused on the middle school years as a crucial time for civic education impact. To have any effect on students, it must be legitimate to teach political education in early adolescence rather than historical/geographical facts via undemocratic rote memorization in a closed classroom. Using current events discussions in classes is very effective, especially when using case studies of democratic, authoritarian, and multicultural societies.

It is necessary in schools to discuss nationalism, militarism, racism, patriotism, religious fundamentalism, and other potential threats to democracy. The red-shirted anti-democrats may have momentarily retreated from the left side of the stage, but they reappeared wearing brown and black uniforms from the right wing, still posing an anti-democratic threat today. In civics lessons, we must expose the falsity of the 'guided democracy' claim and emphasize the key criteria for a democratic system and citizen competence.

We also realize that while we reviewed some Western research indicating that civic education can make a difference, we do not know if this is a universally applicable generalization since not enough cross-national research has been conducted to verify, refute, or qualify this important finding. That is, many school systems may be quite similar cross-nationally, with less variance than internal or domestic school comparisons and variations. However, applying uniform civic education reforms across the board to several countries makes little sense unless the teachers who will teach a new curriculum choose to do so, adapt it to local circumstances, and receive appropriate training, materials, and support to effect the changes. National differences and cultural variations can easily destroy a tolerance curriculum unless careful planning precedes its implementation. The study of political culture indicates that schools serve different socialization functions in various societies. We indicated that some of these basic issues are survival, discrimination, and conscience factors; all are important for even the initiation of truly democratic and egalitarian reforms in India, for example. To try to superimpose any Western curriculum reforms on a third world country (such as India) would be as hopeless as it will be fruitless. Even working with Eastern European cultures is a long, tedious process in which Western educators can only serve as advisors (for example, the actual case of helping Ukrainians in Kiev implement for themselves a Dutch social studies and civic education program, while adapting it to meet local needs and conditions).

Teaching Tolerance and Anti-Authoritarianism

We have enough information about racism and multiculturalism in several countries and experimental materials produced in the West to try out some of this content cross-nationally, particularly in its least expensive or intrusive forms (by asking all dark-eyed, darker-skinned, or red-bandana-wearing students to behave or be treated in certain ways for one day to teach effects of prejudice/stereotyping). One problem with socialization or curriculum research is that only the rich countries get to learn about these findings since the poorer ones cannot afford to buy the books or never find the time to read and implement the appropriate reforms or technology suggested to them.

While we have sound theories for how to directly combat authoritarianism from Altemeyer's experiments, this innovative method needs to be more broadly tried to ascertain its utility in other settings. At any rate, it is worth a try. Meanwhile, we suggest teaching both about democracy and its authoritarian opposite since both are important along with other topics such as humanism and tolerance. We also suggested networking about how to combat the 'enemies of freedom' who are interested in reforming schools in their own right-wing, fundamentalist image. Both the politics of education and politics and education themes are useful to civic education reformers since exposing the hidden curriculum and democratizing the school and classroom are as important as creating national standards, examinations, or goals. Both sets of issues (micro and macro) are equally important.

An anti-authoritarianism curriculum is needed to explore authoritarian theory, regimes, and personality characteristics (a three-level analysis). Our description of these separate facets of authoritarianism cross-nationally is substantiated in detail with our discussion of authoritarianism at the macro (regime) and micro (individual) levels. We described the characteristics of authoritarianism at both levels which may be summarized under the terms militaristic fascism on the one hand and aggression-submission-convention on the other. These characteristics of both regimes and political persons can be seen daily since they are paraded through newspapers and TV (without analysis and *ad nauseum*) on a regular basis.

All the major institutions in society (including churches, mass media, and schools) need to work on deliberately improving interethnic relations and accepting national minorities living in our midst as full-fledged citizens. This is as true of the Baltic republics with their Russian minorities as it is of Slovakia, the FRG, Hungary, and the Czech Republic with their 'Gypsy' minorities. The high degree of anti-Semitism in some of these eastern countries (despite the absence of Jews) is another example of an authoritarian element which needs significant attention since authoritarianism thrives on hatred of the 'other', 'parasites', 'outsiders', and 'strangers' supposedly living off the 'hard-working' citizenry. What is especially dangerous for peace in the area is the lack of respect from many of these regimes (in Slovakia, Serbia, Croatia, Belorussia, Russia) for the international community whether represented by the UN, NATO, OSCE, or the EU. This situation does not bode well for decreasing authoritarianism and increasing democratization in the eastern and southeastern European region.

Democracy and the Curriculum

Multiethnic or divided nations, religious violence and civil war, and external pressures on democratic states are problems many countries face today. We discussed these matters and social democratic values, the inevitability of a reformed market capitalism and its links to democracy, and democratic transitions from military rule. All are important and help formulate and detail the basic elements of a democracy curriculum that deserves to be taught.

There is enough work to do cross-nationally on anti-Semitism, anti-Romany, ethnic nationalism, militarism, stereotyping, racism, anti-multiculturalism, and threatening attitudes to keep the next generation of political scientists, psychologists, and civic educators fully employed. The kinds of school reforms we proposed also should involve the hidden curriculum, classroom climate, and school reorganization. Civic education can make a difference as we have shown. The current focus on geographic and historical factual learning is part of an undemocratic trend to decrease citizen participation and competence in the West. It needs to be offset in a systematic way by groups committed not to counterpropaganda, but to a philosophy of radical reconceptualism: liberation, enlightenment, agency, progressive reform, emancipation, equal opportunity, anti-hegemony, excellence, humanism, teamwork, multiculturalism, resistance, pluralism, pragmatism, reconstructionism, and practical globalism.

While educators are free to take their own stands on a national curricula and national testing, both of these trends in the absence of a new democratic/anti-authoritarian civics curriculum seem to be very dangerous tendencies, especially since their support mainly comes from the right-wing and religious fundamentalists in many countries. Fortunately, these efforts cost money and the forces of fascism are so anti-government that they want reform, but often do not want to pay for it. Perhaps, then, these efforts will fall of their own weight much as the America 2000 Bush/Clinton era education proposal is likely to do since its goals are unrealistic, unattainable, and irrelevant even for the year 1950, not to speak of 2000 and the third millennium.

RECENT DISCUSSIONS OF AUTHORITARIANISM, DEMOCRACY, AND EDUCATION

Of the eight countries which our study and the latest Freedom House report (Karatnycky, Motyl, and Graybow, 1999) have in common, one (Belorussia) is rated as not free, three (Ukraine, Russia, and Croatia) as partly free, and four (Estonia, Hungary, Lithuania, and Poland) as free nations. These countries are categorized respectively as consolidated autocracies, transitional governments, and consolidated democracies. Serbia/Yugoslavia was excluded from the analysis, but it would most likely fit into the unfree group. In general, our analysis is corroborated by other ongoing studies; the dangerous autocratic and undemocratic trends we noted (in countries such as Russia, Belorussia, and Croatia, if not in Ukraine) have continued. With Tudjman's (former president of Croatia) death in 1999, his fracturing HDZ party is freeing up the electoral system, allowing new political coalitions to form, and encouraging free and fair elections to become the rule rather than the exception. In terms of adopting Western political and economic standards, both Croatia and Russia have made 'contradictory progress'. For example, Yeltsin was replaced by Vladimir Putin (a former KGB functionary, hard-line nationalist, and militarist). Belorussia operates under the virtual dictatorship of President Lukashenka, whose major political objectives appear to be maintaining the parliamentary dominance of the Communist Party as well as consummating a political and economic union/merger with Russia. Even in Austria in 2000, an alliance between conservative and neo-Nazi parties was designed to unseat the long-dominant Social Democrats.

Five other parallel and supportive studies also help us understand the role right-wing authoritarianism plays in everyday American life (Hilliard and Keith, 1999), the biological and evolutionary basis for political authoritarianism throughout history and the need for democratic indoctrination in today's world (Somit and Peterson, 1997), and the divided relationship between authoritarianism and the anti-ecology/environmentalist movement among members of Congress and US media luminaries such as Tom DeLay and Rush Limbaugh, respectively (Milburn and Conrad, 1996). The latter study also attributed childhood punishment as the source for punitive adult political attitudes, displacement, projection and denial; hated objects are homosexuals, minorities, abortionists, prisoners, and military enemies.

Two recent studies contribute to our understanding of authoritarianism both as an international phenomenon and as a root cause for prejudice, anti-Semitism, nationalism, xenophobia, anti-Roma, -immigrant, -democratic, and -multiculturalist attitudes and behaviors. One example is the regional comparisons we made between Eastern Europe and other world regions regarding basic political attitudes and behaviors (Meloen and Farnen, 1999, pp. 277-304). The other ten chapters in that book focused on the other political values just mentioned. A special issue of the political psychology/socialization journal, *Politics, Groups and the Individual* (Zick, 1999), reviewed the subject across the international spectrum.

FUTURE PROSPECTS

New Programs and Research Initiatives

Group planning and mutual support are necessary ingredients for successful curriculum reform. While we looked at the results of some of the Western European only or joint Western-Eastern European conferences, we see that many of the conceptual pieces are in place, others are quite commendable in terms of systemic suggestions, but few are very practical for ensuring real educational reform in any immediate or positive way. These conferences need to be rethought, to focus on fundamentals (such as public knowledge, skills, behaviors, and morals) and how to build teams to implement them, not just to meet, socialize, and theorize together. It has proved to be very difficult to inspire civic educational reform in eastern Germany, even with massive western German help, so one can only imagine how difficult it will be to do so elsewhere, even under UNESCO or Council of Europe auspices.

Among the principal matches and comparisons between our research and recent political socialization/education findings are the following suggestions. First, we advocated the study of politics, society, and educational policy or the politics of/and education to show that schools should not be depoliticized with respect to democracy and multiculturalism. Second, an international conference should be called to critique findings and initiate a jointly sponsored international research, publication, conference, and coordination schedule. This could eliminate duplication of effort and establish a common international agenda. Third, more national, international, and global research should be conducted on questions as to what political views may be modified in school and when they are most malleable (presumably in the middle school years), whether students can be helped to accept democracy and anti-authoritarianism for themselves rather than through indoctrination, and how we can encourage ethnic and racial minorities to improve their political education and participant orientations through schooling. Fourth, we can jointly critique useful models of analysis (such as those described in Chapter 1 and Farnen, 1990) which can inform us of systematic components needed to be examined in such reform efforts. For example, there are US, Swedish, Dutch, German, and other civic education models which provide a basis for the democratic reconceptualization of political education and politics. Fifth, we recommended expanding group work, using ethnographic studies, changing political socialization research agenda, reconsidering critical studies and reconceptualization critiques of the schools, and developing new civics materials on militarism, nationalism, internationalism, authority, and democracy to enhance civic participation and citizen competence. Should we all decide to promote 'strong' (not 'weak') democracy in the future, this is surely a worthwhile common goal to take with us into the 21st century.

Appendix: International Survey of Attitudes toward Democracy, Authority, Equality, and Multiculturalism

The survey had two parts: survey questions and background information.

QUESTIONNAIRE

For statements 1 through 47, respondents were to circle a number on a 7-point scale (1 = agree completely; 2 = agree; 3 = agree somewhat; 4 = undecided, no opinion; 5 = disagree somewhat; 6 = disagree; 7 = disagree completely).

1. Democracy by far is the best form of government for our country and people.
2. The majority should abolish minority rights if they choose to do so.
3. It will do us all a lot of good if people of all races, nationalities, religions, and classes attend private or government-run schools together everywhere in our country.
4. It is socially beneficial for laws in our country to require employment of a specified percentage of people in order to reflect important characteristics, such as race, religion, class, gender, and ethnicity.
5. If our government has to economize, cutting the military budget should be a high priority.
6. The best way to prevent a war is to make sure that one is at least as powerful as one's possible opponent.
7. It should be allowed to use the army to maintain law and order.
8. Most people do not know what is good for them.
9. It may be necessary to outlaw or ban certain political parties/groups who are likely to cause public disorder or trouble.
10. Our political institutions are the best in the world.
11. Regardless of what some people say, there are certain races, nationalities, or religions that just will not properly mix with our way of life.
12. Our true and traditional way of life is disappearing so fast that we may have to use force to save it.
13. People who hate our way of life should have a chance to be heard in public.
14. Freedom of speech does not justify someone's teaching foreign or disloyal ideas in our schools.
15. Patriotism and loyalty to our established ways of life are the most important requirements for good citizenship.

196

16. Our way of life is about as good as any other.
17. Although it may be true about fine race horses, there are not any breeds of people who are naturally better than others.
18. There should be laws against marriage between persons of different races.
19. When it comes to things that count most, all races, religious groups, and nationalities are pretty much alike and equal.
20. We certainly owe respect to the higher classes of people in our society, especially when the honor and positions they have come from birth, family, tradition, and custom.
21. We owe unquestionable respect to the better people in our society when their status and prestige come from hard work.
22. Our schools ought to teach us more about promoting individual freedom, popular participation, keeping the peace, and achieving economic equality and justice for all.
23. Our schools already teach us too much about other lands, peoples, cultures, and races.
24. Our schools ought to teach us more about the United Nations, comparative government, and keeping the peace through international organizations and peacekeeping alliances.
25. With respect to minority languages and cultures, our schools ought to prohibit such languages for individual learning, classroom instruction, and separate school subjects.
26. With respect to members of minority groups, parents of minority children should become partners with the schools by helping to determine school curricula and policies and by becoming more directly involved in the schools (e.g., by teaching a course).
27. Concerning teaching and testing methods in the schools, students should be grouped by ability, should learn basic facts, and should take competitive subject examinations so everybody knows where they stand in a course and teachers can be held accountable.
28. Concerning teaching and testing methods in our schools, process is more important than content so that students are active, involved, and critical learners and so that assessment of results is based on less formal means, including student self-assessment.
29. Concerning history, social studies, and civic education, teaching about other countries' history, government, cultures, and peoples is far less important than teaching about patriotism, our nation's glorious history, and our outstanding military achievements.
30. Concerning history, social studies, and civic education, we should eliminate isolationist, provincial, and nationalistic themes from the curricu-

    lum so that students can learn more about international topics (such as the UN, EEC, PLO, OAU, CSCE, GCC, and OPEC).

31. It is a moral duty to care about the needy.
32. People can be divided into two distinct classes: the weak and the strong.
33. One should always be concerned about the wishes of the minorities in our society.
34. Familiarity breeds contempt.
35. Young people sometimes get rebellious ideas, but as they grow up, they ought to get over them and settle down.
36. Our society can only make further social progress if the power is no longer shared among a small elite.
37. Most of our social problems would be solved if we could somehow get rid of the immoral, crooked, and feebleminded people.
38. What this country needs most, more than laws and political programs, are a few courageous, tireless, devoted leaders in whom the people can put their faith.
39. Political power should be decentralized as much as possible.
40. A person who has bad manners, habits, and breeding can hardly expect to get along with decent people.
41. Nowadays, more and more people are prying into matters that should remain personal and private.
42. Although there are differences between people, there is no reason to grant more influence to some than to others.
43. It is a pity that politics are made by small groups of influential people.
44. Sex crimes (such as rape and attacks on children) deserve more than mere imprisonment; such criminals ought to be publicly whipped or worse.
45. People should be directly involved when decisions are made that concern all.
46. If people would talk less and work more, everybody would be better off.
47. Every individual has a right for self-determination.

Respondents used a 9-point scale to indicate how they viewed each person (1 = admire very much; 5 = undecided, no opinion; 9 = dislike very much).

48. Ronald Reagan (United States of America)
49. Mao Tse Tung (Communist China)
50. Franklin D. Roosevelt (United States of America)
51. Michail Gorbachev (Soviet Union)
52. Dwight D. Eisenhower (United States of America)
53. Karl Marx (Germany)
54. Martin Luther King, Jr. (United States of America)

55. Adolf Hitler (Nazi Germany)
56. John F. Kennedy (United States of America)
57. Joseph Stalin (Soviet Union)
58. Nelson Mandela (South Africa)
59. Napoleon (France)
60. Saddam Hussein (Iraq)
61. Mohandas Mahatma Gandhi (India)

PERSONAL INFORMATION

Respondents provided background information by filling in an answer or circling the appropriate number.

1. I was born in the following year: 19 ___
2. I am a: 1-Female; 2-Male
3. The place where I mainly grew up was a: 1-Farm; 2-Rural Town; 3-Suburb; 4-City; 5-Large City
4. My parents are in the following social class: 1-Working; 2-Lower middle; 3-Upper middle; 4-Upper
5. My father's highest educational level was: 1-Primary school; 2-High school; 3-College/university
6. I get most of my public affairs information from: 1-Radio; 2-TV; 3-Newspapers; 4-Word of mouth; 5-Magazine

To determine how respondents described themselves (that is, self-ratings), they were asked to circle the appropriate number on a 7-point scale (1 = left characteristic applies best; 4 = undecided, no opinion, both apply; 7 = right characteristic applies best) which appeared between opposite traits.

7.	Political	Not Political
8.	Liberal	Conservative
9.	Right-Wing	Left-Wing
10.	Anti-Authoritarian	Authoritarian
11.	Religious	Not Religious
12.	Internationalist	Isolationist
13.	Militarist	Pacifist
14.	Equalitarian	Elitist
15.	Multiculturalist	Nationalist
16.	Cosmopolitan	Provincial

References

Adorno, T., E. Frenkel-Brunswik, D. Levinson, R. Sanford (1950). *The Authoritarian Personality*. New York, NY: Harper & Row.

Albinski, M. (1959). *De onderwijzer en de cultuuroverdracht* (The Teacher and the Transfer of Culture). Assen, the Netherlands: Van Gorcum.

Alexander, L. (September 1992). *International Education Comparisons*. Washington, DC: US Department of Education.

Alfert, F. (1959). 'A Multiple Score Personality Test Administered to German and Austrian Students: Cross-Cultural vs. Intra-Cultural Differences', pp. 37-46 in *Journal of Social Psychology*, Vol. 50.

Almond, G. and G. Powell (1996). *Comparative Politics Today*, 6th ed. Reading, MA: Addison Wesley.

Altemeyer, B. (1981). *Right Wing Authoritarianism*. Manitoba, Canada: University of Manitoba Press.

Altemeyer, B. (1988). *Enemies of Freedom*. London, UK: Jossey Bass.

Altemeyer, B. (1996). *The Authoritarian Specter*. Cambridge, MA: Harvard University Press.

Anyon, J. (1981). 'Social Class and the Hidden Curriculum of Work', pp. 317-41 in H. Giroux, A. Penna, and W. Pinar (eds.) *Curriculum and Instruction*. Berkeley, CA: McCutchan.

Arnett, M. (1978). 'Attitudinal Correlates of the Least Preferred Co-Worker Score', p. 962 in *Psychological Reports*, Vol. 43.

Athanasiou, R. (1968). 'Technique Without Mystique: A Study of Authoritarianism in Engineering Students', pp. 1181-8 in *Educational Psychological Measurement*, Vol. 28.

Ayers, J. and M. Rohr (1977). 'Another Examination of Authoritarianism and College Major', p. 828 in *Psychological Reports*, Vol. 41, No. 3.

Banks, A. (ed.) (1995 and 1997). *Political Handbook of the World*. Binghamton, NY: CSA Publications.

Banks, A., A. Day, and T. Muller (eds.) (1997). *Political Handbook of the World: 1997*. Binghamton, NY: CSA Publications.

Barber, J. (1995). *The Book of Democracy*. Englewood Cliffs, NJ: Prentice-Hall.

Bayer, J. (April 1995). "Gesprach mit Ralf Dahrendorf' (Conversation with Ralf Dahrendorf), pp. 503-11 in *Sinn und Form*, Vol. 47, No. 4.

Bethlehem, D. (1985). *A Social Psychology of Prejudice*. London, UK: Croom Helm.

Blackburn, G. (1985). *Education in the Third Reich: Race and History in Nazi Text Books*. Albany, NY: State University of New York Press.

Bracey, G. (October 1997). 'The Seventh Bracey Report on the Condition of Public Education', pp. 120-36 in *Phi Delta Kappan*, Vol. 79, No. 2.

Brigham, J. (December 1993). 'College Students' Racial Attitudes', pp. 1933-67 in *Journal of Applied Social Psychology*, Vol. 23.

Brown, R. (1965). 'The Authoritarian Personality and the Organization of Attitudes', pp. 477-546 in R. Brown (ed.) *Social Psychology*. New York, NY: Free Press.

Bútorová, Z., M. Bútora, I. Dianiška, M. Dobrovodsky, Z. Fialová, P. Frič, O. Gyarfásová, I. Radičová, and T. Rosová (March 1993). *Current Problems of Slovakia After the Split of the CSFR*. Bratislava, Slovakia: Centre for Social Analysis.

Corretero, M. and J. Voss (1994). *Cognitive and Instructional Processes in History and the Social Sciences*. Hillsdale, NJ and Hove, UK: Lawrence Erlbaum.

Christie, R. and P. Cook (1958). 'A Guide to Published Literature Relating to the Authoritarian Personality through 1956', pp. 171-99 in *Journal of Psychology*, Vol. 45.

Christie, R., J. Havel, and B. Seidenberg (1958). 'Is the F-Scale Irreversible'?, pp. 143-59 in *Journal of Abnormal and Social Psychology*, Vol. 56.

Christie, R. and M. Jahoda (1954). *Studies in the Scope and Method of 'The Authoritarian Personality': Continuities in Social Research*. Glencoe, IL: Free Press.

Collier, D. (1993). 'Bureaucratic Authoritarianism', pp. 96-8 in J. Krieger (ed.) *The Oxford Companion to Politics of the World*. New York, NY and Oxford, UK: Oxford University Press.

Connell, R. (1971). *The Child's Construction of Politics*. Melbourne, Australia: Melbourne University Press.

Csepeli, G. (1989). *Structures and Contents of Hungarian National Identity*. Frankfurt am Main, FRG: Peter Lang Verlag.

Csepeli, G. (1994). 'Children of a Paradise Lost', pp. 246-59 in G. Csepeli, D. German, L. Kéri, and I. Stumpf (eds.) *From Subject to Citizen*. Budapest, Hungary: Hungarian Centre for Political Education.

Danigelis, N. and J. Cultler (September 1991). 'An Inter-Cohort Comparison of Changes in Racial Attitudes', pp. 383-404 in *Research on Aging*, Vol. 13, No. 3.

Day, A., R. German, and J. Campbell (1996). *Political Parties of the World* (4th ed.). New York, NY: Cartermill Publishing.

Dekker, H. (1996). 'Democratic Citizen Competence', pp. 386-410 in R. Farnen, H. Dekker, R. Meyenberg, and D. German (eds.) *Democracy, Socialization, and Conflicting Loyalties in East and West*. London, UK: Macmillan and New York, NY: St. Martins Press.

Dekker, P. and P. Ester (1987). 'Working-Class Authoritarianism: A Re-Examination of the Lipset Thesis', pp. 395-415 in *European Journal Political Research*, Vol. 15.

Dekker, P. and P. Ester (1992). 'Authoritarianism and Beliefs About the Unemployed', pp. 13-41 in *Politics and the Individual*, Vol. 2, No. 1.

Dekker, P. and P. Ester (1993). *Social and Political Attitudes in Dutch Society: Theoretical Perspectives and Survey Evidence*. Rijswijk, the Netherlands: Social and Cultural Planning Office and The Hague, the Netherlands: VUGA.

Dekker, H. and L. Jansen (1994). 'In Search for an Explanation of Anti-German Attitudes Among Dutch Schoolchildren', pp. 105-22 in G. Csepeli, D. German, L. Kéri, and I. Stumpf (eds.) *From Subject to Citizen*. Budapest, Hungary: Hungarian Center for Political Education.

Dekker, H., D. Malová, and R. Theulings (1996). 'What Makes a Slovak a Nationalist?', pp. 139-64 in R. Farnen, H. Dekker, R. Meyenberg, and D. German (eds.) *Democracy, Socialization, and Conflicting Loyalties in East and West*. London, UK: Macmillan and New York, NY: St. Martins Press.

Dillehay, R. (1978). 'Authoritarianism', pp. 85-127 in H. London and J. Exner (eds.) *Dimensions of Personality*. New York, NY: Wiley & Sons.

DiTella, T. (1995). 'Military Rule and Transition to Democracy', pp. 836-41 in S. Lipset (ed.) *The Encyclopedia of Democracy*, Vol. 3. Washington, DC: Congressional Quarterly.

Duckitt, J. (1992). 'Education and Authoritarianism among English- and Afrikaans-Speaking White South Africans', pp. 701-8 in *Journal of Social Psychology*, Vol. 132.

Dunham, J. (1973). 'Authoritarian Personality Traits among Students', pp. 40-5 in *Educational Research*, Vol. 16, No. 1.

Eckhardt, W. (1991). 'Authoritarianism', pp. 97-124 in *Political Psychology*, Vol. 12, No. 1.

Eisinga, R. and P. Scheepers (1989). *Ethnocentrisme in Nederland* (Ethnocentrism in the Netherlands). Nijmegen, the Netherlands: ITS.

Ekehammar, B., I Nilsson, and J. Sidanius (1989). 'Social Attitudes and Social Status: A Multivariate and Multinational Analysis', pp. 203-8 in *Personality and Individual Differences*, Vol. 10.

Ellison, C. and D. Powers (June 1994). 'The Contact Hypothesis and Racial Attitudes Among Black Americans', pp. 385-400 in *Social Science Quarterly*, Vol. 75, No. 2.

Enyedi, Z., F. Erös, and Z. Fabian (1997). *Authoritarianism and the Political Spectrum in Hungary*. Discussion Paper Series. Budapest, Hungary: Collegium Budapest, Institute for Advanced Study.

Erös, F., Z. Fabian, Z. Enyedi, and Z. Fleck (1996). *Prejudices, Authoritarianism, and Political Attitudes during the Post-Communism Transformation (1994)*. Survey Research Department, Institute of Psychology, Hungarian Academy of Sciences, Budapest, Hungary.

Europa Yearbook (2 vols.) (1995). London, UK: Europa Publications, Ltd.

Farnen, R. (1990). *Integrating Political Science, Education, and Public Policy*. Frankfurt am Main, FRG: Verlag Peter Lang.

Farnen, R. (1993a). 'Cognitive Maps: The Implications of Internal Schemata (Structures) versus External Factors (Content and Context) for Cross-National Political Research', pp. 212-91 in G. Cespeli, L. Kéri, and I. Stumpf (eds.) *State and Citizen: Studies on Political Socialization in Post-Communist Eastern Europe*. Budapest, Hungary: Institute of Political Science.

Farnen, R. (ed.) (1993b). *Reconceptualizing Politics, Socialization, and Education*. Oldenburg, FRG: University of Oldenburg BIS.

Farnen, R. (1993c). 'Reconceptualizing Politics, Education, and Socialization', pp. 376-459 in R. Farnen (ed.) *Reconceptualizing Politics, Socialization, and Education*. Oldenburg, FRG: University of Oldenburg BIS.

Farnen, R. (ed.) (1994a). *Nationalism, Ethnicity, and Identity: Cross-National and Comparative Perspectives*. New Brunswick, NJ and London, UK: Transaction Publications.

Farnen, R. (1994b). 'Nationality, Ethnicity, Political Socialization, and Public Policy: Some Cross-National Perspectives', pp. 23-102 in R. Farnen (ed.) *Nationalism, Ethnicity, and Identity: Cross-National and Comparative Perspectives*. New Brunswick, NJ and London, UK: Transaction Publications.

Farnen, R. (1994c). 'Nationalism, Ethnicity, National Identity, and Multiculturalism: Concluding Observations', pp. 443-62 in R. Farnen (ed.) *Nationalism, Ethnicity, and Identity: Cross-National and Comparative Perspectives*. New Brunswick, NJ and London, UK: Transaction Publications.

Farnen, R. (1994d). 'Political Decision Making, Problem Solving, and Eduation', pp. 129-52 in S. Miedema, G. Biesta, B. Boog, A. Smaling, W. Wardekker, and B. Levering (eds.) *The Politics of Human Science*. Brussels, Belgium: VUB Press.

Farnen, R. (1996). 'Nationalism, Democracy, and Authority in North America and Europe Since 1989', pp. 39-105 in R. Farnen, H. Dekker, R. Meyenberg, and D. German (eds.) *Democracy, Socialization, and Conflicting Loyalties in East and West*. London, UK: Macmillan and New York, NY: St. Martins Press.

Farnen, R. (1997a). 'The Present as Seen from the Past', pp. 3-12 in R. Farnen and H. Sünker (eds.) *Politics, Sociology, and Economics of Education: Interdisciplinary and Comparative Perspectives*. London, UK: Macmillan and New York, NY: St. Martins Press.

Farnen, R. (1997b). 'Politics, Education, and Paradigmatic Reconceptualism: US Critical Theory in the 1990s', pp. 15-43 in R. Farnen and H. Sünker (eds.) *Politics, Sociology, and Economics of Education: Interdisciplinary and Comparative Perspectives*. London, UK: Macmillan and New York, NY: St. Martins Press.

Farnen, R. (1997c). 'Summary/Conclusions: The Future as Seen from the Present', pp. 229-48 in R. Farnen and H. Sünker (eds.) *Politics, Sociology, and Economics of Education: Interdisciplinary and Comparative Perspectives*. London, UK: Macmillan and New York, NY: St. Martins Press.

Farnen, R., H. Dekker, R. Meyenberg, and D. German (eds.) (1996). *Democracy, Socialization, and Conflicting Loyalties in East and West*. London, UK: Macmillan and New York, NY: St. Martins Press.

Farnen, R. and D. German (1996). 'Central and Eastern European Elite Perspectives on Political, Communications, Educational, Economic, and Environmental Changes (1989-92', pp. 106-36 in R. Farnen, H. Dekker, R. Meyenberg, and D. German (eds.) *Democracy, Socialization, and Conflicting Loyalties in East and West*. London, UK: Macmillan and New York, NY: St. Martins Press.

Farnen, R. and D. German (May 1997). 'Transitions to Democracy: Elite Perspectives on Political Change in Central and Eastern Europe from 1989 to 1997'. Paper delivered to the International Political Science Association Research Committee on Political Socialization and Political Education and Comenius Centre for Education and Democracy, 20-5 May 1997, Charles University, Prague, Czech Republic.

Farnen, R. and D. German (May 1998). 'Elite Perspectives on Ethnic Tolerance/Conflict, Nationalism, and Civic Education in Central and Eastern Europe (1993-6)'. Paper delivered to the IPSA/RCPSE Round Table Conference, 19-23 May 1998, Brussels, Belgium.

Farnen, R. and H. Sünker (eds.) (1997). *Politics, Sociology, and Economics of Education: Interdisciplinary and Comparative Perspectives*. London, UK: Macmillan and New York, NY: St. Martins Press.

Fauts, J. (November/December 1993). 'Multicultural Education and the Idols of the Mind: Why Multicultural Education is Under Attack', pp. 356-8 in *Social Education*.

Forbes, H. (1985). *Nationalism, Ethnocentrism, and Personality*. Chicago, IL: The University of Chicago Press.

Fratczak-Rudnicka, B., J. Garlicki, R. Holly, V. Martinez, T. Ulinski, R. Zelichowski (1994). 'Warsaw Students' Knowledge and Opinions Concerning the European Community', pp. 270-97 in G. Csepeli, D. German, L. Kéri, and I. Stumpf (eds.) *From Subject to Citizen*. Budapest, Hungary: Hungarian Centre for Political Education.

Freedom House Survey Team (1993, 1995, 1998). *Freedom in the World: The Annual Survey of Political Rights and Civil Liberties 1992-1993, 1994-1995, 1997-1998*. New York, NY: Freedom House.

Fromm, E. (1941/1965). *Escape from Freedom*. New York, NY: Avon Books.

Fukurai, H. and J. Alston (1992). 'Sources of Neo-Nationalism and Resistance in Japan', pp. 207-23 in *Journal of Contemporary Asia*, Vol. 22, No. 2.

Fukuyama, F. (1992). *The End of History and the Last Man*. London, UK: Penguin Books.

Gabennesch, H. (1972). 'Authoritarianism as a World View', pp. 857-75 in *American Journal of Sociology*, Vol. 77.

Gann, L. and P. Duigan (1986). *The Hispanics in the United States*. Boulder, CO: Westview Press.

Giroux, H. (1993). *Living Dangerously: Multiculturalism and the Politics of Difference*. New York, NY and Frankfurt am Main, FRG: Peter Lang.

Goldstein, K., and S. Blackman (1978). *Cognitive Style*. New York, NY: Wiley & Sons.

Granberg, D. and G. Corrigan (1972). 'Authoritarianism, Dogmatism and Orientations toward the Vietnam War', pp. 468-76 in *Sociometry*, Vol. 35, No. 3.

Greenberg, H., and D. Fare (1959). 'An Investigation of Several Variables as Determinants of Authoritarianism', pp. 105-11 in *Journal of Social Psychology*, Vol. 49.

Greenburg, E. (1969). 'Black Children and the Political Socialization System: A Study of Socialization to Support', pp. 108-28 in C. Bell (ed.) *Growth and Change*. Encino, CA: Dickinson Publishing.

Grift, W. van der, W. de Vos, and J. Meloen (1991). *Antisemitisme en autoritarisme onder scholieren* (Anti-Semitism and Authoritarianism among High School Students). Utrecht and De Lier, the Netherlands: Rijksuniversiteit Utrecht/Anne Frank Sticting. Academish Boekencentrum.

Gupta, D., A. Jongman, and A. Schmid (1993). 'Creating a Composite Index for Assessing Country Performance in the Field of Human Rigths: Proposal for a New Methodology', pp. 131-62 in *Human Rights Quarterly*, Vol. 15.

Hagendoorn, L. (1993). 'Authoritarianism, Education, and Democracy', pp. 181-99 in G. Csepeli, L. Kéri, and I. Stumpf (eds.) *State and Citizen*. Budapest, Hungary: Institute of Political Science, Hungarian Center for Political Education.

Hamilton, M. and P. Mineo (1996). 'Personality and Persuasability: Developing a Multidimensional Model of Belief Systems', pp. 49-68 in *World Communication*, Vol. 25, No. 2.

Hartford Courant (8 October 1995). '*Washington Post* Poll on Race Shows Images are Distorted', p. A11.

Hastings, B. (1996). ' Right Wing Authoritarianism and Social Issues Among Contemporary College Students', pp. 85-98 in *Politics, Groups and the Individual*, Vol. 6, No. 1.

Hein, J. (August 1994). 'Migrant to Minority: Army Refugees and the Societal Construction of Identity in the United States', pp. 281-306 in *Sociological Inquiry*, vol. 64, No. 3.

Held, D. (1993). 'Democracy', pp. 220-4 in J. Krieger (ed.) *The Oxford Companion to Politics of the World*. New York, NY and Oxford, UK: Oxford University Press.

Hesselbart, S. and H. Schuman (1976). 'Racial Attitudes, Educational Level and a Personality Measure', pp. 108-14 in *Public Opinion Quarterly*, vol. 40, No. 1.

Hibbing, J. and E. Theiss-Morse (March 1996). 'Civics is Not Enough: Teaching Barbarics in K-12', pp. 57-62 in *PS: Political Science and Politics*, Vol. 29, No. 1.

Hilliard, R. and M. Keith (1999). *Waves of Rancor*. Armonk, NY and London, UK: M.E. Sharpe.

Hirshberg, M. (1994). 'Apolitical Patriotism: The New Zealand National Self-Image'. (Unpublished manuscript.) Christchurch, New Zealand: Department of Political Science, University of Canterbury.

Hogan, H. (1970). 'A Symbolic Measure of Authoritarianism', pp. 215-9 in *Journal of Social Psychology*, Vol. 82.

Holly, R. (1994). 'The Chinese Portrait of Poland's Neighbor', pp. 236-54 in R. Holly (ed.) *Political Transformation of the System*. Warsaw, Poland: Institute of Political Science (PAN).

Hopf, C. (1993). 'Authoritarians and Their Families', pp. 119-43 in W. Stone, G. Lederer, and R. Christie (eds.) *Strength and Weakness; The Authoritarian Personality Today*. New York, NY: Springer.

Hunter, B. (ed.) (1994-5). *Statesman's Yearbook* (131st ed.). New York, NY: St. Martin's Press.

Huntington, S. (1996). *The Clash of Civilizations and the Remaking of World Order*. New York, NY: Simon & Schuster.

Ichilov, O. (ed.) (1998). *Citizenship and Citizenship Education in a Changing World*. London, UK and Portland, OR: The Woburn Press.

Inglehart, R. (1997). *Modernization and Post-Modernization*. Princeton, NJ: Princeton University Press.

Inglehart R.,M. Basañez, and A. Moreno (1998). *Human Values and Beliefs: A Cross-Cultural Sourcebook*. Ann Arbor, MI: The University of Michigan Press.

Jankowski, M. (1986). *City Bound: Urban Life and Political Attitudes Among Chicano Youth.* Albuquerque, NM: University of New Mexico.

Jenness, D. (1990). *Making Sense of Social Studies.* New York, NY: Macmillan.

Jennings, M. (1993). 'Education and Political Development Among Young Adults', pp. 1-24 in *Politics and the Individual,* Vol. 3, No. 2.

Kaltsounis, T. (January/February 1997). 'Multicultural Education and Citizenship Education at a Crossroads: Searching for Common Ground', pp. 18-22 in *Social Education.*

Karatnycky, A., A. Motyl, and C. Graybow (1999). *Nations in Transit 1998.* New Brunswick, NJ and London, UK: Transaction Publishers.

Kausikan, B. (1993). 'Asia's Different Stand', pp. 268-75 in G. Hastedt (ed.) *One World, Many Voices.* Englewood Cliffs, NJ: Prentice-Hall.

Kirscht, J. and R. Dillehay (1967). *Dimensions of Authoritarianism: A Review of Research and Theory.* Lexington, KY: University of Kentucky Press.

Knutson, J. (1974). 'Psychological Variables', in *Political Recruitment.* Mimeographed Report. Berkeley, CA: The Wright Institute.

Koralewicz, J. (1992). 'Authoritarianism and Degree of Confidence in Political Leaders and Institutions in Poland, 1984'. Paper presented to the IPSA/RCPSE and Polish Academy of Sciences Conference on 'Political Consciousness and Civic Education During the Transformation of the System', 30 November to 3 December 1992, Institute of Political Studies, Warsaw, Poland.

Krauthammer, C. (1 March 1992). 'Fascism is Buchanan's Cause, Not Anti-Semitism', p. B4 in *Hartford Courant.*

Krieger, J. (ed.) (1993). *The Oxford Companion to Politics of the World.* New York, NY and Oxford, UK: Oxford University Press.

Kurian, G. (3 vols.) (1988). *World Education Encyclopedia.* New York, NY: Facts on File Publications.

Lambley, P. (1980). *The Psychology of Apartheid.* London, UK: Secker & Warburg.

Länteenmaa, J. (1995). 'Youth Culture in Transition to Post-Modernity: Finland', pp. 230-5 in L. Chisholm, P. Büchner, H. Krüger, and M. du Bois-Reymond (eds.) *Growing Up in Europe.* Berlin, FRG and New York, NY: Walter de Gruyter.

Lausitz, U. (1995). 'Contradictions of Modern Childhood Within and Outside School', pp. 221-7 in L. Chisholm, P. Büchner, H. Krüger, and M. du Bois-Reymond (eds.) *Growing Up in Europe.* Berlin, FRG and New York, NY: Walter de Gruyter.

Lawrence, J. (1970). 'White Socialization, Black Reality', pp. 418-37 in A. Wilcox (ed.) *Public Opinion and Political Attitudes.* New York, NY: Wiley & Sons.

Lawson, E. (1996). *Encyclopedia of Human Rights* (2nd. ed.). Washington, DC and London, UK: Taylor & Francis.

Lederer, G. (1982). 'Trends in Authoritarianism: A Study of Adolescents in West Germany and the United States Since 1945', pp. 299-314 in *Journal of Cross-Cultural Psychology,* Vol. 13, No. 3.

Lederer, G. (1983). *Jugend und Autorität: Über den Einstellungswandel zum Autoritarismus in der Bundesrepublik Deutschland un den USA* (Youth and Authority: Changing Attitudes on Authoritarianism in Germany and the USA). Opladen, FRG: Westdeutscher Verlag.

Lederer, G. (1993). 'Authoritarianism in German Adolescents', pp. 182-98 in W. Stone, G. Lederer, and R. Christie (eds.) *Strength and Weakness: The Authoritarian Personality Today.* New York, NY: Springer.

Lederer, G. and A. Kindervater (1995). 'Internationale Vergleiche' (International Comparisons), pp. 167-88 in G. Lederer and P. Schmidt (eds.) *Autoritarismus und Gesellschaft: Trendanalysen und vergleichende Jugenduntersuchungen 1945-1993* (Authoritarianism and

Society: An Analysis of Trends and Comparative Youth Research 1945-1993). Opladen, FRG: Leske and Budrich.

Lederer, G. and P. Schmidt (eds.) (1995). *Autoritarismus und Gesellschaft: Trendanalysen und vergleichende Jugenduntersuchungen 1945-1993* (Authoritarianism and Society: An Analysis of Trends and Comparative Youth Research 1945-1993). Opladen, FRG: Leske and Budrich.

Lee, R. and P. Warr (1969). 'The Development and Standardization of a Balanced F-Scale', pp. 109-29 in *Journal of General Psychology*, vol. 81.

Leo, J. (24 January 1994). 'A Sunny Side on Race', p. 24 in *US News and World Report*.

LeVine, R. and D. Campbell (1972). *Ethnocentrism: Theories and Conflict, Ethnic Attitudes and Group Behavior*. New York, NY: Wiley.

Libo, L. (1957) 'Authoritarianism and Attitudes toward Socialized medicine among Senior Medical Students', pp. 133-6 in *Journal of Social Psychology*, Vol. 46.

Liebhart, E. (1970). 'Socialization im Beruf' (Socialization on the Job), pp. 715-26 in *Kölnischer Zeitschrift für Soziologie und Sozial Psychologie*, Vol. 22, No. 4.

Lijphart, A. (1993). 'Consociational Democracy', pp. 188-9 in J. Krieger (ed.) *The Oxford Companion to Politics of the World*. New York, NY and Oxford, UK: Oxford University Press.

Lijphart, A. (1995). 'Multiethnic Democracy', pp. 853-65 in S. Lipset (ed.) *The Encyclopedia of Democracy*, Vol. 3. Washington, DC: Congressional Quarterly.

Lind, G., J. Sandberger, and T. Bargel (1982). 'Moral Judgment, Ego Strength, and Democratic Orientations: Some Theoretical Continuities and Empirical Findings', pp. 70-110 in *Political Psychology*, Vol. 3, Nos. 3-4.

Lindgren, H. and E. Singer (1963). 'Correlates of Brazilian and North American Attitudes toward Child Centered Practices in Education', pp. 3-7 in *Journal of Social Psychology*, Vol. 60.

Linz, J. (1995). 'Authoritarianism', pp. 103-6 in S. Lipset (ed.) *The Encyclopedia of Democracy*, Vol. 3. Washington, DC: Congressional Quarterly.

Lipset, S. (1959). 'Democracy and Working Class Authoritarianism', pp. 482-501 in *American Sociological Review*, Vol. 24.

Lipsitz, L. (1965). 'Working Class Authoritarianism: A Re-Evaluation', pp. 103-9 in *American Sociological Review*, Vol. 30, No. 1.

MacKay, J. (1993). *State of Health Atlas*. New York, NY: Simon & Schuster.

Makiya, K. (Spring 1994). 'From Beirut to Sarajevo: Can Tolerance be Born of Cruelty?', pp. 20-6 in *New Perspectives Quarterly*, Vol. 11, No. 2.

Martin, W. (1989). *Problem Employees and Their Personalities*. New York, NY: Quorum Books.

Martoccia, C. (1964). 'Authoritarianism and College Major', p. 510 in *Psychological Reports*, Vol. 15.

McFarland, S. and S. Adelson (July 1996). 'An Omnibus Study of Personality, Values, and Prejudice'. Paper presented to the annual meeting of the International Society for Political Psychology, Vancouver, British Columbia.

McFarland, S., V. Ageyev, and M. Abalakina (1993). 'The Authoritarian Personality in the United States and the Former Soviet Union: Comparative Studies', pp. 199-228 in W. Stone, G. Lederer, and R. Christie (eds.) *Strength and Weakness: The Authoritarian Personality Today*. New York, NY: Springer Verlag.

McFarland, S., V. Ageyev, and M. Abalakina (July 1990). 'The Authoritarian Personality in the USA and USSR: Comparative Studies'. Paper presented to the 13th Annual Meeting of the International society of Political Psychology in Washington, DC.

McFarland, S., V. Ageyev, and N. Djintcharadze (February 1996). 'Russian Authoritarianism Two Years After Communism', pp. 210-17 in *Personality and Social Psychology Bulletin*, Vol. 22, No. 2.

McFarland, S. and C. Sparks (1985). 'Age, Education and the Internal Consistency of Personality Scales', pp. 1692-1702 in *Journal of Personality and Social Psychology*, Vol. 49, No. 6.

McGinn, N. (November 1996). 'Education, Democratization, and Globalization: A Challenge for Comparative Education', pp. 341-57 in *Comparative Education Review*, Vol. 40, No. 4.

Meloen, J. (1983). *De autoritaire reactie in tijden van welvaart en crisis* (The Authoritarian Response in Times of Prosperity and Crisis). Amsterdam, the Netherlands: University of Amsterdam, unpublished dissertation.

Meloen, J. (1986). 'The Dynamic Sociopolitical and Economic Influence on Authoritarianism: The Construction of an Empirical Time-Series Model', pp. 62-71 in M. Brouwer, J. van Ginneken, L. Hagendoorn, and J. Meloen (eds.) *Political Psychology in The Netherlands*, The Nijmegen Papers. Amsterdam, the Netherlands: Mola Russa.

Meloen, J. (1991a). 'The Fortieth Anniversary of "The Authoritarian Personality": Is There New Evidence to Consider the Authoritarian Personality to be the Backbone of "Left" as well as "Right-Wing" Dictatorships?', pp. 119-27 in *Politics and the Individual*, Vol. 1, No. 1.

Meloen, J. (1991b). 'Anti-authoritarianism and Political Activism', pp. 261-6 in *South African Journal of Psychology*, Vol. 21, No. 4.

Meloen, J. (1993). 'The F Scale as a Predictor of Fascism: An Overview of 40 Years of Authoritarianism Research', pp. 47-69 in W. Stone, G. Lederer, and R. Christie (eds.) *Strength and Weakness: The Authoritarian Personality Today*. New York, NY: Springer Verlag.

Meloen, J. (1994a). 'A Critical Analysis of Forty Years of Authoritarianism Research: Did Theory Testing Suffer from Cold War Attitudes?' pp. 127-65 in R. Farnen (ed.) *Nationalism, Ethnicity, and Identity: Cross-National and Comparative Perspectives*. New Brunswick, NJ and London, UK: Transaction Publishers.

Meloen, J. (1994b). 'State Authoritarianism Worldwide: A 170 Nation Global Indicators Study'. Paper presented at the RCPSE International Political Science Association (IPSA) World Congress, 22-26 August 1994, Berlin, FRG.

Meloen, J. (1996). 'Authoritarianism, Democracy and Education: A Preliminary Empirical 70-Nation Global Indicators Study', pp. 20-38 in R. Farnen, H. Dekker, R. Meyenberg, and D. German (eds.) *Democracy, Socialization and Conflicting Loyalties in East and West: Cross-National and Comparative Perspectives*. London, UK: MacMillan and New York, NY: St. Martins Press.

Meloen, J. (1998). 'Fluctuations of Authoritarianism in Society: An Empirical Time Series Analysis for the Dynamic Socio-Political and Economic Influence on Authoritarianism in American Society, 1954-1977', pp. 107-32 in *Social Thought & Research*, Vol. 21, Nos. 1 and 2.

Meloen, J. (1999 in press). 'The Political Culture of State Authoritarianism' in S. Renshon and J. Duckitt (eds.) *Political Psychology: Cultural and Cross-Cultural Perspectives*. London, UK: MacMillan and New York, NY: St. Martins Press.

Meloen, J. and R. Farnen (1999). 'Democratic, Authoritarian, and Multiculturalist Attitudes in Eastern Europe', pp. 277-304 in Z. Enyedi and F. Erös (eds.) *Authoritarianism and Prejudice*. Budapest, Hungary: Osiriskindó.

Meloen, J., R. Farnen, and D. German (1994a). 'Authoritarianism and Democracy', pp. 123-52 in G. Csepeli, D. German, L. Kéri, and I. Stumpf (eds.) *From Subject to Citizen*. Budapest, Hungary: Hungarian Center for Political Education.

208   *Democracy, Authoritarianism, and Education*

Meloen, J., R. Farnen, and D. German (1994b). 'Authoritarianism, Democracy, and Symbolic Political Leadership in the New World Order', pp. 255-81 in R. Holly (ed.) *Political Consciousness and Civic Education During the Transformation of the System.* Warsaw, Poland: Institute of Political Studies, Polish Academy of Sciences.

Meloen, J. G. van der Linden, and H. de Witte (1994). 'Authoritarianism and Political Racism in Belgian Flanders: A Test of the Approaches of Adorno et al., Lederer, and Altemeyer', pp. 72-108 in R. Holly (ed.) *Political Consciousness and Civic Education During the Transformation of the System.* Warsaw, Poland: Institute of Political Studies, Polish Academy of Science.

Meloen, J., G. van der Linden, and H. de Witte (1996). 'A Test of the Approaches of Adorno et al., Lederer, and Altemeyer of Authoritarianism in Belgian Flanders: A Research Note', pp. 643-56 in *Political Psychology,* Vol. 17, No. 4.

Meloen, J. and C. Middendorp (1991). 'Authoritarianism in The Netherlands: Ideology, Personality or Subculture', pp. 49-72 in *Politics and the Individual,* Vol. 1, No. 2.

Meloen, J. and J. Veenman (1990). *Het is maar de vraag . . . Onderzoek naar responseffecten bij minderhedensurveys* (It's Only the Question . . . An Investigation into Response Effects in Minority Surveys). Lelystad, The Netherlands: Vermande.

Merelman, R. (June 1980). 'Democratic politics and the Culture of American Education', pp. 319-32 in *American Political Science Review,* Vol. 74, No. 2.

Merelman, R. (March 1996). 'Symbols as Substance in National Civics Standards', pp. 53-7 in *PS: Political Science and Politics,* Vol. 29, No. 1.

Middendorp, C. (1978). *Progressiveness and Conservatism: The Fundamental Dimensions of Ideology Controversy and Their Relationship to Social Class.* The Hague, The Netherlands: Mouton Publishers.

Middendorp, C. (1991). *Ideology in Dutch Politics: The Democratic System Reconsidered.* Assen, The Netherlands: Van Gorcum.

Middendorp, C. and J. Meloen (1990). 'The Authoritarianism of the Working Class Revisited', pp. 257-67 in *European Journal of Political Research,* Vol. 18.

Middendorp, C. and J. Meloen (1991). 'Social Class, Authoritarianism and Directiveness: A Reply to Ray', pp. 213-20 in *European Journal of Political Research,* Vol. 20.

Milburn, M. and S. Conrad (1996). *The Politics of Denial.* Cambridge, MA and London, UK: MIT Press.

Milgram, S. (1974). *Obedience to Authority: An Experimental View.* New York, NY: Harper & Row.

Molnar, T. (1995). *Authority and Its Enemies.* New Brunswick, NJ: Transaction Publishers.

Monroe, K., G. Almond, J. Gunnell, I. Shapiro, G. Graham, B. Barber, K. Shepsle, and J. Cropsey (March 1990). 'Nature of Contemporary Political Science: A Round Table Discussion', pp. 34-43 in *P.S.: Political Science and Politics.,* Vol. 23, No. 1.

National Standards for Civics and Government (1994). Calabasas, CA: Center for Civic Education.

NCSS (September 1992) National Council for the Social Studies. 'Curriculum Guidelines for Multicultural Education', pp. 274-94 in *Social Education,* Vol. 56.

Oesterreich, D. (July 1993). 'Right Wing Extremism, Racism, and Authoritarianism: A Comparison Between the East and the West'. Paper presented to the XVIth Annual Scientific Meeting of the I8nternational Society for Political Psychology, Cambridge, MA.

Ovortrup, J. (1995). 'Childhood in Europe: A New Field of Social Research', pp. 7-20 in L. Chisholm, P. Büchner, H. Krüger, and M. du Bois-Reymond (eds.) *Growing Up in Europe.* Berlin, FRG and New York, NY: Walter de Gruyter.

Pantic, D. (1994). 'Changes in Political Socialization in Serbia', pp. 370-92 in G. Csepeli, D. German, L. Kéri, and I. Stumpf (eds.) *From Subject to Citizen*. Budapest, Hungary: Hungarian Centre for Political Education.

Patrick, J. (May 1997). 'Global Trends in Civic Education', pp. 1-3 in *Methodology*, Vol. 1, No. 1 (http://civnet.org/journal/issue1/patrick.htm).

Peabody, D. (1961). 'Attitude Content and Agreement Set in Scales of Authoritarianism, Dogmatism, Anti-Semitism and Economic Conservatism', pp. 1-11 in *Journal of Abnormal Social Psychology*, Vol. 63.

Perioe, S. (1970). 'Authoritarianism, Anti-Nominalism and Affiliation among College Students' pp. 325-6 in *Proceedings of the 78th Annual Convention, American Psychological Association*.

Pervin, L. (1990). *Handbook of Personality*. New York, NY and London, UK: Guilford Press.

Peterson, S. (1990). *Political Behavior: Patterns in Everyday Life*. Newbury Park, CA: Sage Publications.

Phoenix, A. (1995). 'Difference and Differentiation: Young Londoners' Accounts of Race and Nation', pp. 173-87 in L. Chisholm, P. Büchner, H. Krüger, and M. du Bois-Reymond (eds.) *Growing Up in Europe*. Berlin, FRG and New York, NY: Walter de Gruyter.

Photiadis, J. (1962). 'Education and Personality Variables Related to Prejudice', pp. 269-75 in *Journal of Social Psychology*, Vol. 58.

Plant, W. (1966). 'Changes in Intolerance and Authoritarianism for Sorority Women Enrolled in College for Two Years', pp. 79-83 in *Journal of Social Psychology*, Vol. 68.

Popov, N. (1995). *The Russian People Speak: Democracy at the Crossroads*. Syracuse, NY: Syracuse University Press.

Povrzanovic, M. (1995). 'War Experiences and Ethnic Identities: Croatian Children in the Nineties', pp. 29-39 in *Collegium Antropologicum*, Vol. 19, No. 1.

Prezeworski, A. (1993). 'Socialism and Social Democracy', pp. 832-9 in J. Krieger (ed.) *The Oxford Companion to Politics of the World*. New York, NY and Oxford, UK: Oxford University Press.

Raaijmakers, Q., W. Meeus and W. Vollebergh (1986). 'Dutch Adolescents, Their Level of Education and Their Political Intolerance', pp. 114-9 in M. Brouwer, J. van Ginneken, L. Hagendoorn, and J. Meloen (eds.) *Political Psychology in The Netherlands*. Amsterdam, The Netherlands: Mola Russa.

Ray, J. (1976). 'Do Authoritarians Hold Authoritarian Attitudes?', pp. 307-25 in *Human Relations*, Vol. 29.

Ray, D., B. Brock-Utne, B. Franco, R. Ghosh, M. Haavelsrud, A. Ibrahim, M. Karlekar, N. London, R. Malisa, M. Vallejo, V. Parizek, D. Radcliffe, D. Tran, N. Voskresenskaya, and Z. Navzhao (1994). *Education for Human Rights*. London, Ontario, Canada: UNESCO: International Bureau of Education.

Rényi, J. and D. Lubeck (January 1994). 'A Response to the NCSS Guidelines on Multicultural Education', pp. 4-6 in *Social Education*.

Rigby, K. (1984). 'Acceptance of Authority and Directiveness as Indicators of Authoritarianism: A New Framework', pp. 171-80 in *Journal of Social Psychology*, Vol. 122, No. 2.

Rigby, K. (1987). 'An Authority Behavior Inventory', pp. 615-25 in *Journal of Personality Assessment*, Vol. 51, No. 4.

Riggs, F. (1998). 'Glossary of Terms Used in this Issue', pp. 311-30 in *International Political Science Review*, Vol. 19, No. 3.

Roe, R. (1975). *Links en rechts in empirisch perspectief* (Left and Right Wing in an Empirical Perspective). Ph.D. dissertation, University of Amsterdam, Amsterdam, The Netherlands.

Rokeach, M. (1960). *The Open and Closed Mind*. New York, NY: Basic Books.

Rose, R. and C. Haerpfer (1993). *Adapting to Transformation in Eastern Europe: New Democracies Barometer II*. Glasgow, Scotland: Centre for the Study of Public Policy, University of Strathclyde.

Rourke, J. (1995). *International Politics on the World Stage*. Guilford, CT: Dushkin Publishing Group, Brown and Benchmark Publishers.

Russet, B. and H. Starr (1994). *World Politics*. New York, NY: W. H. Freeman and Co.

Sander, W. (1994). *Strengthening Democracy Through Political Education*. ERIC Document ED 385487.

Sanford, R. (1973). 'Authoritarian Personality in Contemporary Perspective', pp. 139-70 in J. Knutson (ed.,) *Handbook of Political Psychology*. San Francisco, CA: Jossey Bass Publishers.

Scheepers, P. A. Felling, and J. Peters (1992). 'Anomie, Authoritarianism, and Ethnocentrism: Update of a Classic Theme and An Empirical Test', pp. 43-59 in *Politics and the Individual*, Vol. 2, No. 1.

Schlesinger, Jr., A. (September/October 1997). 'Has Democracy a Future?', pp. 2-12 in *Foreign Affairs*, Vol. 76, No. 5.

Schmidt, P. and M. Berger (July 1993). 'Changes in Authoritarianism and Left-Right Orientation Among East and West German youths: Results of a Two-Wave Panel Study'. Paper presented at the XVIth Annual Scientific Meeting of the International Society of Political Psychology, Cambridge, MA.

Sears, D. and J. McConahay (1970). 'Racial Socialization, Comparison Levels, and the Watts Riot', pp. 568-81 in A. Wilcox (ed.) *Public Opinion and Political Attitudes*. New York, NY: Wiley & Sons.

Sears, D. and N. Valentino (March 1997). 'Politics Matters: Political Events as Catalysts for Pre-Adult Socialization', pp. 45-66 in *American Political Science Review*, Vol. 91, No. 1.

Shaver, J., H. Hofmann, and H. Richards (1971). 'The Authoritarianism of American and German Teacher Education Students', pp. 303-4 in *Journal of Social Psychology*, Vol. 84.

Sherwood, J. (1966). 'Authoritarianism and Moral Realism', pp. 17-21 in *Journal of Clinical Psychology*, Vol. 22, No. 1.

Shils, E. (1954). 'Authoritarianism: "Right" and "Left"', pp. 24-49 in R. Christie and M. Jahoda *Studies in the Scope and Method of "The Authoritarian Personality": Continuities in Social Research*. Glencoe, IL: The Free Press.

Siber, I. (1991). 'Review of Research on the Authoritarian Personality', pp. 21-8 in *Politics and the Individual*, Vol. 1, No. 1.

Siber, I. (1994). 'Political Socialization and Social Changes in Croatia', pp. 358-69 in G. Csepeli, D. German, L. Kéri, and I. Stumpf (eds.) *From Subject to Citizen*. Budapest, Hungary: Hungarian Centre for Political Education.

Sidanius, J. (1978). 'Intolerance of Ambiguity and Sociopolitical Ideology: A Multidimensional Analysis', pp. 215-35 in *European Journal of Social Psychology*, Vol. 8.

Sidanius, J. (1984). 'Political Interest, Political Information Search, and Ideological Homogeneity as a Function of Sociopolitical Ideology', pp. 811-28 in *Human Relations*, Vol. 37, No. 10.

Sidanius, J. (1985). 'Cognitive Functioning and Sociopolitical Ideology Revisited', pp. 637-61 in *Political Psychology*, Vol. 6, No. 4.

Sidanius, J., R. Brewer, E. Banks, and B. Ekehammar (1987). 'Ideological Constraint, Political Interest, and Gender: A Swedish American Comparison', pp. 471-92 in *European Journal of Political Research*, Vol. 15.

Sidanius, J. and B. Ekehammar (1976). 'Cognitive Functioning and Sociopolitical Ideology: A Multidimensional and Individualized Analysis', pp. 205-16 in *Scandinavian Journal of Psychology*, Vol. 17.

Sidanius, J., B. Ekehammar, and J. Lukowsky (June 1983). 'Social Status and Sociopolitical Ideology Among Swedish Youth', pp. 395-415 in *Youth and Society*, Vol. 14, No. 4.

Sigelman, L. and S. Welch (March 1993). 'The Contact Hypothesis Revisited: Black-White Interaction and Positive Racial Attitudes', pp. 781-95 in *Social Forces*, Vol. 71, No. 3.

Simpson, E. (1971). *Democracy's Stepchildren*. San Francisco, CA: Jossey-Bass.

Simpson, M. (1972). 'Authoritarianism and Education: A Comparative Approach', pp. 223-34 in *Sociometry*, Vol. 35.

Sniderman, P., P. Tetlock, and R. Peterson (1993). 'Racism and Liberal Democracy', pp. 1-28 in *Politics and the Individual*, Vol. 3, No. 1.

Somit, A. and S. Peterson (1997). *Darwinism, Dominance, and Democracy*. London, UK and Westport, CT: Praeger.

Steeh, C. and H. Schuman (September 1992). 'Young White Adults: Did Racial Attitudes Change in the 1980s?', pp. 340-67 in *American Journal of Sociology*, Vol. 98, No. 2.

Stone, W., G. Lederer, and R. Christie (1993). *Strength and Weakness: The Authoritarian Personality Today*. New York, NY: Springer Verlag.

Stuart, I. (1965). 'Field Dependency, Authoritarianism and Perception of the Human Figure', pp. 209-14 in *Journal of Social Psychology*, Vol. 66.

Szabo, M. (1991). 'Political Socialization in Hungary', pp. 59-78 in H. Dekker and R. Meyenberg (eds.) *Politics and the European Younger Generation: Political Socialization in Eastern, Central, and Western Europe*. Oldenburg, FRG: University of Oldenburg BIS.

Todd, E. (1985). *The Explanation of Ideology: Family Structures and Social Systems*. Oxford, UK: Basil Blackwell.

Todd, E. (1987). *The Causes of Progress: Culture, Authority, and Change*. Oxford, UK: Basil Blackwell.

Tomlinson, S. (1993). 'White Pupils' Views of Ethnic Minorities in England', pp. 263-72 in *International Journal of Group Tensions*, Vol. 25, No. 3.

Torney, J., A. Oppenheim, and R. Farnen (1975). *Civic Education in Ten Countries*. New York, NY: Wiley & Sons and Stockholm, Sweden: Almqvist & Wiksell.

Toth, O. (1995). 'Political-Moral Attitudes Amongst Young People in Post-Communist Hungary', pp. 189-94 in L. Chisholm, P. Büchner, H. Krüger, and M. du Bois-Reymond (eds.) *Growing Up in Europe*. Berlin, FRG and New York, NY: Walter de Gruyter.

Tumin, M. (1961). *An Inventory and Appraisal of Research on American Anti-Semitism*. New York, NY: Freedom Books.

UNDP (1991, 1994, 1996). United Nations Development Programme. *Human Development Report 1991, 1994, 1996*. Oxford, UK: Oxford University Press.

UNESCO (October 1995). *Curriculum Development: Civic Education in Central and Eastern Europe*. Vienna, Austria: Kulturkontakt.

VanDyke, V. (1988). *Introduction to Politics*. Chicago, IL: Nelson-Hall Publishers.

Vanhanen, T. (1997). *Prospects of Democracy: A Study of 172 Countries*. London, UK: Routledge.

Völgyes, I. (1993). 'Political Culture in Eastern Europe: Re-examining the Formative Roles of Socialization After the System Change of 1989-1990', pp. 84-104 in G. Csepeli, L. Kéri, and I. Stumpf (eds.) *State and Citizen*. Budapest, Hungary: Institute of Political Science, Hungarian Center for Political Education.

Vollebergh, W. (1991). 'The Limits of Tolerance'. Dissertation Abstract. Utrecht, The Netherlands: ISOR, University of Utrecht.

Vollebergh, W. (1994). 'The Consolidation of Educational Differences in Authoritarianism in Adolescence', pp. 57-71 in *Politics and the Individual*, Vol. 4, No. 1.

Vollebergh, W. (1996). 'Identification with Social Groups and Intolerance Among Dutch Adolescents', pp. 304-30 in R. Farnen, H. Dekker, R. Meyenberg, and D. German (eds.) *Democracy, Socialization, and Conflicting Loyalties in East and West*. London, UK: Macmillan and New York, NY: St. Martins Press.

Voss, J., D. Perkins, and J. Segal (1991). *Informal Reasoning and Education*. Hillsdale, NJ: Lawrence Erlbaum.

Wagner, A. (1990). 'The OECD Study on Education for Cultural and Linguistic Minority Children: Innovative Schools'. Paper presented to the International Sociological Association World Congress, July 9-13, 1990 in Madrid, Spain.

Ward, D. (1986). 'Comments on Cognitive Functioning and Sociopolitical Ideology Revisited', pp. 141-7 in *Political Psychology*, Vol. 7, No. 1.

Watts, M. (1996). 'Polarization and the Development of Political Ideology in Germany: Race, Values, and Threat', pp. 165-94 in R. Farnen, H. Dekker, R. Meyenberg, and D. German (eds.) *Democracy, Socialization, and Conflicting Loyalties in East and West*. London, UK Macmillan and New York, NY: St. Martins Press.

Whitehind, L. (1993). 'Democratic Transitions', pp. 224-7 in J. Krieger (ed.) *The Oxford Companion to Politics of the World*. New York, NY and Oxford, UK: Oxford University Press.

Willis, P., A. Bekenn, T. Ellis, and D. Whitt (1988). *The Youth Review: Social conditions of Young People in Wolverhampton*. Aldershot, UK: Avebury, Gower.

Winter, D. (1996). *Personality*. New York, NY: McGraw Hill.

de Witte, H. (1996). 'Unskilled Blue Collar Workers: Bourgeois and/or Authoritarian? Results from a Small Scale Survey in Belgium', pp. 1-13. Leuven, Belgium: Higher Institute for Work.

Wrightsman, L. (1997). *Social Psychology*. 2nd ed. Monterey, CA: Brooks/Cole.

Zick, A. (ed.) (1999). 'Special Issue on Authoritarianism', *Politics, Groups, and the Individual*, Vol. 8, Nos. 1 and 2.

Index of Names

214   *Democracy, Authoritarianism, and Education*

Index of Subjects